After Capital

Theory, Culture & Society

Theory, Culture & Society caters for the resurgence of interest in culture within contemporary social science and the humanities. Building on the heritage of classical social theory, the book series examines ways in which this tradition has been reshaped by a new generation of theorists. It also publishes theoretically informed analyses of everyday life, popular culture, and new intellectual movements.

EDITOR: Mike Featherstone, *Goldsmiths, University of London*

SERIES EDITORIAL BOARD

Roy Boyne, *University of Durham*

Nicholas Gane, *University of Warwick*

Scott Lash, *Goldsmiths, University of London*

Couze Venn, *Goldsmiths, University of London*

The Theory, Culture & Society book series, the journals *Theory, Culture & Society* and *Body & Society*, the TCS website and related conferences, workshops, and other activities now operate from Goldsmiths, University of London. For further details please contact:

e-mail: tcs@sagepub.co.uk
web: http://tcs.sagepub.com/

Recent volumes include:

Risk Society
Ulrich Beck

The Tourist Gaze 3.0
John Urry and Jonas Larsen

Consumer Culture and Postmodernism, Second Edition
Mike Featherstone

The Body and Society, Third Edition
Bryan S. Turner

Simmel on Culture
David Frisby and Mike Featherstone

Globalization
Roland Robertson

Economies of Signs and Space
Scott Lash and John Urry

Formations of Class & Gender
Beverley Skeggs

The Body and Social Theory, Third Edition
Chris Shilling

The Consumer Society, Revised Edition
Jean Baudrillard

Couze Venn

After Capital

Los Angeles | London | New Delhi
Singapore | Washington DC | Melbourne

Los Angeles | London | New Delhi
Singapore | Washington DC | Melbourne

SAGE Publications Ltd
1 Oliver's Yard
55 City Road
London EC1Y 1SP

SAGE Publications Inc.
2455 Teller Road
Thousand Oaks, California 91320

SAGE Publications India Pvt Ltd
B 1/I 1 Mohan Cooperative Industrial Area
Mathura Road
New Delhi 110 044

SAGE Publications Asia-Pacific Pte Ltd
3 Church Street
#10-04 Samsung Hub
Singapore 049483

Editor: Natalie Aguilera
Assistant editor: Delayna Spencer
Editorial assistant: Eve Williams
Production editor: Katherine Haw
Copyeditor: Chris Bitten
Proofreader: Rebecca Storr
Indexer: Couze Venn
Marketing manager: Susheel Gokarakonda
Cover design: Wendy Scott
Typeset by: C&M Digitals (P) Ltd, Chennai, India
Printed in the UK

© Couze Venn 2018

First published 2018

Apart from any fair dealing for the purposes of research or private study, or criticism or review, as permitted under the Copyright, Designs and Patents Act, 1988, this publication may be reproduced, stored or transmitted in any form, or by any means, only with the prior permission in writing of the publishers, or in the case of reprographic reproduction, in accordance with the terms of licences issued by the Copyright Licensing Agency. Enquiries concerning reproduction outside those terms should be sent to the publishers.

Library of Congress Control Number: 2018932208

British Library Cataloguing in Publication data

A catalogue record for this book is available from the British Library

ISBN 978-1-5264-5012-8
ISBN 978-1-5264-5013-5 (pbk)

At SAGE we take sustainability seriously. Most of our products are printed in the UK using responsibly sourced papers and boards. When we print overseas we ensure sustainable papers are used as measured by the PREPS grading system. We undertake an annual audit to monitor our sustainability.

'This extraordinary work synthesises, extends and originates a vast range of scholarship and critical thought. In doing so, it offers the most concise yet most comprehensive account of the crisis of our times, and of the very nature of capitalism as such, to have been produced for many years. Couze Venn is one of the great unsung intellectual heroes of our age; how many other thinkers are able to synthesise post-structuralist philosophy and postcolonial theory with Marxist political economy and critical ecology, without a trace of superficiality in their approach to any of these sources? How many would even dare to try? This is an invaluable book for anyone who wants to think politically about the state of the world today, inside or outside the academy, in any discipline.'

Jeremy Gilbert, Professor of Cultural and Political Theory, University of East London

'*After Capital* takes the risky path that our bleak circumstances demand. This thoughtful and learned intervention boldly spells out protocols for a new way of living. Moving between critique and urgent, unsentimental speculation, Couze Venn identifies the novel habits required to sustain life beyond the war, waste and squalor of contemporary capitalism.'

Paul Gilroy, Professor of American and English Literature, Kings College, University of London

'*A tour de force*. It is difficult to overstate the importance of this book – not only for the present but for many generations to come.'

Valerie Walkerdine, Professor, Cardiff University

'I could not recommend a better book to those interested not only in the interdependence of the multiple crises (environmental, economic and political) that we are currently entangled in, but also in alternative visions for the future. *After Capital* is outstanding scholarship that daringly and passionately articulates new conceptual frameworks that makes clear the potential of a post-capitalist and post-anthropocentric cosmopolitics of the commons to make life after capital something to look forward to.'

Dr Tiziana Terranova, University of Naples, L'Orientale

'With typical depth and thoughtfulness, Couze Venn explores and untangles the intricately woven and mammoth issues that we face today. Erudite and scholarly, these pages are a revelation and guide in our complex and uncertain times.'

Dr Dave Beer, Reader, York University

The book is dedicated to my wife Francesca for the years of constant and unfailing emotional sustenance, love and intellectual companionship. The loving support of our close family, Scarlett Thomas, Rod Edmond, Sam Ashurst, Hari Ashurst-Venn and Nia Ashurst-Venn has sustained me through the long process of writing; they have been a constant source of encouragement, comfort and fun. It is dedicated also to Francesca's and my granddaughter Ivy, in the hope that the world she inherits from us is a liveable and happy one, to be shared amongst all equally as the greatest gift.

Contents

About the Author x
Acknowledgements xi

    Introduction
    The State of the World: Convergent Crises   1

1 New Mechanisms of Dispossession: Property,
    Inequality and the Debt Society   24

2 In the Shadow of Tipping Points: The Political
    Economy of Climate Change   52

3 Colonialism, Dispossession and Capitalist Accumulation:
    A Decolonial History of the Present   64

4 From Liberalism to Neoliberalism: A Dissident Genealogy   86

5 Towards a World in Common   108

6 New Foundations for Postcapitalist Worlds   123

References 144
Index 157

About the Author

Couze Venn is Emeritus Professor in the Media and Communications Department, Goldsmiths, University of London, and Associate Research Fellow at the Johannesburg University. He was a founder member of the *Ideology & Consciousness* Collective in 1976. He is a co-author of *Changing the Subject: Psychology, Social Regulation and Subjectivity* (Methuen, 1984 and Routledge, 1998), author of *Occidentalism. Modernity and Subjectivity* (Sage, 2000), *The Postcolonial Challenge: Towards Alternative Worlds* (Sage, 2006), co-author of *Inequality, Poverty, Education* (Palgrave, 2014). He is the Managing Editor and Reviews Editor of *Theory, Culture & Society*, Reviews Editor of *Body & Society*. His many papers have appeared in *Ideology & Consciousness, Theory, Culture & Society, Body & Society, Subjectivity, New Formations, Critical Arts, Parallax, Social Identities, Political Geography, PsychCritique*. He has edited or co-edited special issues and sections on Michel Foucault (with Tiziana Terranova), Affect (with Lisa Blackman), Problematizing Global Knowledge (with Mike Featherstone et al.), Cosmopolis (with Mike Featherstone et al.), Rethinking Race. His research interests include decolonial theory, cultural theory, contemporary philosophy, science and technology studies, the critique of capitalism.

Acknowledgements

This book has taken much longer to complete than I had anticipated. Along the way many friends and colleagues have offered comments and generous encouragements without which this book would never have seen the light of day. Several aspects of the book have been developed over the years, through talks and seminars to which colleagues had kindly invited me, and in a number of journal articles. Key arguments were tried out at a plenary lecture for the Radical Foucault Conference in 2011 organised by my friend Jeremy Gilbert. Jeremy has also read early drafts of chapters and provided valuable comments and advice when I needed reassurance about the overall project. The problem of debt in today's financial capitalism was presented in 2012 at the TCS seminar on property at the University of Naples l'Orientale, organised by colleagues there, principally Tiziana Terranova and Iain Chambers. The analysis in Chapter 3 extends a position I developed in an article in *Theory, Culture & Society* in 2009 – 'Neoliberal political economy, biopolitics and colonialism'; Chapter 4 has benefited from the research which Francesca and I did for our book *Inequality, Poverty, Exclusion* (Palgrave Macmillan, 2014); and Chapter 6 draws from my paper in *Body & Society* in 2010 – 'Individuation, relationality, affect: Rethinking the human in relation to the living'.

I have discussed ideas and shared early drafts with the Changing the Subject book group, Julian Henriques, Wendy Hollway, Cathy Urwin and Valerie Walkerdine. Their intellectual and emotional support and enthusiastic comments and inputs helped me reorganise the arguments and have a better sense of what I needed to foreground. Cathy has since died and we all miss her greatly.

My colleague and friend Mike Featherstone has offered all manner of support over the years, providing me with opportunities to test and disseminate many ideas through articles in the journals he edits, as well as through the Theory, Culture & Society Book Series. He has been a rock on whom I have relied a lot.

Robert Rojek at Sage has skilfully steered the book through the hazards of the publishing machine. Thank you Robert.

Special thanks are due to Dave Beer, Jeremy Gilbert, Paul Gilroy, Chris Miles, Lynne Segal, Tiziana Terranova, Vron Ware. Their confidence in the project and their comments have sustained me and helped me rework my arguments.

Other colleagues and friends provided much valued suggestions and encouragement. Some have read chapters at different points in the process of writing and I have tried to incorporate their suggestions where necessary. They are Lisa Blackman, Ryan Bishop, Andy Conio, Neal Curtis,

Acknowledgements

Simon Dawes, Heike Doring, Nick Gane, Yasmin Gunaratnam, Sunil Manghani, Matt Merefield, Dimitris Pappadopoulos, John Phillips, Bev Skeggs and Tomoko Tamari. I am grateful also to my colleague Sheila Sheikh whose kindness and support has been invaluable. Dr Lydon has nursed me through serious health problems.

Thanks are due to the team at SAGE – Katherine Haw, Delayna Spencer, Susheel Gokarakonda who have been helpful, patient and indulgent, making the task of completion less stressful than it could have been, and the copyeditor, Christine Bitten has ironed out the kinks.

Introduction
The State of the World: Convergent Crises

This book is an intervention at a moment when the world seems more fraught with danger than at any time in history. The all too visible signs are the converging crises concerning the global economy, the environment, the depletion of non-renewable resources, increasing violences and the breakdown of social cohesion; they threaten a perfect storm in the near future. A profusion of analyses has emerged that challenge the status quo to argue that the magnitude of the task requires drastic transformations in practices, ways of life and expectations which underlie the problems. For many, the crash of 2008 stands as the signifier forewarning of the dangers inherent in the witches brew concocted from the rapacious plunder of the earth, the degradation of the environment, the pollution of habitats, the massive increase in inequality worldwide, and the assimilation of the state within capital. The destructive consequences have brought into focus the fragility of much that the dominant orthodoxy thought solid and enduring, exposing the illusion of a triumphant and benign capitalism and foregrounding both the limits of planet-earth as well as the vulnerability of democratic institutions.

Whilst one can identify capitalism and the way of life associated with it as the underlying cause, the present study goes further by seeking to establish the linkages whereby these correlated crises can be seen to be the culmination of tendencies in process for at least two centuries. It therefore presents a genealogy of the mechanisms whereby the emergence of predatory economic systems fixated on ever increasing commodification and privatisation of all existing resources from land to knowledge and life itself has gradually intensified the iniquities and risks incipient in economies and socialities premised on dispossession and ceaseless growth and class, racial and gender oppressions. It develops arguments for breaking with these mechanisms and the discourses that authorise them; it thus clears the ground for imagining alternatives that increase the possibility of avoiding the coming of the worst.

Yet, the search for possible radical solutions is thwarted by the failure to find common ground amongst those trying to overcome the fragmentation of oppositional politics at a time when the forces maintaining existing relations of power and destructive ways of being are stronger than ever. These forces have become more organised politically, institutionally and discursively, able so far to recruit supporters across categories of class, gender and race. A worrying aspect for democratic politics is that their appeal has been particularly strong amongst many workers who have experienced the domination of global finance in the form of increasing precarisation, marginalisation and loss of self-esteem, and for those for whom an authoritarian and exclusionary populism holds out the hope of better times to come.

The question therefore is: What analysis of the crises and what narratives of possible alternatives could break through the stuckness that makes one fear for the future? This is the question which underlies the project elaborated in *After Capital*. A central argument running through the different chapters is that if the crises are dynamically interconnected, as many believe they are, the implication suggests a call for a new perspective and a new kind of politics that would encompass both older struggles around equality and social justice and new sectional interests that currently are often divisive and disconnected. The arguments in the book propose a politics of the commons allied to a cosmopolitical project oriented towards an emancipatory goal. As I explain below, this involves a challenge to existing property regimes and asymmetrical relations of power and wealth underlying zero-sum or win/lose economies such as capitalism. It also involves promoting values of equality, liberty, conviviality and fundamental rights as the basis for ways of being that respect all creatures and the limits of the planet. Such a shift prompts an engagement with the problem of reconstituting ontological, epistemological and ethical foundations adequate for this project, as I outline in the final chapter.

In the light of the wealth of information now continuously accumulating in the public domain, the visible aspects of the crises I am highlighting have become only too familiar, as they have been widely discussed in academic writings and disseminated by dissident or oppositional movements, groups and media.[1] In spite of the divergent standpoints, one area of agreement amongst a broad spectrum of analysts is that the response to the fall-out from the crash promoted by governments and policy-makers, operated through regulatory mechanisms such as the IMF, central banks and existing inter-governmental protocols, agreements and agencies such as the WTO and NAFTA, essentially instrumentalises a strategy of transferring risks and wealth from the poorer, more vulnerable and less powerful sections of the world's populations to a rich minority.

Indeed, as I show in the next chapter, analyses developed in the aftermath of the crash have demonstrated why and how the 'neoliberal' management of the economy through the promotion of private accumulation, flexible regulation and short-term fiscal and monetary strategies primarily benefits global corporations and owners of capital.[2] As we know, the result has been to trigger a vicious circle of insurmountable debts, national deficits, mafia and feral economies, and increasing destitution, adding to the ongoing problems of diminishing resources, climate change and overloaded ecologies. The overriding goal of profit maximisation has even found ways of turning a crisis into a profit-generating occasion, as Mirowski in *Never Let a Serious Crisis Go to Waste* (2013), Naomi Klein in *This Changes Everything: Capitalism vs. Climate Change* (2014), and others have described. This mindset has even instituted new forms of trading such as those relating to carbon emission and capture, typified in claims such as one made (before Trump) by the US chief climate negotiator that 'no one is better positioned to win big in the multi-trillion dollar low-carbon energy innovation than the United States', a claim that attests to the interests in turning climate change into an investment opportunity.[3] It must be said that matters have become more complicated with the policies which the Trump Administration has embarked upon, particularly regarding the regressive approach to the regulation of emissions, the curtailment of research into global warming, and instituting measures that further damage the lives of the precariat, and not just in the USA. But no amount of disinformation can dissolve the fact of diminishing resources, climate change and growing inequalities.

The dominant or mainstream approach to the situation has not only worsened the problems whilst extracting even more wealth from the general public through austerity programmes, as, notably, Joseph Stiglitz in *The Price of Inequality* (2013) and Mark Blyth in *Austerity: The History of a Dangerous Idea* (2013) have shown: it has enabled corporations and the rich elites to 'confiscate' what remains of common wealth, as Stengers has starkly put it in *Aux temps des catastrophes* (2009). Her analysis finds support in Nancy MacLean's (2017) investigation of the 'new right' or neocon's well prepared stealth programme for this kind of transfer of wealth to the already very rich. This expropriation includes not only natural resources such as land, water, forests, mineral deposits, and so on but also the accumulated treasury of know-hows invested in social, cultural, educational, environmental and technological institutions and processes – mislabelled as 'capital' – that are regarded as 'infrastructure' or 'externalities'. The opportunities for further private capital accumulation had already followed in the wake of the emergence of financial capitalism coupled to the deployment of new information technologies functioning as instruments for the capture of wealth and data; the austerity option is simply another turn of the screw in the process of pauperisation.

Yet, as I discuss in the next chapter, and as Blyth (2013) argues, the introduction of austerity measures is the consequence of the growth of institutions 'too big to fail', and 'too big to bail'. He makes the point that

> The cost of bailing, recapitalizing, and otherwise saving the global banking system has been ... between 3 and 13 trillion dollars. Most of that has ended up on the balance sheet of governments as they absorb the costs of the bust, which is why we mistakenly call this a sovereign debt crisis when in fact it is a transmuted and well-camouflaged banking crisis. (Blyth, 2013: 5)

This view finds support amongst many experts, notably Stiglitz (2013) or Curtis (2013), who have all established that the strategies for saving capitalism in effect have transferred the costs of bailout onto the state and the people. Besides, as I go on to show, the banking crisis has conveniently helped capital to consolidate its grip on the apparatuses of power worldwide.

It is this situation of state-assisted dispossession that has increased support for the view that the transformations necessary to prevent the coming of the worst require a break with existing economies and the apparatuses and discourses that sustain them, notably, the primacy of the model of growth as 'the arrow of time' exemplified in the process of modernisation as 'development' which today is driven by global competition for profit maximisation heedless of the accumulation of problems (Stengers, 2009: 9–11). It requires a break also with the prioritisation of private property and private interest over the general interest and common good. The implications mean that critiques of capitalism must target existing ways of life, socialities, subjectivities and the unequal relations of power inscribed in and sustained through them.

There are other reasons for advocating radical transformations in the way we live. This is because, since the emergence of industrial capitalism some two centuries ago, the same forces driving incessant accumulation and growth have so transformed the planet and its systems that many scientists argue it is appropriate to think about the effects in terms of the (problematic) concept of Anthropocene, which they claim signals the start of a new geological age (Zalasiewicz et al., 2017; see also Crutzen, 2002; see Jason W. Moore, *Capitalism in the Web of Life*, 2015, for a critique of the relation between capitalism and Anthropocene through concepts such as Capitalocene; also Claire Colebrook, *Death of the PostHuman*, 2014). There are clearly many significant transformations of the planet which require analysis in terms of enduring any long-term impact. For instance, amongst the signs of epochal change Sam Wong (2016) picks out the following as key markers: global warming and its effects, such as the fact that 'global sea levels are higher than at any point in the last 115,000 years' (Wong, 2016: 14); carbon emission rates due to fossil fuel burning which are 'higher than in the preceding 65 million years' (Wong, 2016: 14); the production of materials previously unknown in their elemental form has proliferated, particularly aluminium, 500 million tons of which have now been produced, and plastics, the annual production of which is 500 million tons, to which one should add the billions of tons of concrete produced so far; the increase in levels of nitrogen and phosphorus in soils which has doubled in the last hundred years due to intensive farming; the geological changes resulting from deforestation, farming, drilling, mining, landfills, dam-building and coastal reclamation; radioactive isotopes produced in the development of nuclear weapons; and evidence of the extinction of many species due to all the above. Recently, evidence identifying the formation of new minerals (208 crystalline compounds catalogued by Robert Hazen) further supports the recognition of geological change due to human activity (cited in Whyte, 2017, referencing a paper in *American Mineralogy*) – though it must be said that the question of an Anthropocene age remains open. Equally, one should include the destructive consequences due to the massive amount of other chemical and biochemical pollutants provoking diseases as well as altering the biome, resulting in such phenomena as loss of biodiversity, bee colony collapse and severe decline in other pollinators, notably, flying insects (Hallmann et al., 2017), with adverse effects for food production.

In addition, it is crucial to highlight the effects of plastics since researchers have added the notion of 'Plasticene' to draw attention to the biophysical mutations due to the effects of plastics on rocks and particularly the oceans where an estimated 5.25 trillion pieces of plastic weighing over 260,000 tonnes float at sea; more recent estimates multiply these figures depending on the measuring techniques. The evidence shows that a new ecosystem – a 'plastisphere' – which passes into the food chain through fish, and can have pathogenic as well as epigenetic consequences (Reed, 2015: 28; see also Gabrys et al., 2013, *Accumulation: The Material Politics of Plastics*). The point to note is that the addition of the concept of Plasticene alongside that of Anthropocene makes visible our total dependence on a carbon economy, that is, not just oil and gas but the mass of polymers and polycarbonates which the petrochemical industry derives as by-products of oil, particularly the many forms of plastic and their ubiquitous presence and manifold uses, both good (e.g medical equipments) and bad (e.g packaging), in the world we have made. The point about these anthropogenic effects is not that human activity is having transformive consequences for the planet and its ecological and geophysical systems, since all living things do so and have done so for millennia, but the scale and speed of these transformations, outpacing the ability of many species to cope, as many scientists are arguing. A striking study that demonstrates the complex intertwinement of natural and human ecologies with economic, political and cultural processes is that of Anna Tsing's account of the travels and travails of the Matsutake mushroom in *The Mushroom at the End of the World: On the Possibility of Life in Capitalist Ruins* (2015). It is a story of the manifold feed-back and feed-forward loops and intersections across geographies and habitats that make vividly concrete the network of correlations and effects, including destructive ones, that bind all creatures and the planet in the web of life.

Of course, the crucial dimension of the crises in the public's mind, apart from growing inequalities, concerns climate change now that all the main indicators of global average temperature show that a rise of 1°C had already been reached at the end of 2015 (Le Page, 2015a: 8; see also Wadhams' *A Farewell to Ice*, 2016). This stage in global warming supports the agreement amongst scientists that global surface temperatures will likely rise more than 2°C before the end of the century, since such a rise is already locked in due to current greenhouse gas emissions (GHG – carbon dioxide and methane, though there are more destructive but under-reported ones such as HFC-23), and that new targets for reductions in GHG are about ways of possibly keeping the increase to this figure rather than the more likely higher figure (the details are examined in Chapter 2).

We know too that the COP 21 climate conference in Paris in December 2015 optimistically agreed to limit global warming to less than 2°C above pre-industrial times, ideally targeting a rise of 1.5°C. But many scientists argue that actions proposed at COP 21 do not go far enough to achieve this target since 'the emissions cuts promised by countries are still wholly insufficient' (Le Quere, cited by Le Page, 2015a: 8). The Trump Administration's abandonment of the Clean Power Plan and its rejection of the anthropogenic explanation simply adds to this prognostic, especially given that the USA is responsible for 25% of world emission since the industrial revolution. Indeed, to achieve the 1.5°C target, there would need to be zero emissions after 2050 as well as a massive programme of carbon capture, or 'negative emissions' amounting to 500 giga tons by 2100, using a variety of technologies. This goal would require the development of a 'whole new industry' which is yet to emerge (Pearce, 2016: 30–33), prompting the view that only a revolutionary shift in how power is generated, distributed and used would avoid increases beyond 2°C by the end of the century (Le Page, 2015a). Indeed, some analysts suggest 1.5°C will be reached in the next 10 years unless effective action is taken now, especially by the big emitters (Holmes, 2017). Given that the main emitters are cars, coal and cows (the 3Cs) – and I would add another C, namely, capitalism – the enormity of the task becomes evident.

The urgency is driven by the fact that the epochal effects of climate change – though denied or downplayed by powerful forces, as MacLean (2017) and Monbiot (2017) have revealed – are now well understood, such as extreme weather, the melting of polar ice, the warming of oceans and the rise in sea levels, the diminishing availability of arable land, the growth of unsustainable habitat and a mass of other anthropogenic changes affecting the ecology and geology of the earth (detailed in Chapter 2). It is not an anti-science attitude alone that motivates this denial, but what the abandonment of fossil fuels would mean for the now dominant economies and for existing ways of life. Indeed, to take one obvious example, how would armies manage without oil, i.e. without fuel for aircrafts, bombers, tanks, armoured vehicles, etc.? Thus, without transformations in current technologies and the way we live, including prevailing relations of power and property, it is increasingly argued by many that the world would experience the beginning of a 'sixth great mass extinction', possibly including humans.[4]

These issues are examined in Chapter 2 where I develop a political economy of climate change in line with my argument that all the developments I have noted are interconnected and that capitalism as a specific form of a market economy is at the root of the merging of crises. It is therefore necessary to uncover these linkages as a key step towards establishing the basis for transcending our toxic socio-economic systems and the underlying values and assumptions, and to propose instead a politics grounded in the idea of postcapitalist commons. It is important to stress that the question of commons or the common is more than just a matter of transformations in the processes of production, for it involves fundamental changes touching every aspect of society and how we relate to each other. Basically, the shift in perspective expresses the view that the politics of the common implies a challenge not only to existing regimes of power and property and to the category of things that can be privately owned, but, as I have noted, it primarily involves developing the ontological, epistemological and ethical standpoints that could inform postcapitalist alternatives that would prioritise values of solidarity, conviviality, generosity, and propose a fundamental rethink of the place of humans in the scheme of things (established in Chapter 6).

Obstacles to change

The main problem when one turns to the question of alternatives is the extent to which the structural, institutional, technological, discursive, 'ideological' and subjective dimensions of the issues that arise act as so many and complex barriers at the level of practical action. To start with, we are faced with the fact that, in spite of all the signs indicating that 'the gods have failed' (Elliott and Atkinson, 2008), decision-makers across the world share with the pervasive 'neoliberal orthodoxy' (Glyn, 2007) the conviction that not only is capitalism not broken but that it is the only rational system we have, and that, once mended, a new improved and more careful capitalism will emerge from the crisis able to provide solutions to all the environmental, resource, economic and social problems. This conviction, or excuse, has dictated that the approach to current crises must rely on market fixes such as austerity programmes, front-loading debt on the state and ordinary citizens, and market-based or purely technical 'solutions' to climate change. As critics of market fixes have been proclaiming, the slashing of expenditure on social protection and welfare, programmes of 'liberalisation', the 'offshoring' of production, financial transactions, and capital-holding corporations (Urry, 2014a), and the off-loading of risks and responsibilities to less powerful or compliant nations are intensifying inequalities and endangering the basis of democracy. Besides, the same forces promoting reliance on the rationality of the market also account for the failure so far to implement effective and binding action to tackle climate change and global environmental destruction.

The process of systematic dispossession is being achieved through stratagems such as harvesting tangible and intangible assets of public sectors on the mythical grounds of the greater efficiency of the private sector; securing new forms of enclosures, typically of land and raw materials in the poorer countries, particularly in Africa through the operation of what Burgis (2015) calls 'the looting machine'. Transnational corporations and sovereign capital holders routinely participate in this new scramble for Africa. In many ways, and as I show in Chapter 3, it is the continuation by other means of strategies of wealth capture put in place in the period of colonialism and that provided conditions for the consolidation of capitalism (see also Williams, 1964 [1944]; Amin, 1977; Braudel, 1986; Gilroy, 1993; Arrighi, 1994; Venn, 2006a, amongst a long list of those who have explored the connections binding colonialism and capitalism). Today the strategies operate through geo-politico-economic and technical dispositifs of military power, soft power, client states, structural adjustments, technological transfer and so on which have built upon previously established colonial regimes (Venn, 2006a).

Furthermore, sovereignty now operates through stratagems that target the control of territory not through colonial appropriation but through various means, that include purchase, licensing agreements for extracting minerals, corrupt dealings with politicians and officials, inciting fear amongst indigenous inhabitants as in the Amazon basin, and so on (see also, Stuart Elden's 2009 wider analysis of the spatial dimension of power in *Terror and Territory*). I will argue in the next chapter that these mechanisms ensuring the transfer of wealth have become hard-wired in finance capitalism, notably through flows of money and assets that further institutionalise the role of debt in the process. They are part of the neoliberal approach for managing the global economy which is applied across nations, for instance, exemplified in the measures forced upon Greece by the Troika of the European Central Bank, the European Commission and the IMF.

The pervasive character of the mindset framing these approaches is neatly summarised by Dardot and Laval (2010: 5, 6) in *La nouvelle raison du monde* when they argue that 'neoliberalism' has succeeded in securing a grip on the forms of our existence, operating

> sometimes in its political form (the conquest of power by neoliberal forces), sometimes in its economic form (the expansion of global financial capitalism), sometimes in its social form (the individualisation of social relations at the expense of collective solidarities, the extreme polarisation between rich and poor), sometimes in its subjective form (the emergence of a new subject, the development of new psychic pathologies).

One should add the manufacture of consent through the manipulation of information by governments and most media outlets, mostly owned by conglomerates keen to foster ignorance and myths serving existing regimes of property and power.

This understanding of neoliberalism as a mobile form of governance emphasises its strategic and pragmatic character. Besides, the attitudes, values and understandings inscribed in the discourse of neoliberalism are revealed in its watchwords such as value for money, competition, targets, audit, 'the market', compliance, resilience and other incantations of management-speak. These values have been disseminated not just through the economy and the political system, but underlie interventions targeting all aspects of society: the conduct of citizens, social and educational policy, the administration of law, the approach to environmental and resource problems, new techniques for producing a docile workforce through precarisation, the economisation of knowledge, invasive techniques of surveillance, the suppression of dissent, and so on. As Foucault has explained, these areas, namely, 'population, technology, training and education, the legal system, the availability of land, climate' (Foucault, 2008: 141), are precisely those targeted in the neoliberal strategy aiming to construct the framework that ensures that a market economy founded in principle on competition can intervene with efficacy to establish a neo-biopolitical governmentality supporting the general economisation of society benefiting capital.

In the background of such strategies one finds the necessity by corporations and financial institutions to reduce risks whilst pursuing accumulation, a condition for which is the acquisition of material and intangible assets and collateral by any means necessary. This stratagem helps to sustain the exponential growth in the value of money-capital, an escalation driven by the trade in derivatives and other rent-seeking mechanisms operating through informational and cybernetic technologies, as I will explain in Chapter 1. Of course, the kind of strategic decisions I am summarising would not have been possible without the unequal relations of power that have become embedded in state and quasi-state institutions operating across the globe to authorise and legitimise them.

An important dimension of these developments is not only the widespread recognition that the toxic mix I am describing has bankrupted many states, seriously damaged environments and increased suffering worldwide: it is the fact that they have created an oligarchy of transnational corporations that excercise control over the levers of power through 'the nexus between economics and politics' (Stiglitz, 2013: lvi). In his analysis, Stiglitz shows why the current crisis is the direct consequence of political and economic forces and mechanisms working together in the interest '(O)f the 1%, for the 1%, by the 1%' (2013: xxxix). And recently Naomi Klein and her team, in *This Changes Everything*, have produced a mountain of evidence that backs up the kind of points I have signalled, powerfully arguing for the linkages between climate change, 'market fundamentalism', 'deregulation of the corporate sector', and the 'stranglehold over our economy, our political process, and most of our major media outlets' by an elite minority 'enjoying more unfettered political, cultural, and intellectual power than at any point since the 1920s' (2014: 18).[5]

How they do so is well worth a closer look, for it reveals the insiduous, highly organised, yet flexible manner in which global relations of economic and geopolitical power operate. Basically, power is exercised by means of interconnecting 'small-world networks' of decision-makers, think-tanks, and conglomerates linking finance, industry, and media, operating as a hub of elites. A crucial property of small-world networks is that they have a high degree of connectivity amongst the hubs or nodes, enabling information to be exchanged quickly between two or more unconnected points whilst minimising intermediate points, thus minimising noise and energy expenditure (for example and for similar reasons, the brain operates according to a small-world network – Tsonis and Tsonis, 2004).[6] In the case of corporate power, the networks form a 'super entity' of highly connected corporations that control global finance and circumscribe decision-making across business sectors, as Coghlan and MacKenzie (2011) report, summarising a study by the Swiss Federal Institute of Technology. This study shows that just 147 corporations control 40% of the 43,060 corporations surveyed, doing so through interlocking directorates, share ownership in each other, agenda setting, and so on, and by way of establishing the decision-making framework, that is, by setting the rules of the game and the agenda shaping business activity across all sectors. The fact that 40% of the megacorporations are mostly financial institutions adds weight to the argument that the outstanding feature of the new economic order is the creation of new rent-seeking mechanisms and a (related) debt society to feed the accumulative machine at the cost of the radical erosion of liberty and democracy.

Besides, the interconnections are characterised by complexity, requiring the kind of management that relies on cybernetic systems, as I examine in the next chapter by reference to Lyotard's analysis in *The Postmodern Condition* (1984 [1979]). It also requires the establishment of systems for the control of information as a central feature of the 'relationship between the politics of information and the practices of capital accumulation' (Gilroy, 1993: 7). Today this relationship is instrumentalised in the form of 'big data', metrics and social media, and through the ownership of data and software by very few 'providers', and increasingly through the extension of the latter's activities into marketing and sales.

Regarding the strategies whereby this kind of power is maintained, we are witnessing a tighter correlation between the vertical top down organisation of political power, the vertical distribution of wealth, and the horizontal integration of what Deleuze and Guattari called 'apparatuses of capture' (1998: 437–448); today the latter include the central role of the debt economy and the control of information as I will show in Chapter 1. I would point out also that the verticality of power is de-territorialised and mobile, being globally organised as I noted above. It is clear therefore that these transformations are not reducible to a simple reiteration of established hierarchies, but institute quite new strategies for the capture of wealth-power operating in the interest of an elite of individuals and corporations. They announce a new form of sovereignty which is essentially anti-democratic and totalitarian in orientation.

The concentration of power which this analysis and those of Stiglitz and Klein describe points to the deep-seated roots of the obstacles to change. They are the built-in resistance relating to the fact that many institutional and political structures, and economic, legal, informational and geopolitical assemblages and arrangements have been set up precisely to preserve dominant economic and political relations of power. Thus, on the one hand, it is easy to understand the hostility to change on the part of those who benefit most from the existing composition of economic and political power, for example, through cashing in on the lucrative contracts and initiatives generated by the 'liberalisation' of the apparatuses of social security and the welfare state that today we associate with austerity programmes and the shrinking of the state. One could note also the new opportunities to profit from commodity shortages and the fall-out due to climate change (Mirowski, 2013; Klein, 2014: 9, amongst others). The beneficiaries are the same corporations, expert advisers, and holders of capital for whom 'disaster capitalism' (Klein, 2008) and the 'war economy' (Marazzi, 2008) are occasions for profit and accumulation. Geopolitical interests are a crucial dimension of these reconstitutions of politico-economic power.[7]

Yet, on the other hand, one must also recognise that the reluctance of ordinary people to break with existing lifestyles and socio-political and economic systems relates to several factors operating in various combinations: the fears arising from increasing precarity and insecurity due to the structural effects of financial capitalism; the subjective attachments invested in existing ways of living, and a feeling of ontological security embedded in the familiar; a mixture of acquiescence, ignorance and resignation feeding into the sense that the room for manoeuvre for individuals and disparate groups is limited; and the adoption of coping strategies that displace the problem onto oneself by assuming responsibility for one's poverty. The subjective aspects of these strategies are revealed in Arlie Hochschild's studies of the coping mechanisms and the emotional responses to insecuritisation and the pressures arising from the deterioration of working conditions due to corporate search for profit maximisation (Hochschild, 2012 [1983]). More recently, her analysis of precarisation and its connection to the rise of the new Right is instructive in pointing to what she calls 'magical' thinking on the part of those who have lost out in the fall-out, for instance, those who are tempted to put their trust in a strong leader promising the return of good times (Hochschild, 2016).

Today the 'apparatuses of capture' include the manufacture of distrust, suspicion and disorientation, for example 'fake news', the denigration of scientists or expert knowledge, as well as the deployment of stealth tactics to try to garner support for policies that actually further disadvantage the specific constituencies targeted for 'capture' by New Right projects (see MacLean, 2017; Monbiot, 2017). It would appear therefore that the goal of private accumulation as overriding value has presided over the formation and recruitment of pliable subjectivities and the mobilisation of key developments such as information technologies and the internet, to serve a neo-biopolitics of population that supports the infernal machine for the dispossession of liberties, rights and common wealth, apparently operating beyond democratic control. Resistance to these forces has taken many forms, sometimes regressive, such as the rise of authoritarian populisms, but also the resurgence of emancipatory politics.

In addition to resistances in the context of these politico-economic relations of power and interests, the problem of change has to contend with the fact that specific contradictions and temporal, spatial and scalar disjunctures and conflicts have emerged with the new phase of transnational corporate capitalism that have significantly reduced the scope of governments and international bodies to take effective action to address global problems such as the confluence of crises I am examining. The temporal disjucture arises from the fact that the objectives of these corporations are driven primarily by their interest in the maximisation of profit over the short term and in maintaining or improving market share, an objective bound up with the workings of the stock market by which even their longer-term investments must abide. Yet, measures to tackle problems such as climate change, environmental degradation, and increasing inequalities, and initiatives to transform the agricultural and manufacturing bases to serve 'sustainability', as well as the need to effect necessary changes in attitudes and values, all require the reconstitution over the long term of capabilities, institutions, subjectivities, processes of decision-making and so on. The spatial or territorial disjuncture concerns the fact that corporations and conglomerates operate on a global scale with scant regard for the better interest of any particular country, whilst infrastructure investments in capabilities and know-hows and all the things which equip a people for particular ways of life, that is, much of what can be called enlarged or expanded commons, have been and require the accumulation of collective resources and assets at the level of every state (developed in Chapter 5; see also Amartya Sen and Martha Nussbaum's *The Quality of Life*, 1993). It should be said that some infrastructural projects in poorer and weaker countries are funded by global or sovereign capital as part of the strategy of soft power aiming to secure trading advantages and the control of mineral and other resources.

These temporal and spatial disjunctures correlate with geographies and temporalities of power (Elden, 2007); they feed into each other and inscribe conflicting values and goals at the level of the state. Furthermore, new informational technologies, by speeding up the global circulation of communications and money (amongst other flows) have introduced a new scale in the speed and location of events and transactions; they have thus intensified the indeterminacies inherent in the inter-dependent systems. Together, the temporal, spatial/territorial and scalar dimensions of the problems add to the already complicated set of inter-dependencies and feed-back loops characterising phenomena such as growing inequalities and destitution or complex systems such as the climate and biomes. They further impede radical change, evidenced for example in the difficulties encountered in achieving binding and effective protocols amongst nations at the various climate summits since the Kyoto Protocol (1992). These obstacles account for the inadequate progress made by states to address the range of problems I have identified at the start or those underlined in many IPCC Reports and countless scientific assessments of the plight of the environment and resources. These hazards and problems are well known, having been widely disseminated for some time in a massive literature.[8]

The question of obstacles to change depends also on the fact that the dynamics of complexity and inter-dependencies are poorly understood because of the dominance of mechanistic or piecemeal approaches that individualise the systems and processes involved instead of foregrounding perspectives that are grounded in concepts of relationalities, metastability and associated milieux.[9] The advantage of anti-mechanistic approaches is that they are consistent with the standpoint of a post-anthropocentric cosmopolitics that extends our understanding of the co-constitution of humans and the world by recognising the effects of all creatures on the habitats we all co-habit.[10] And so, besides resistances to change that are ingrained in the economic relations of power and in habits of thought, the indeterminacies and messiness relating to the complexity of the processes involved in the convergence of crises mitigate against radical interventions and provide an opportunistic excuse for maintaining the status quo. The result is the piecemeal approach to the problems of systemic crisis that turn out to be counter-productive because of unintended consequences, for example, the development of biofuels for energy generation that uses up land needed for crops (Le Page, 2015a: 11), or the case of GMO crops produced by agribusiness that damage habitats and biomes due to the systemic use of pesticides and insecticides, and that adversely affect biodiversity, as the analysis in Isabelle Stengers shows (2009: 50ff). Not surprisingly, these risky experiments are generally tried out first in the 'postcolony' and weak states and are driven by corporations whose primary goal is the protection and pursuit of their own interests rather than those of ordinary farmers and consumers, for example, preventing farmers from re-using seeds from their GM crops.

Elements for a postcapitalist agenda

Yet many studies, even from the point of view of a possible reform of capitalism, have started to demonstrate the intimate connections binding the range of systems noted above into a complex whole. They thus make visible the apparatuses and relays that pragmatically and efficatiously join together the parts. Increasingly, such studies identify neoliberal capitalism as the source of developments that have in recent decades aggravated the intrinsic fragility of things. A notable example is that of Donovan and Hudson whose influential heterodox analysis, *From Red to Green?* (2011) emphasises the 'symbiotic relationship' binding resource depletion, ecosystem damage, and the financial market. They conclude from this basis that the ransacking of global resources to support the financial sector is producing what they describe as an environmental 'credit crunch' that will be as destructive as the economic one.

Donovan and Hudson's prognostic is echoed by Amy Larkin in *Environment Debt* (2013) where she argues that capitalism's free-loading on natural resources, whilst passing the costs onto the public in the form of 'externalities', is creating a mounting environmental crisis that will bankrupt existing economic systems. Earlier, but in the same vein, Tim Jackson (2009) in *Prosperity without Growth* had attributed the underlying cause of growing scarcity, ecological degradation, and increasing levels of inequality to the model of ceaseless economic growth and its mistaken association with greater prosperity. A radical ecological and wider standpoint is developed by Isabelle Stengers in *Au temps des catastrophes* (2009: 9–15) to make similar points about the irresponsibility of the growth imperative 'identified with progress' and driven by a particular view of 'development' as the 'arrow of time', a perspective which is pushing the world towards barbarity (2009: 17). The effects of the imperative of competition and accumulation on the drive for growth, and the consequences for pauperisation, climate change and resource depletion, are an important dimension of those prognoses that I will discuss in Chapters 1 and 2.

What is interesting about these analyses from a variety of disciplines is not just the now ubiquitous indictment of rapacious capitalism, but the vocabulary signalling a standpoint that radically decentres and relocates the human with respect to the world, informed by concepts such as symbiosis, reciprocity, contingency, compossibility, commonalities, and generally, a sense of 'continuities between humans and non-humans' in the form of 'associated bodies' (Naess, 1993; Venn, 2010; Descola, 2011: 82). Such a vocabulary rhymes with the concept of life which is founded on the ontology that understands being to be essentially being-with and being-more-than-one. This standpoint opens towards different and postcapitalist foundations for principles of social justice and ethical conduct, allied to a politics of the common which the obstacles I have summarised prevent from emerging (established in Chapters 5 and 6 that elaborate my earlier analyses in Venn, 2010, 2014). A fundamentally different basis for approaching what is at stake in the convergence of crises is implicated in this shift.

It follows from the arguments I have been outlining that the issue of finding long-term solutions must pass through the critique of the discourses and the relations of force which have authorised the practices, the beliefs and values, the laws and institutions, which over the course of the 'long twentieth century' (Arrighi, 1994) have naturalised capitalism and the mythical 'free market' economy as the most efficient, rational and sensible system for the allocation, distribution, development and evaluation of human, technical and natural resources (on the free market as myth, see Chang, Thing 1 in *23 Things They Don't Tell You About Capitalism*, 2010). Indeed, the mechanisms put in place within a neoliberal framework to escalate the unequal distribution of wealth and resources nationally and globally – through what could be called the Great Disinheritance – have now become hard-wired into technical, legal, economic, political, military, geo-politico-economic and discursive dispositifs that, through their aggregate effects nationally and globally, have secured the autonomisation of the process of accumulation. This mobile assemblage functions as scaffolding upholding the current varieties of capitalisms, including sometimes uneven combinations of neo-feudal, dynastic, 'traditionalist' and 'modern' social orders: capitalism is nothing if not pragmatically versatile with respect to relations of power.

So, how do we challenge or break with existing relations of power and forms of life that have become dominant or 'hegemonic', that is, taken for granted because their contingent and constructed character has become invisible, thus making them function as common sense in everyday discourse?

We could start by recognising that the authority of this dominant social order and the regime of truth that underwrites it derive not only from the institutional, discursive and subjective supports put in place within the framework shaped by neoliberal thought: it is the result of the sustained effort by think-tanks and pressure groups such as the Mont Pelerin Society, the Heritage Foundation, the American Legislative Exchange Council, the Adam Smith Institute, the Ayn Rand Institute, and many others whose prime objectives have been to disseminate neoliberal and neo-classical political economy and their regime of truth in 'mainstream' economic teaching and across policy-making bodies in governments worldwide. Opposing its doctrine requires a gestalt switch.

The implication for critique is the formulations of a new conceptual framework that starts by establishing why the co-constitutive, co-dependent, symbiotic, complex and fragile character of all living things should be the foundation for grounding more equitable ways of life consistent with the limits that the planet imposes, and with an ethics that could provide common ground for a postcapitalist world, key elements of which are trailed in Jeremy Gilbert's *Common Ground* (2014), Dardot and Laval's *Commun* (2014), and Venn (2010). The issues are fundamental and go to the heart of what is at stake in postcapitalist alternatives. The approach I shall develop foregrounds the view that organisms and entities form complex interactive and inter-dependent ecosystems that reach provisional and fragile states of stability, depending on the particular composition of their conditions of possibility; in other words, they are metastable. It is in the light of this perspective that I have argued that a postcapitalist project must involve a radical reconstitution not only of economies, socialities and technologies, but equally of the subjectivities that now are imbricated in ways of being and their material, institutional and discursive supports, including attitudes to the earth and to non-human animals, that tie humans in social relations that close off post-anthropocentric and post-solipsistic alternatives. The question of subjective change is perhaps the most intractable and intransigent of the problems because of the investments people make in the familiar and the habitual, in what appears safe, or in divisive identity politics. So, adding to the task of critique, one needs to recognise the long and difficult process of technical and subjective reconstitution, difficult because it will take generations and requires that we question so much of what we have come to take for granted as 'natural', inevitable, efficient, 'modern', 'progressive', desirable, or right.

However, incipient aspects of alternative ontologies that support more convivial relationships concerning humans and the living world generally already exist amongst a number of indigenous people in many parts of the world. Though they have their limitations from the point of view of a new politics of commons, they point to the longevity of counter-hegemonic values and they signal attitudes to the earth that extend the scope of conviviality. Of course such indigenous communities are ever under threat from agribusiness, big landowners, the extractive industries, and technologies that favour accumulation. Nevertheless resistance to the forces of capital have led to initiatives promoted by movements such as the Landless Workers Movement (MST from 1984) in Brazil (now with over a million members), the Landless Peoples' Movement in South Africa and elsewhere from 2001, the Via Campesina Movement from 1993, now spreading across continents, that seek land reform and sustainable agriculture which could at least in principle be harnessed within a broad postcapitalist standpoint. Issues of land ownership, co-operative production and a decolonial politics deriving from a different perspective of the human/nature relationship, for example in the analyses of Walter Mignolo (2011), Philippe Descola, and others, are foremost in such contestations. Clearly, a postcapitalist politics of commons involves much more, as I show in Chapters 5 and 6.

The problems noted above prompt us to establish a new political and economic agenda around basic questions such as: Who owns, and who should own, the earth? What could replace existing regimes of property? How would one reconstitute or reappropriate commons and extend commons and 'common pool resources' (CPRs, investigated in Elinor Ostrom's work, *Governing the Commons*, 1990); how should the commoners organise their management at the different scales of the local, the national and the transnational? It is worth noting here that, besides Ostrom's critique of Garrett Hardin's 'Tragedy of the commons' (1968), the research on CPRs that she describes and synthesises covers thousands of cases, thus showing that collective forms of owning, maintaining and collaboratively managing the large varieties of commons studied already thrive in many parts of the world, though they mostly do not threaten capitalism and are largely ignored in mainstream/orthodox economic analyses. Notable examples include Denmark where 'three quarters of wind turbines are co-owned by local communities' (Lawrence, 2017: 32). Lawrence notes also that in Germany some local municipalities are buying back their local grids, so that these local communities now own and profit from the renewable energy infrastructure. These thriving commons point to the potentialities for similar developments across the world.

Examples of other initiatives within the scope of enlarging commonly held resources include the idea of a Library of Things, such as those in Toronto, Sacramento and in London; they can be expanded to include other necessities that can be shared. Another initiative that resonates with ideas of creative commons and CPRs is the case of the Viome factory in Greece where a group of workers took over a production plant whose parent company had gone bankrupt in the wake of the economic crisis in Greece and decided to relaunch production but within a non-hierarchical organisational structure of decision-making and work practices. They have organised themselves as a democratic collective, and have operated successfully with support from the local community (Chakrabortty, 2017: 29). One could note also that remnants of post-Enclosures commons have survived even in Europe, for example, in the Fells of the Lake District in England which James Rebanks (2015) describes in his enlightening account of shepherds' work and lives there. The existence of such commons recalls the open field system of cultivation that had existed in England for centuries before Norman dispossession and the Enclosures. What is striking about this and many other cases, for instance involving indigenous practices, is the implicit or tacit ecological understanding of the fragile and mobile relationship between habitats, farming and human lives which the collectives or commoners share, and that is enacted in their evolving collaborative practice as they adapt to new conditions and knowledges.

Of course, in many places collectively owned resources are increasingly under threat because of misappropriations by corporations and kleptocracies – a neo-colonial manoeuvre clearly evident in new forms of enclosure spreading across Africa and South America, often accompanied by campaigns of intimidation and terror (see for instance Elden's analysis of territory and terror, 2007 and also Gilbert's analysis of commons and appropriation, 2014: 164, 165; and Dardot and Laval's *Commun*, 2014, which have affinities with the perspective I develop in Chapter 6). These acts of dispossession are underwritten by technocratic epistemologies that serve exploitation, and regimes of truth that deride or commandeer indigenous and customary knowledges through biopiracy (Shiva, 2002, and what Mignolo, 2011, calls 'epistemicide').

Clearly, the answers to the questions I am posing are eminently practical, though guided by the kind of fundamental principles I have sketched. The reason is that, on the one hand, the problems which now confront us regarding the growing chasm between the superrich and the rest as well as impending scarcities of land, water, minerals, spaces for living, and so on, arising from the effects of global financial capitalism, climate change, global warming and the exhaustion of essential resources are unprecedented and require unprecedented responses. Thus we should be inventing new methods for producing food and the necessities of life, for instance, by deploying energy technologies based on ambient energy sources (examined in Chapter 6 by reference to the future as ambient). Equally, we would need to draw from new knowledges about materials, biological activity, ecologies, bodies and so on in order to invent renewable means and conditions of existence. An implication is likely to be the emergence of new ways of living in relatively self-sufficient commons, but as part of networked and collaborative polities functioning within wider webs of support activities and services. The fact is that the probable breakdown of existing political systems when the tipping points are reached by mid-century will require creative approaches to regulatory systems, at both the local and the global levels, that, optimistically, would be experimental, self-reliant, democratic, inclusive and flexible within the context of a politics of commons and the guardianship of the earth. The alternative, as many fear, is a descent into barbarity.

On the other hand, collaboration amongst diverse communities and polities, both local and transnational, would be fraught with obstacles without a broad agreement on a number of fundamental principles that could operate as the framework for what one could call the regulative idea of a cosmopolitical commonality, that is, an idea of the common that refuses zero-sum economies as well as the exclusions and inequalities legitimated on the basis of differences of one kind or another (Derrida, 1997a; Venn, 2002, 2006a: 161–171, and 2014; also Latour, 2005). None of this would be possible without all of the world's accumulated stock of knowledge and know-how being considered as part of a common inheritance, since most knowledges are collaboratively produced (Strathern, 2004) or depend on disciplinary fields established through the effort of countless contributors over time.[11] Deployed in education and training, this common stock would be essential for equipping a people for the processes of adaptation, adoption, invention, research, sharing and protection of the world's living and non-living resources that will be necessary for survival in hostile conditions.

In view of these points, other questions appear, such as: What accounting practice and system of valuation can one invent to take proper account of common resources and the value of socio-cultural and environmental goods now mismeasured according to capitalist accounting practices and normally bracketed as so-called 'externalities' by firms – the critical accounting perspectives developed by authors such as Miranda Joseph (2014) are examined in the next chapter. What is to happen to the state, or how are common interests to be reorganised and secured in new forms of democratic institutions? And, given the global character of the crises, what transnational agreements, regulatory systems, institutions and principles can be put into place to secure effective action? What are the implications for forms of governance grounded on the absolute guarantee of liberty, positive freedoms and respect for all creatures? What technologies and their management are appropriate for new ways of life that manage existence within the limits of the planet and with regard to the ecological entanglement and plasticity of all living things? What are the implications of a post-anthropocentric ontology? And, the question underlying all the other questions: what does it means to 'live well with and for others in just institutions' (Ricoeur, 1992: 351).[12] Finally, what system of values and what ways of life allow for the incalculable, i.e. the affective, spiritual or noological, and aesthetic dimensions of existence that make life worth living?

The analysis in the book will show that what is at stake is not only opposed visions of a just society, but quite incommensurable understandings of what it means to be human at all, implying a struggle over conflicting perceptions of what is possible and what is equitable, thus a struggle over disjunct political philosophies and imaginaries. Equally, it is a struggle about defending hard-won political spaces and protecting socio-cultural common wealth such as free public libraries and spaces, as well as about opening up new spaces for inventing ways of being which have not and, indeed, could not have existed before, since the technical, environmental and cultural conditions of possibility for such a future were absent.

But before the more philosophical issues can be addressed, the chapters that follow will examine in greater detail the nature of the problems trailed in this Introduction and establish the grounds for decoupling ideas of well-being, prosperity and the just society from capitalism and its logic of growth, as well as from other exploitative and unethical forms of society. A longer historical, or *longue durée*, approach, will be deployed to reveal the role played by liberal political economy, biopolitical governmentality, colonialism, historically specific property regimes, and an economistic environmental politics in the formation of the ensemble of apparatuses whereby political, economic and psychological strategies and forces have managed to maintain existing relations of power, secure a hold on the minds and purses of the majority of people, and provoke the crises we are addressing. Equally, the task involves the problematisation or recuperation of a whole range of concepts such as those of liberty, freedom, fundamental rights, value, ownership, democracy, the social bond and 'sustainability' that had historically served dissident struggles as part of radical democratic agendas but that today, in their corrupted or in their mediatised forms, are often mobilised to prop up capital.

Outline of chapters

In the Introduction, I have tried to show that the current conjuncture of crises linking the economy to environmental damage, climate change, resource depletion, and rising destitution across continents is the culmination of a long history of dispossession and exploitation against a background of struggles for equality, liberty and social justice. The dynamics at play have now brought the world to a point of unpredictable transition in which democratic institutions and values are the stakes. An argument outlined here and developed throughout the book points to the worsening of stressors brought about by the ascendency of neoliberalism and its prioritisation of corporate interests and private accumulation at the expense of the common good. Related to this, I noted that finance capitalism, supported by cybernetic technologies, has been central to the developments that have accelerated the ravages of the planet and deepened the unequal relations of power between capital and labour worldwide. A longer history of capitalism is signalled to highlight the model of unending growth as a crucial element installed at the heart of the linkages. The key role which colonialism and its contemporary legacies have played in sustaining both capitalism and liberal governmentality from the time of the industrial revolution is underlined; today, new mechanisms of dispossession reiterate this process of wealth transfer from the poor and the subjugated to a rich elite globally and locally. I have suggested that the most likely scenario for a liveable future is that of a politics of commons or the common that radically challenges existing zero-sum economies and existing property regimes and forms of governance, and that dethrones the anthropocentric and phallogo-ethnocentric privileges that are complicit with existing systems of oppression. The implications of this narrative are elaborated in the chapters that follow; this includes in the final, more theoretical, chapter the alternative ontological, epistemological and ethical standpoints that could serve as the basis for the transformations that would inform ways of life that respect the limits of the planet and relocate the place of the human in the scheme of things.

Chapter 1 – New Mechanisms of Dispossession: Property, Inequality and the Debt Society – starts by examining the changes in the global economy which underlie the 2008 crash in order to point to the systematic and complex character of the stressors leading up to it. It identifies capitalism in terms of its distinct property regime according to which everything can be commodified, a process whose dominant aim is the private accumulation of wealth. It shows how recent shifts in the relationship between the state and capital, correlated to shifts in the relation of power and wealth between owners and non-owners of capital, private interest and general or common interests and goods, have hardened the domination of capital. It establishes that the key mechanism inscribing these shifts is the emergence of a debt society nourished by rent-seeking devices, and characterised by a recomposition of the relation between finance, debt and capital assets, facilitated by information technologies. The debt economy, through its informationalisation and circulation in financial circuits of capital, alongside fiscal and monetary policies, has the effect of autonomising the transfer of wealth from the majority of people to a rich minority. This point is further elaborated by making visible the decisive mutations in apparatuses or dispositifs of dispossession whereby forms of general equivalence founded on information, money and the market have intensified the process of appropriation through the distortion of value introduced by derivatives, and through the emergence of a debt society. It highlights the role of the state in facilitating this process, and thus points to the extent to which the interests of capital have become so commanding that they now determine policy across all sectors of society.

An important aspect of the analytical apparatus is the argument that the consolidation of neoliberalism as the political arm of financial and corporate capitalism has been legitimated through a neo-biopolitical governmentality that institutes a realignment of the population into the us/them, friend/enemy divide underlying the pathologisation of the 'losers' and the militarisation of society; such a shift undermines the idea of the common good. The chapter points to the claim, developed across several chapters, that the elimination of the ethical basis of 'good government' in favour of a utilitarian and amoral management of population and resources to suit the interests of transnational corporations and geopolitical forces has fundamentally eroded the basis of democratic polities.

Chapter 2 – In the Shadow of Tipping Points: The Political Economy of Climate Change – summarises key evidence showing the anthropogenic character of global warming and climate change. It reviews ongoing plans by the extractive industries that are bound to accelerate the destruction of habitats, increase pollution and lead to further geophysical transformations worldwide, accompanied by species extinction, land grabs and conflicts, most visibly in Africa, South America and parts of Asia. These developments illustrate the essential connection binding capitalism, neoliberal political economy, climate change and the model of ceaseless growth; they have contributed to the intensification in the convergent crises the book examines.

Chapter 3 – Colonialism, Dispossession and Capitalist Accumulation: A Decolonial History of the Present – begins with an overview of the present state of the world in terms of the features that underlie both the confluence of crises and the inability or reluctance of governments to take effective action to implement the changes necessary to tackle the problems. It argues for a longer genealogy of capitalism in order to uncover the less visible and often neglected processes that have been instrumental in producing the current state of affairs. The vital role which colonialism and its contemporary legacies have played in sustaining both capitalism and liberal and now post-liberal governmentalities from the time of the industrial revolution is underlined. Today, the strategies of dispossession operate through different agencies and instruments to reconstitute the process of the expropriation and uphold global inequalities of wealth and power. Foucault's concept of 'the discourse of race war' is deployed to analyse the discourses that have historically legitimated subjugation and dispossession and the violences intrinsic to them.

A key argument is that such discourses are inscribed in liberal and neoliberal political economy and philosophy and have served to underpin (varieties of) capitalism and their respective governmentalities. The historical analysis goes on to show that the us/them divide underlying forms of subjugation is ingrained in the biopolitics of population which these governmentalities institute in the form of imperial governance or coloniality of power. An important inference is that coloniality as the model of the oppressive form of power that enables exploitation and servitude is the exemplary embodiment of this divide. The chapter makes the case that the neoliberal prioritisation of generalised competition as a ruling idea promotes this form of power and thus universalises the militaristic logic that today shapes geopolitico-economic relations; this logic of power thus reiterates and generalises colonial relations of domination.

Chapter 4 – From Liberalism to Neoliberalism: A Dissident Genealogy – develops an account that brings to light the differences in value inscribed in social and economic policy that divided 'radical' liberal reformers in the 19th century from utilitarian liberals in terms of a moral economy that sought a balance between private interests and the general interest or common good, and in terms of the essential role of the state in ensuring this balance. The analysis of the post-Enlightenment and emancipatory ambition that motivated the enduring conflicts encompassing class, gender and race struggles helps to pinpoint what was at stake politically and ethically, and what neoliberalism breaks with by reference to a politics of the present and with regard to its abnegation of responsibility for the vulnerable. This is elaborated in the section, 'From Adam Smith to Milton Friedman: Alas poor Beveridge'.

Chapter 5 – Towards a World in Common – proposes the idea of enlarged or postcapitalist commons as counter to capitalism and its property regime and system of values. In the period of liberal governmentality, the state undertook to construct and reorganise 'infrastructures' as a central component of the strategy for improving the productivity of resources, including labour. The resultant public works encompassed social and environmental policies, affecting health, hygiene, reproduction, education, training, urban redevelopment, transport, land management, public amenities and services. Though primarily intended to benefit business interests and meet reason of state, such public works and amenities were the aggregate product of a whole community's labour, paid for by means of general taxation, and should be regarded as forms of common pool resources, enhancing the capabilities of the people as a whole and conditioning the wellbeing of all. Their status as common wealth, that is, as collectively held goods and resources, should grant them the quality of an inalienable inheritance. Their increasing privatisation in neoliberal times is thus a process of disinheritance that impoverishes everyone.

Chapter 6 – New Foundations for Postcapitalist Worlds – addresses the philosophical and theoretical issues concerning the foundations which could inform postcapitalist societies. It presents perspectives which support a post-anthropocentric ontology by reframing the relationship of self/other, the human and the world, and mind/body/world, in terms of the essential co-implication and co-constitution of all forms of life in sustaining existence in common. This ontology asserts the idea of being as fundamentally being-with and as relational; it thus prioritises a position that decentres the human in relation to non-human beings and world. It is argued that such a standpoint is consistent with an ethics that recomposes ideas of solidarity and conviviality to include all creatures. The chapter draws out the implications for an epistemology that rejects the claim of the autonomous unitary subject as the privileged and rational agent of history and knowledge. It displaces the question of agency onto the terrain of an ethics of responsibility for the other that foregrounds the problem of answerability with respect to individual action, or the 'who' of action. This standpoint avoids the pitfalls of a 'flat ontology' and the confusions associated with the 'posthuman'. The chapter underlines the argument that responsibility is beholden to a history of responsibility, a view that implicates an apprenticeship in learning to live in convivial ways of being. Together these arguments support postcapitalist economies and socialities based on commons and ecologically grounded technologies within the scope of the collective and democratic management of the planet's resources. The book is thus located in the conceptual space of a 'to come' that holds out the hope of avoiding the coming of despotisms and inhuman socialities and that promotes the possibility of ways of life that enable one to live well with and for others in just societies.

Notes

1 For example, the many radical websites such as Antipode, Soundings, the Canary, openDemocracy, and many more, and examined in a growing archive of new forms of resistance, for example, in Graeber (2011); Conio (2015); Hessel (2010); Mason (2012).

2 Indicatively, Stengers, 2009; Tett, 2010; Roubini and Mihm, 2010; Stiglitz, 2010 and 2013; Curtis, 2013; Dardot and Laval, 2014; Atkinson, 2015.
3 'Upfront' in *New Scientist*, 3045, 31 October 2015.
4 Report of a study at Stanford, Princeton and Berkeley, June 2015; see also Stengers, 2009; Colebrook, 2014; Kolbert, 2014; Moore, 2015.
5 The USA has been at the forefront of this reconstitution of capital, as Panitch and Gindin (2013) have shown.
6 Or, more likely, according to a fractal web of nested small-world networks, i.e., a galaxy.
7 The emergence of a 'super entity' of global corporations, though subject to complex and uneven dynamics, and the dominance of informationalised financial capitalism which allows global capital to circulate more freely and faster explain why notions of so-called 'free trade' and the 'free market' are no longer operative for capitalism; they were never 'free' anyway (Polanyi, 2001 [1944]) though they remain useful in political rhetoric. Competition too needs to be similarly rethought in terms of discourses that cover over the actual machinery of capital accumulation, as I examine in Chapter 1.
8 For example, apart from IPCC Reports, the Brundtland Commission 1987, regarding climate change, and Wilkinson and Pickett (2009, 2010) regarding the effects of poverty and inequality.
9 Metastability is understood as a property of complex systems characterised by the fact that their point of equilibrium is altered whenever any element of the complex whole is changed or a new organism inserted into it. See also the work of Bateson (1980), Simondon (2005), Stiegler (2007), and others which I discussed in Venn (2010).
10 See, for example, Latour (2003); Stengers (2009); Haraway (2016), and the 'deep ecology' perspective.
11 The problems of the 'ownership' of knowledge, whether generated by research and development or inscribed in indigenous knowledges are dealt with in Chapters 5 and 6 where the notion of commons that I develop goes beyond the limitations of the concept of 'general intellect' tied to production (Marx, Grundisse) or the idea of 'cognitive capitalism' (Hardt and Negri, 2011) which neglects craft and tacit knowledges of all kinds, and knowledge of how to live embedded in a culture.
12 From a different point of view, this question invokes principles and a politics committed to keeping clear and wide the margin between the human and the inhuman, particularly since the latter is immanent in the former, as Lyotard claims in *The Inhuman* (1993), but it's a margin that's eroded in times of social turbulence.

1
New Mechanisms of Dispossession: Property, Inequality and the Debt Society

Financialisation, neoliberal capitalism and the new regime of accumulation

This section will make visible the dynamics that connect the commodification of debt, the reconstitution of the state according to the model of the enterprise and its accounting practice to better serve the interests of capital, and financialisation as the nexus linking the different components of the new economy. It develops a longer historical approach to argue that, with the new system of value grounded in the commodification in principle of everything from land to debt, knowledge and life, a new modality of capitalism is emerging. This new composition of capital is authorised by neoliberal discourse functioning as a diffused political philosophy and political economy that provides it with a vocabulary of justification and the values and rationality that can be strategically and pragmatically deployed in its support. I shall be arguing that this phase in the evolution of capitalism as a zero-sum game has intensified and institutionalised the turbulent pressures driving the various crises identified in the Introduction. It will become clear too that the genealogy of accumulation and growth is in correlation with a genealogy of exploitation and resource use secured by harnessing technological advances in the service of capital.

To chart the changes, let us start with the now familiar analysis of Marazzi who in *The Violence of Financial Capitalism* underlines the fact that the incentive for the changes was coming from the search for profit maximisation, arguing that the latter, through 'financial engineering' (2010: 44), had resulted in the 'reduction in the cost of labor, attacks on syndicates, autonomization and robotization of entire labour processes, delocalization in countries with low wages, precarization of work, and diversification of consumption models. And precisely financialization' (2010: 31).

It is a view which finds support in Roubini and Mihm's account in the wake of the 2008 crash when they explained how,

> decades of 'market fundamentalism' laid the foundation for the meltdown, as so-called reformers swept aside banking regulations established in the Great Depression, and as Wall Street firms found ways to evade the rules that remained ... (B)anks increasingly adopted compensation schemes like bonuses that encouraged high-risk, short-term leveraged betting ... They effectively

shifted negative consequences away from traders and bankers ... (they were) part of a larger epidemic of moral hazard. (Roubini and Mihm, 2010: 268)

They pick out the key role of 'shadow banking' in the making of the crisis: 'These "banks" were also nonbank mortgage lenders, conduits, structured investment vehicles, monoline insurers, money market funds, hedge funds, investment banks and other entities' (2010: 34), often operating outside regulatory protocols. They make the point that speculative borrowing and lending inside the shadow banking system leading up to the crash was boosted by the Commodity Futures Modernisation Act in the USA in 2000 that 'declared huge swathes of the derivatives market off-limits to regulation' (2010: 75). For example, one of the instruments being deregulated and placed off-balance sheet was credit default swaps (CDSs) that, once 'liberated', reached 'a notional value of $60 trillion by 2008' (ibid.).

From an historical point of view, it is instructive to recall Karl Polanyi's observation that financial innovations have been a central component in every crisis which has beset Europe for centuries (Polanyi, 2001 [1944]). This is underlined in Roubini and Mihm's analysis when they point to the many other examples and the similarities between them, for example, the fact that most 'begin with a bubble ... (which) often goes hand in hand with the excessive accumulation of debt, as investors borrow money to buy into the boom ... asset bubbles are often associated with excessive growth in the supply of credit' (Roubini and Mihm, 2010: 17ff.). They note in that respect the 'tulip mania' of 1630, the John Law Mississippi Company in 1719, the South Sea Company bubble of 1720, and global crashes such as in 1825, which led to the new Poor Law Acts of 1834 and the workhouse in England (Ashurst, 2010), the 'global meltdown' of 1873 and the Great Crash of 1929. It could incidentally be argued that the austerity programmes adopted by many countries to address the current crisis may well lead to new outsourced forms of workhouse. Although major technological innovations such as that of the railroads or the creation of the Internet are sometimes important factors too, as they point out, the 'most destructive booms-turn-bust have gone hand in hand with financial innovations' (2010: 8).

As we know, the institutions and measures put into place after the great depression – notably the Bretton Woods institutions (World Bank and IMF), central banks acting as lender of last resort, the Basel Capital Accord stipulating the ratio of capital to assets for banks, etc. – were supposed to help regulate markets to prevent such crashes and mitigate the effects of minor contractions in the world market. But, as Roubini and Mihm stress, 'market fundamentalism' dictated a phase of deregulation, whilst 'new structures of incentives and compensation ... channelled greed in new and dangerous directions' (Roubini and Mihm, 2010: 32). The crucial element to add to the brew is debt-financed consumption which not only 'fuelled economic growth' (2010: 18) but also fed into the vicious cycle of borrowing and spending by the population at large, creating 'irrational euphoria' oblivious of the risks (2010: 14). The exemplar of this irresponsibility is the case of loans given to NINJAs (borrowers with no income, no jobs, no assets) that were sanitised and leveraged by financial institutions, and contributed to the mountain of unsecured loans leading up to the crash.

Amongst other familiar features of the new apparatus of financial capitalism one finds the following: financial instruments such as derivatives and the futures market, much of it now automated through algorithmic and high frequency trading of securities (HFT, algo trading), facilitated by new electronic and cybernetic technologies (with a helping hand from the USA which legislated to protect traders in derivatives from oversight, as I just noted), hedge funds and private equity acquisitions that harvest or asset-strip the profitable parts of companies and load debts on them. One should signal also the activities of 'vulture' funds, i.e., a more rapacious or parasitic species of hedge funds that buys up debts, including sovereign debts in poor countries, to extract crippling repayments. Generally, these financial instruments involve the leveraging of assets, often insecure, often in the form of 'real estate', and credit or debt facilitated by the new techniques of informationalisation and the mathematics of chaos and probabilities that became part of the securitisation game (Roubini and Mihm, 2010: 33). As I argue later on, derivatives operate as the mechanism whereby the modes of general equivalence instituted in terms of money, information and the market are exemplarily co-articulated. One should foreground also the technological dimension of these economic transactions, since the technical supports of financial systems tend to be neglected although they should play an important part in the analysis of these systems and crises, for example, with regard to cybernetic technology today or relating to the role of the ticker tape and telegraphic communication in the 1929 crash. All these systems and apparatuses or dispositifs are the gears of the accumulative machine, operating through forms of rent-seeking devices for the creation and harvesting of 'surplus'.

The history of their recent emergence goes back to 1970 in response to 'the crisis of capital accumulation', as Harvey (2005: 14ff.; 2010) has shown by reference to diminishing returns on capital. The new techniques and practices introduced as part of financial capitalism can thus be viewed as a response to this situation. Indeed, as Michael Lewis reveals in *The Big Short* (2010), the invention of instruments like the derivatives that drive transactions in the financial market was planned and organised from the 1990s precisely with profit maximisation as the overriding concern. The vehicles for this were the complicated schemes for packaging financial products or 'synthetics' based on debt. Similarly, Gillian Tett in *Fool's Gold* (2009) and *The Silo Effect* (2015) points out that the arcane technical character of synthetics were well beyond the grasp of leading bankers who inhabited the 'silo' created by the new financial paradigm dominating markets; they were of course happy to collect on the fortunes that were generated without heed of the consequences.

New Mechanisms of Dispossession

A revealing example of the kind of complexity at the heart of financialisation is the extent to which the mathematics of complexity, chaos and probability is being used by quantity analysts or 'quants' to produce new financial models and trading algorithms that are able to explain patterns, instabilities and performance relating to markets more accurately than according to the still dominant equilibrium theory and Chicago School economics. For example, Mark Buchanan (2014) draws a parallel between financial models and the meteorological models developed to address extreme weather, as well as those used in physics relating to processes endowed with feed-back, to claim that the current assumptions underlying mainstream economic theory are founded on delusions. Equally, Weatherall (2013) has argued that the application of the mathematics of complexity is effective in dealing with probability calculations on the financial market because they follow power–law distributions similar to those applying to systems like the weather. He too points out that this approach is completely different from the equilibrium model which financial institutions like the European Central Bank still rely upon and that upholds austerity programmes (see also the demolition of this model by Blyth, 2013; Stiglitz, 2013; Klein, 2014; Krugman, 2015, and many others). And in *An Engine, Not a Camera: How Financial Models Shape Markets*, Donald MacKenzie (2006) makes the important point that the new mathematical models do not simply describe or reflect an independently existing economic state of affairs but instead make possible the proliferation of practices like derivatives.

A fascinating illustration of these new mechanisms and their inherent risks concerns the use of the Black-Scholes equation in finance 'to value European options, that is, the right to buy or sell an asset at a specified time in the future. Remarkably, it is identical to the equation in physics that determines how pollen grains diffuse through water' (Forshaw, 2013: 22). The equation, refined by Scholes and Merton (who received the Nobel Prize for their work in 1997), prompted them to set up a hedge fund in 1994 to trade in derivatives; it made billions but crashed in 1998 with $4.6 billion debt which required a bailout to protect the financial system from the fall-out (Luyendijk, 2015). Yet, the use of these new instruments became ubiquitous; and we know the disastrous consequences (see, for example, Mackenzie and Vurdubakis' 2011 analysis of problems with coding in financial operations). The point is that Black-Scholes and similar models for options pricing used in risk management are subject, like all dynamic systems characterised by complexity, to initial conditions or initial state of the system, and to metastability – what economists call volatility. In the case of economic activity, these conditions include human inputs, which are variable and capricious, and framed by politics, for example, assessments of geo-economico-political situations affecting markets (Knorr-Cetina and Bruegger, 2002), and fiscal and monetary policies such as austerity, etc. The problem is that whilst the link between the models and economic activity is subject to feed-back loops and unpredictability, a disconnect exists between the reality of the systems experiencing points of crisis and the simplistic models, the dogmatism, or the cynical opportunism determining policy framed by bankrupt economic theories and political agendas.

An important aspect of the new financial system is that the invention and trading of derivatives – collateralised debt obligations (CDOs), credit default swaps (CDSs), collateralised loan obligations (CLOs) and the like – on the world financial markets not only generates value well in excess of the value of the original assets, but also its predominance in the circulation of capital deepens uncertainties in the system and distorts the whole question of value. Today, in their autonomised form, notably through 'algo trading', these 'products' of what Marazzi calls 'financial engineering' not only operate as virtual stocks that in turn autonomise the creation of value, they also introduce new systemic risks. The latter are unavoidable anyway since the probabilistic functions embedded in the algorithms include both 'benign' as well as 'savage' or 'wild' chance or risk, as Benoit Mandelbrot has explained in *Fractales, hasard et finance* (1997: 58–65); these embedded risks result in the likelihood of a 'flash crash', for instance, the major crash of 6 May 2010 and the lesser one of 8 July 2015. Nowadays algorithmic technology increasingly by-passes human traders by selecting the best combination of stock to invest in by holders of capital, doing so via software that searches through the market index to pick the best combination at any given time (Adee, 2017: 22). One analyst has put the value derived over the last three years from these 'passive funds' at about $1.3 trillion whilst managed funds lost $250 billion (ibid.).

The distortion of value is all the more disturbing in light of the fact that the value of derivatives-related trading is several times the value of world GDP, as Lee and LiPuma (2002), Arnoldi (2004), Venn (2006a and 2006b), and others have underlined. Many recent estimates put the ratio at about 10 to 1; for instance, the Bank of International Settlements reckons the value of derivatives to have been $691 trillion at the end of 2014, whilst GDP for 2014 was $78 trillion (World Bank, 2014). This ratio by comparison makes the sphere of production far less significant in generating profits for holders of capital – yet this asymmetry forces sectors of production to reduce costs and increase 'productivity' to compete with or feed into the financial sector because of their sensitivity to their share value on the stock markets. It has been argued that the reliance of value-creation on informational technologies announces the emergence of cybernetic capitalism (Robins and Webster, 1988), but my concern is about the processes whereby such knowledges are recruited or produced in the service of capital. For sure, power/knowledge dynamics are involved, but also a whole history of property regimes, as well as a history of what Foucault called 'technologies of the social', thus relating to subject formation, and a history of subjugation to add to the mix alongside the forms of resistance that constantly intervene to alter the dynamics and nourish the hope of an emancipation.

One needs to add the following for a fuller picture of financialisation as the new process creating value for capital: the privatisation of social services and their downgrading to minimise costs; the externalisation of the cost of administration onto the (online) purchaser or client; the harvesting of 'free labour' by means such as using ever more powerful techniques for extracting information from 'big data' collected from consumers' internet purchasing activity and from crowdsourcing and the monetisation of social media. Another important component to foreground is the invention of managerial compensation schemes dreamt up to incentivise managers by inflating rewards for top executives and thereby bind them to the principle of 'shareholder value maximisation'. Elements of this strategy were developed specifically to align the interests of executives with the drive for growth to feed the imperative of profit maximisation, as Chang has explained (2010: 17). The flip side of this stratagem is the reduction in the cost of labour, including through setting targets and expectations that can only be met by capturing the unpaid labour time extracted from employees, particularly in the so-called 'knowledge economy' via informational technologies that electronically impound employees' 'free time'. And of course, financial capitalism operates in an environment of sophisticated transnational systems and schemes that institute strategies of pricing, ownership and investments to enable corporations and holders of capital to avoid, or at least minimise, tax payments and social responsibility (Roubini and Mihm, 2010; Shaxson, 2012; Stiglitz, 2013, and many others). It is important also to keep in view the colonial establishment of many of these mechanisms and rules of the game; this includes the support of compliant power elites (the kleptocracies) helping corporations and sovereign funds in their search for safe havens for routing transactions in order to by-pass regulatory and taxation regimes. Equally, financial capitalism has encouraged the interpenetration of licit and illicit economic transactions to the benefit of mafia capitalism. As I go on to show, these are all part of the network of instruments that together establish the parameters of the debt society.

It has become clear that these new practices driving capitalism, including the principle of 'shareholder value maximisation' fixated on short-term cycles dominated by profit maximisation, have transformed the relation between capital and labour (Glyn, 2007), worsened working and living conditions for most people, and amplified the imbalances and the destructive tendencies inherent in the global economy, as Chang (2010: 17–19) and Roubini and Mihm (2010) show. The view that the acceleration of dispossession directly relates to the predominance of financial capitalism is further supported by studies of inequality such as in Wilkinson and Pickett's (2010) *The Spirit Level* where they detail the negative impact of neoliberal strategy for income distribution and argue that: 'the truth is that the major changes in income distribution in any country are ... (due to) changes in institutions, norms, and political power ... Differences in pre-tax earnings rise, tax rates are made less progressive, benefits are cut, the law is changed to weaken trade union powers and so on' (2010: 243). The evidence they have gathered shows that 'almost all the problems which are common at the bottom of the social ladder are more common in more unequal societies', making such unequal societies 'social failures' (2010: 18).

Whilst the innovations in financial capitalism as well as the consequences of current fiscal and monetary policy are now common knowledge, what is still disputed are the motivations for the changes and the knowing disregard by decision-makers of the destructive effects for large sections of the world's population. What I want to examine at this point are not so much the details of the changes, but two broader features: on the one hand, the relations of force that worked to institutionalise the conditions for financial capitalism to grow into a self-serving economy, and, on the other hand, the structural changes in the economy and in the role of the state introduced to try and immunise capital against the new risks associated with financialisation. A feature to emphasise is the fact that the apparatuses or dispositifs set up to try and protect capital from these risks require the active support of the state as enabling agency, particularly by providing the collateral against these risks, for example, through Quantitative Easing and the transfer of public assets into private holdings.

Harvey's (2005) account of the emergence of neoliberalism provides a clue regarding motivations when he highlights the structural and political forces that from the 1970s were responding to shifts in the redistribution of wealth in the post-war period, produced by the welfare state system – itself a feature of post-war socio-political settlement – that had resulted in a narrowing of the gap between the richer and poorer sections of populations. The question of capital accumulation and the politics of wealth redistribution can thus be seen to have been at the heart of the strategic shifts relating to contemporary politico-economic reconstitution, bound up with the pressures coming from anti-socialist, anti-redistributionist and anti-Keynesian discourses and manoeuvres deployed by think-tanks and pressure groups. Amongst such groups, one can pick out the key role of the Mont Pelerin Society which was established to promote ordo- and neoliberal economic doctrines against socialist social policy (see the analysis by Mirowski and Plehwe, 2009, in *The Road From Mont Pelerin*). Their anti-socialist arguments were elaborated in influential works, notably, Friedrich Hayek, *The Road to Serfdom* (2010 [1944]), and Milton Friedman, *Capitalism and Freedom* (2002 [1962]); their arguments and the analysis of neoliberal discourse in Foucault's *Birth of Biopolitics* (2008) and the implications for a genealogy of contemporary capitalism will be examined in Chapter 4.

And so, when one relocates the 2008 crisis in terms of a history of struggles and transformations relating to ideas of a just or equitable society, the political and economic calculations driving the shifts in the global economy become more apparent. This is evidenced in Stiglitz's analysis of neoliberal economic strategy in *Globalization and its Discontents* (before the 'credit crunch') when he argues that the decades-long course of action instituting the changes shows that '... the "free marketeers" went further in [liberalization] with disastrous consequences for countries that followed their advice ... the enormous risks ... were borne by the poor, while evidence that such liberalization promoted growth was scanty at best' (2002: ix, x). A related point is that many studies have demonstrated that the 'liberalisation' of the financial sector such as the Big Bang of 1986, besides introducing endemic chaotic turbulence in the economy, has resulted in the distortion or even dampening of productive activity in many countries, further weakening workers' economic power. Recent evidence is provided in the report by Raymond Torres and colleagues whose research into world employment patterns establishes a link between inequality, the precarisation of labour and poverty (Torres, 2015). The point to underline regarding the new financial and trading apparatuses put in place is that 'The system that failed so miserably didn't just happen. It was created. Indeed, many worked hard … to ensure that it took the shape that it did. Those who played a role in creating the system and managing it – including those who were so well rewarded by it – must be held accountable' (Stiglitz, 2010: xxiv).

This has not happened, unsurprisingly, since those who exercise the greater economic and political power on the world stage are precisely those who should be held to account. Besides, they continue to exercise decision-making power through the range of geopolitical, legal, trade and other organisations and institutions that, through their operation, protect the existing relations of power whilst making it possible for those who have already been 'well rewarded' to now benefit from the fall-out arising from the crises. I noted in the Introduction how corporate power today is exercised by means of interconnecting 'small-world networks' of decision-makers, think-tanks and conglomerates linking finance, industry and media, operating as hubs of interests and clusters of powers. This kind of overwhelming force explains why financial institutions can allow themselves to generate profits by betting on the risks still embedded in the markets, or by inventing new risky financial vehicles such as Exchange Traded Funds inserted into the architecture of stock markets (ETFs, worth $1.2 trillion in 2011 [Wachman, 2011], rising to $2.971 trillion in 2015 [Rennison, 2015]). Furthermore, the widespread practices associated with financial leverage such as margin trading, or 'gearing', take risks on the assumption of rises in the stock market or specific stocks to cover the interest; however, margin trading (borrowing to buy shares) pushes up stock prices, incites the urge for higher yields, and can create overheating and crashes, as happened with the Shanghai stock market in July and August 2015.

Evidence that the crisis is good for profit-seeking ventures (Mirowski, 2013) is reflected in the relatively healthy if fluctuating state of stock markets, boosted by central banks' gift of billions through 'Quantitative Easing', contrasted, as everyone knows, to the misery heaped on the 99% through austerity. The view that asymmetrical relations of power lie behind the state of the world is underlined in Stiglitz's analysis in *The Price of Inequality* where he shows how the 'money-inequality political/economic nexus' (2013: xxii) has systematically promoted policies that have intensified inequality everywhere as well as producing 'an economic system that is less stable and less efficient, with less growth, and a democracy that has been put into peril' (2013: xli). Austerity programmes have thus reinforced the tendencies towards instability and inequality. Meanwhile, the risks and toxic debts associated with the mechanisms of financial capitalism feeding on leveraged debts and capital inflation continue to cumulate in the system and spread across the whole social body as 'odious debt', leading to further precarisation of workers and the poor. They damage trust in existing institutions and threaten a new massive crash. These developments would not have been possible without the reinforcement of the power of capital, including through the institution of more powerful security regimes that obstruct and delegitimate protest and resistance and invade or insecuritise private lives through technologies of total surveillance, in other words, the soft terror which is integral to what Deleuze (1990) describes as 'societies of control'.

Seen in this light, the question of control and power brings into view the transnational dimension of both the current economic predicament and the key players (the new networked archipelago of elites) in the global economy, for they limit what individual states, especially client states or the weaker ones like Greece currently, can do to reduce state deficits or rebalance national economies. The issue thus highlights the extent to which existing technical, operational and regulatory frameworks at the global level are part of the problem and not part of the solution. Other cases relating to control concern the ability of transnationals to pressurise weaker countries to sell off land, mineral rights and other assets often by dispossessing poor farmers and those who for generations have relied on commonly held resources as their main source of income and food (Allen, 2010; also many reports on land grabbing by Oxfam, Environmental Justice Organisation, Liabilities and Trade [EJOLT] and other agencies).

As a backdrop for the next section on the debt society, I would like to signal the phenomenon of what John Urry (2014a) calls 'offshoring', to describe the corporate strategy of dispersing across the world, particularly in poorer and less powerful states, key aspects of the global economy such as taxes, wealth, industrial production, energy, waste, etc.; a strategy which is transforming national economies, politics and ecologies. The relevant point is the link between the imperative of profit and accumulation and the shifting relationship between two interpenetrating assemblages: transnational and finance corporations on one side, and facilitating or acquiescing states on the other side. Investigations by many authors such as Shaxson (2012), Klein (2014) and Urry (2014a), have shown how the bulk of financial and trade transactions today is routinely placed beyond the reach of the state through subterfuges such as transfer pricing via subsidiaries in tax havens. The process concerns the ability of transnational companies to shelter their profits from tax by routing transactions through shell companies in a tax haven, usually in ex-colonies or dependencies, and that then sell the commodity at greatly inflated prices on to other subsidiaries located at the point of sale in any particular country so that little profit, if any, is technically declared. It is common knowledge now that the major proportion of the world's trade passes through tax havens such as The British Virgin

Islands which has hundreds of thousands of registered companies making and keeping vast fortunes through this trickery. Other tax-avoidance subterfuges include routing transactions through many small companies so that each accounts for but a tiny fraction of sales and profit within a complex structure. Indeed, the evasions operate through many and complex mechanisms, as the Paradise Papers shared by Suddeutsche Zeitung have revealed in November 2017, involving offshore territories such as the Isle of Man, Jersey, Bermuda, the Grand Cayman, law firms such as Appleby, trusts, subsidiaries, lobby groups, accountants.

Of course, transnational corporations that opt not to play this game would quickly go out of business. This explains how – to list well-known cases – Amazon has avoided paying more than a meagre sum as tax on their operations for several years, or AstraZeneca similarly paying no tax in the UK on huge profits in 2013 and 2014 (Chakrabortty, 2015: 35). Indeed, Chakrabortty reveals the extent of collusion between the state and conglomerates in the UK whereby the latter have been allowed to benefit from loopholes (ibid.). The same global artifices have cost 'developing' countries an estimated $1.2 trillion in lost revenue in 2011 (Vallely, 2011: 39). Vallely notes that the Caymans shelter 70% of the world's hedge funds which account for between 30 to 60% of trading on the London and New York stock exchanges (ibid.). To give an idea of the amount of tax the superrich avoid, it has been calculated that the value of funds sequestered in offshore tax havens by the superrich amounts to trillions of dollars, with one past estimate putting the figure at $32 trillion (James Henry, 2012, for the Tax Justice Network, and Reuters). The mobile and globally networked character of these transactions make it difficult for regulatory bodies to significantly alter the relations of force that have so far shaped them, in spite of pious or hopeful declarations.

The debt society

It should be clear from the arguments so far that financialisation occupies a central role in the new forms of accumulation; as Marazzi explains, 'financialization is ... the form of capital accumulation symmetrical with new processes of value production' (Marazzi, 2010: 49). Value is extracted through interest on capital so that money is produced by means of money and generates value 'beyond factory gates', value which is reinscribed in the 'sphere of the circulation of capital' (Marazzi, 2010: 49, 50). Marx as we know analysed this process in terms of 'fictitious capital' (Marx, 1959: Ch. 29, 469) where he contrasted it with 'stocks' (see also Polanyi's discussion, 2001 [1944]: 8ff., and my points in Venn, 2009a); he expressed it in the formula M–M' whereby money-capital (M) begets more money yet by-passing the process of the creation of value via the production of commodity, M–C–M' (Marx, 1970 [1867]: 154–155; see also Arrighi's discussion of this formula, 1994: 5, 6; also the analysis of money by Matthew Tiessen, 2014).

Today, the process involves the commodification and circulation of debt by way of its informationalisation through digital and cybernetic technologies such that all manner of loans, e.g., bank loans, mortgages, credit card purchases, student loans, etc., are converted into leveraged money-capital which then circulates in the form of new financial products alongside other virtualised securities or collateral. Clearly, debt itself takes many forms, and significant differences exist between countries depending on the composition of capital in these countries. Yet, the dual process of virtualisation and securitisation of debt, when leveraged and accelerated through financial engineering, exponentially inflates its value, with effects across the world. The point remains that in today's global economy, debt, and 'rent' from debt in its multiple forms, has become the primary feeder of capital.

A crucial feature of the virtualisation of securities is that these 'products' of virtual capital, particularly from the 1990s, have become detached from a firm relationship to capital assets – as recommended by the Basel Accords regarding liquidity ratios – particularly from the 1990s as authors such as Lewis (2010), Tett (2009), Roubini and Mihm (2010) and Blyth (2013) and others have explained in their accounts of the invention of these instruments (noted above). Thus, they either operate outside the circuit of production, or piggy-back on it via the stock exchange as site of the inflation and harvesting of value. In effect, there are now two circuits in the circulation of capital, one represented by the formula M–D–M', with debt/securitisation (D) as the motor, and the other represented by the familiar M–C–M' relating to accumulation by way of the production of commodities and the related extraction of 'surplus-value'. However, with the domination of the economy by the financial sector, the latter circuit is penetrated by and made subordinate to the former. This process has been structurally secured by recent changes in accounting practices applying to firms, particularly the shift from historical cost accounting (HCA), which prioritises the cost of firms' assets, to fair value accounting (FVA) which prioritises mark-to-market valuation, and thus trading on financial markets, as the basis for setting the value (FVA was institutionalised or 'normalised' by the International Financial Reporting Standards in 2011).

The implications have been explored in critiques of accounting, for instance as developed by Miranda Joseph who in *Debt to Society: Accounting for Life under Capitalism* (2014) explores modes of accounting deployed in the constitution of social relations and in operationalising the link between regimes of accumulation, governmentality and debt (see also Ashurst and Venn, 2014 regarding the role of statistics for biopolitical governmentality from the 19th century as a key measuring tool or metrics of social policy framed by 'value for money'). Joseph's work is in solidarity with the various critiques of audit culture and its functioning as a central mechanism of financial capitalism, for example, Marilyn Strathern's (2000) questioning of audit in relation to accountability and the question of value.[1] Such work echoes analyses which prioritise the standpoint of commons to reframe the question of value, and support approaches which are developing accounting practices appropriate for calculations of environmental 'sustainability', as Jan Bebbington et al. (2014) have been doing.

The point I want to emphasise is that the process of accumulation by means of debt as the basis for extending rent-seeking practices, when added to the other devices for extracting value, further contributes to the destabilisation of value, allowing speculation to run the game. Furthermore, as Lazzarato (2009, 2011) has shown, financialisation recruits every consumer into this machinery every time someone uses a credit card, takes out a bank loan, and so on: 'Through consumption, we unknowingly and habitually maintain a relation with the economy of debt' (2011: 20; also Lazzarato, 2015). Indeed, as I indicated above, this relation is hard-wired into the system through the digital and informational technologies that enable our consumption patterns to be harvested as data and be calibrated to further suture us into the accumulation machine. One should bear in mind here that internet traffic is dominated by a few transversal conglomerates, particularly Amazon and Google, as Andrew Keen (2015) has exposed, though analysis should keep at the forefront the issue of the ownership of software and informationalised knowledge, rather than just the technological capabilities Keen describes.

The state too participates in underpinning the debt economy, exemplified by the policy of Quantitative Easing (QE) as a monetary device both for bailing out, that is, recapitalising, the toxic financial sector, namely, by providing new low-risk opportunities for rent-seeking capital, and as an instrument for transferring the cost and risks of this policy onto the general public who pick up the bill for the consequent state deficit. Basically, QE is the system by which a central bank creates equity by buying securities such as government bonds and financial assets from financial institutions, using electronically created money, i.e. informationalised or virtual money, thus generating new money which in theory is supposed to circulate in the economy. QE increases bond and share prices, which benefit stock holders (corporations and the very rich), though it is supposed to benefit everyone through 'trickle down' via bank lending to boost investment and spending. 'Trickle down' economics, as Stiglitz explains in *The Price of Inequality*, 'has long been discredited ... (whereas) the riches accruing at the top have come at the expense of those down below' (2013: 8); the mythical character of trickle down is exposed in Chang (2010: 137ff., Thing 13).

Furthermore, since interest rates on government bonds in situations of economic crisis are very low, the system means that through QE the largely dysfunctional financial institutions are able to acquire assets cheaply then lend to government and businesses at higher interest rates, generating instant profit and bulking up financial institutions' assets and liquidity. Stiglitz (2013), along with other heterodox critics of recapitalisation, has described it as a gift: 'never in the history of the planet had so many given to so few who were so rich without asking anything in return' (2013: 210). It is a system for immunising capital from risks. The amounts involved so far provide some perspective in relation to austerity policies that aim to recover the cost of bailouts from the people as a whole: in the USA, between November 2008 to the present, the Federal Reserve has bought bonds worth $3.7 trillion; from March 2009 to July 2012, the UK Central Bank has bought government securities worth £375 billion; for the European Central Bank, the total value of QE from 2009 to September 2016 was put at 1.1 trillion Euros (*BBC News*, 2015).

Other counter-productive consequences of the policy of bailouts or QE that feed into the debt economy include the stimulation of inflation in the price of many assets, particularly land and urban buildings or real estate used as collateral (as it is meant to do, as Thomas Piketty points out in *Capital in the 21st Century*, 2014: 244–247), leading to increases in rent and in the national debt. The latter, as we know, has led many states to reduce the deficit through austerity programmes. Yet, it has become clear that programmes such as cutting back public expenditure, selling off public assets, reducing support for the needy, introducing stealth tax on pensions and savings, and extracting a greater proportion of people's income through a whole range of indirect taxes, feed into the institutionalisation of the debt economy. In any case, these measures further depress the economy, which results in lower tax revenue and possible deflation, thereby adding to the pressure to extract even more income from the people as a whole through further direct and indirect forms of taxation. This is despite the arguments and historical evidence which show that the austerity solution doesn't work (Blyth, 2013) – except for the rich, a view shared not only by opponents of neoliberal capitalism but even by heterodox critics like Paul Krugman (2015).

Austerity is thus a form of sub-contracted taxation on people's income, savings and spending undertaken by the state on behalf of capital. It is in effect an indirect tax, the underlying aim of which is dispossession. Furthermore, we know that the burden of cut-backs in services and increases in taxation falls disproportionately on the less powerful and the vulnerable, a fact confirmed by many studies (Atkinson, 2015: Chs 7 and 8; Blyth, 2013). In short, the monetary kid glove of QE hides the fiscal iron fist of austerity. QE and bailouts fatten holders of capital and flatten the precariat. In effect, austerity guarantees the uninterrupted transfer of wealth from the have-nots or have-little to the rich owners of capital and equity. It is not just 'zombie economics' as Blyth (2013), following Quiggin (2012), calls this economic revenant that's periodically unleashed yet has never delivered for non-holders of capital except in inflicting pain: it is the economics of the bully. And it is imposed wherever opposition, such as from unionised labour, is weak or has been disarmed, shackled by laws and prohibitions. It is an integral component of the debt economy. QE and the politics of austerity are not a cure but a poison.

Interestingly, this twist in the logic of capital has a venerable pedigree, since fiscal and monetary measures in times of economic crisis in the last two centuries have tended to follow a tested liberalist and utilitarian recipe whereby 'private losses are socialized, they become the burden of society at large and, by implication, of the national government, as budget deficits lead to unsustainable increases in public debt' (Roubini and Mihm, 2010: 55); benefits are of course privatised, that is, confiscated by the already wealthy, as Marazzi has argued (2010: 48). The scenario in which the poorer and less powerful are made to foot the bill for an economic crash, both directly and through crippling increases in the national debt, has a long tradition, re-invented on the occasion of the regular capitalist crises, as similar policies pursued after the 1825 and 1873 global crashes show (Ashurst, 2010; Roubini and Mihm, 2010). Today, the very rich escape because, as noted above, they have the means to take evasive action and institute protective measures by parking their wealth in tax havens, a situation facilitated by the globalised character of finance capitalism, as Shaxson (2012) amongst others has detailed. Recently, leaked documents in 2016 concerning the offshore activities of Mossack Fonseca provide hard evidence for what economists already knew. QE is thus the tragi-comic incarnation of the economy of debt, animated by the predatory economics of austerity.

A number of important conclusions can be drawn from the institutionalisation and socialisation of debt. First, through the debt economy, neoliberal capitalism is putting into place what is effectively a permanent source of rent generated by the ensemble of apparatuses or dispositifs that I have highlighted. These new instruments of accumulation – digitalised credits, loans and other rent-seeking devices – have become the main drivers of growth. Second, the lasting legacy of the new economic and social order is that the combination of the debt economy, the financialisation-cum-commodification of social services, and the crisis of public debt has so altered the relationship between public and private interests that the question of the general interest or common good can no longer be posed in terms of criteria of value outside those of the enterprise; to do so requires that one challenges and breaks with the values and politics of this new order. Third, a key consequence is the doubling of the state as both lender of last resort (via the central bank) and as debtor of last resort. In effect, the state, via the taxation system, is being repositioned as debt-collector-in-chief. This means not only that debt ends with the state, that is to say, with the people, but it adds weight to my argument that by way of these stratagems the state functions as out-sourced agency operating on behalf of holders of capital to extract value directly from a population. Fourth, the debt economy functions as means for redistributing the risks inherent in financial capitalism from owners of capital to non-owners. In a sense, for capital, the debt economy embodies the fantasy of immunity from risks to ensure that capital always wins, that is, appropriates more wealth. To that extent, the stakes in the emergence of a debt society are not so much 'correct' or good economics as the politics of inequality and a democracy to come.

The role of the state as relay and as agency is absolutely necessary in all this, for the state is the dispositif that has the authority to set levels and forms of taxation, enact supporting laws (including labour and employment laws and laws to authorise the privatisation of common wealth) and determine expenditures on social services and investments in infrastructure. In other words, it is the state that has the power to institute the measures that have enabled the power vested in capital to manage the risks and opportunities to its advantage. Additionally, one needs to consider the role which lobbies, think-tanks and decision-making networks play as intermediaries and facilitators to smooth the way for corporate strategy aiming to minimise or off-load costs and secure advantageous government contracts. And one could add total surveillance as one of the mechanisms whereby the dominant powers try to protect themselves against dissidence and counter-attacks from the body politic resisting the debt economy. Of course, these stratagems are consistent with the repositioning of the state as an enterprise, working according to the model of the enterprise, a development which is one of the key objectives of neoliberalism, as Foucault's analysis (2008), and Dardot and Laval's (2010) more detailed demonstration have established.

This phase in the evolution of capital is the cumulation of a long history of the centrality of debt and its relation to money, revealed in David Graeber's ground-breaking *Debt* (2011), and sign-posted from a different point of view in Susan George's (1988) analysis of 'Third World' debt in *A Fate Worse than Debt*. We find it in Foucault (2003) who highlighted the correlation of indebtedness and prosperity in *Society Must be Defended*, and in Deleuze (1990) whose analysis of 'societies of control' pointed to the shift from disciplinary societies – referencing Foucault – to the rule by the corporation and its machinic logic serving the market that he summarised thus: 'Man is no longer the man confined (l'homme enfermé) in disciplinary milieux, but the indebted man' (1990: 6); as I noted earlier, Deleuze's idea of the indebted 'man' is elaborated in Lazzarato in terms of the neoliberal techniques that constitute this individual (2011). Clearly, asymmetrical relations of power as well as issues of ethics and of ontology are implicated in the new composition of capital and the new relation between state and the polity institutionalised through these developments, for they alter the relation of force between owners and non-owners of property/capital, and they announce the production of a society in which we are all 'debtors, guilty and responsible with respect to capital' as Lazzarato puts it (2011: 11).

From this point of view, one could note that Alain Joxe, in *Empire of Disorder* (2002: 114–116), well before the current crisis, in his arguments concerning the link between 'accelerated poverty' and 'accelerated wealth' in contemporary times (2002: 43), drew attention to the custom amongst the ancient Greeks of the periodic annulment of debt to preserve the social bond, since debt tended to accumulate and lead to conflict. A vital politico-economic issue is at stake here, being played out in many countries (see also my discussion of debt by reference to Joxe in Venn, 2006a: 167). Furthermore, as he points out, the idea of debt has a long association with the idea of sin or 'trespass' in Western Christian church doctrine – though this applies to the Protestant, not Catholic version, as Matthew 6: 7–15 illustrates; this theology of indebtedness makes the punishment of debtors, that is, the 'losers' in zero-sum economic games, through measures that further impoverish them and reduce their freedom of manoeuvre, appear legitimate and moral.

Graeber expresses this relation of indebtedness in even blunter terms when he says that,

> If history shows anything, it is that there's no better way to justify relations founded on violence, to make such relations seem moral, than by reframing them in the language of debt – above all because it immediately makes it seem that it's the victim who's doing something wrong. Mafiosi understand this. For thousands of years, violent men have been able to tell their victims that those victims owe them something. If nothing else, they 'owe them their lives' ... because they haven't been killed. (Graeber, 2011: 5)

Subjugated people in colonial regimes know this only too well. Today, recipients of 'welfare' are made to feel doubly guilty: for being socio-economic 'failures', and for being indebted. Unequal relations of power regarding gender and race follow a similar logic of indedtedness.

Indeed, the reference to the standpoint of 'guilt' in relation to the articulation of debt according to neoliberal political economy and philosophy suggests an homology with the logic of the surveillance society, since that logic assumes that every individual is a potential threat to good order or to the state, that is, always-already guilty and a potential enemy of either the state or capital. The situation suggests the reconfiguration of biopolitics whereby the tropes of them/us, friend/enemy, creditor/debtor, owners/non-owners of capital relay each other to frame a postliberal governmentality anchored in the military mindset of the 'war machine'. An implication of this new imaginary is that the friend/enemy logic of war (Carl Schmitt, in *The Concept of the Political*, 2007 [1932]) would thus be extended to include nearly all citizens, the distinction being decided according to norms of 'normal' or 'healthy' or 'productive' or 'compliant' conduct, with disturbing implications about the place of liberty and fundamental rights in postliberal, postdemocratic societies (see also Deleuze, 1990; Deleuze and Guattari on the 'war machine', 1988: 416–423; or again, Joxe, 2002; Venn, 2006a: 149; Agamben, 1998: Ch.1 on the logic of sovereignty).

I shall discuss this political issue in the chapters dealing with the discourse of liberalism and what Foucault (2003) has examined in terms of the 'discourse of race war', that is, a discourse that operates a radical binary division of a population between 'them and us' consonant with all forms of oppression and exclusion and the unequal relations of power they inscribe. The exemplar of this militaristic logic is evident in the system of rule which emerged from colonial subjugation in the form of an imperial governmentality, that is, a system in which the extrajudicial, or state of exception, is normalised alongside the rule of law to thus authorise the violent suppression of resistance (Venn, 2006a; see also Agamben, 1998 regarding bare life, and 2005 regarding the state of exception). Its extension today across all populations promoted by the dominion of neoliberal political economy acquires new significance when one points out that for Foucault the 'discourse of race war', and the form of power consistent with it, at the limit authorises 'killing' the other as an expression of sovereign might and right, bearing in mind that for him 'killing', or what we could understand as thanatopolitics, includes 'the fact of exposing someone to death, increasing the risk of death for some people, or, quite simply, political death, expulsion, rejection, and so on' (Foucault, 2003: 256); the fate of refugees in many countries today illustrates this militaristic logic.

The point of view I have been developing suggests that the emergence of the debt society and its role in the process of accumulation of wealth completes the long process which began with so-called 'free' market capitalism and governmentality, since it is the means whereby the state finally becomes an agent or client of capital, aligning its interest and mode of operation with those of business and holders of capital (Foucault, 2008; Braudel, 1977, discussed in Venn, 2009a). The sovereignty of capital is thus accomplished: as Braudel claimed, 'Capitalism only triumphs when it becomes identified with the state, when it is the state' (1977: 64, 65). The view developed in this book is that one of the crucial shifts brought about by neoliberalism is precisely this realignment of the relationship connecting sovereignty, authorising discourses and capital, instituted through the state. The state as the diffused site for the exercise and application of political power can thus be regarded as the locus for the coordination of these strategies of power serving capital. I will show in Chapter 4 that the specific articulation of the three dimensions of economic power, political power and authorising discourses, along with ideas of social justice in determining the social order, has been the stakes in the long struggles fought out both within liberalism from Adam Smith, and in relation to socialism, with implications concerning post-capitalist socialities.

These stakes are at the heart of the reasons why the fundamental questioning advocated here raises the possibility of approaches to economies and ways of living that reject prevailing property relations and are instead founded on an enlarged concept of commons that fundamentally challenges the assumptions and value-system supporting capitalism, as well as other politico-economic systems based on inequalities of power and forms of dispossession – the two are intimately linked anyway. Furthermore, the break with existing economies would be in alliance with the project of decoupling the model of growth from the concepts of prosperity and 'development' whilst developing a political and social ecology consistent with new forms of local, state and interstate egalitarian polities; this politics of commons would need to be consistent with the limits which climate/the environment and exhaustible resources impose (Gorz, 1994; Strathern, 2004; Jackson, 2009; Latouche, 2009; Stengers, 2009; Dardot and Laval, 2010 and 2014; Gilbert, 2014; Klein, 2014, amongst authors discussed in the book).

Money, the market, information and the conceptual roots of connected crises

The dissection of the economic crisis above has shown that the shift from liberalism to neoliberalism makes visible the ethical, ontological and epistemological issues which have been the stakes in the underlying political struggles. The implication, as I indicated in the Introduction, is that the elaboration of alternative scenarios for the future must proceed through a longer term approach to the developments which have brought us to the present conjuncture. This involves the reconstruction of the discourses and processes that, in their co-articulated composition, have produced unjust and conflictual socialities, and now with convergent crises, the threat of unliveable ones. This section begins this task, focussing on presenting a conceptual framework that makes sense of the present as part of clearing the grounds for alternatives to capitalism. The analysis will primarily highlight the following interconnected features:

1. A long history of accumulation, trailed in a mass of critiques for a long time, tied to colonialisms, exclusions, racisms and unequal relations of force, with roots in the soil of various forms of subjugations and servitudes, and predating the capitalist period (Venn, 2006a). The interconnections binding together these vectors of dispossession are outlined in Foucault's 'counterhistory of race struggle' where he argues that the emergence of a 'discourse of race war' has enabled the victors to enact a 'binary perception and division of society and men: them and us ... the masters and those who must obey them, the rich and the poor ... the despots and the groaning people' (Foucault, 2003: 74). This binary division has come to be inscribed in the juridico-political discourses that authorise the deployment of the force of law to justify 'acts of violence, confiscations, pillage, and war taxes' levied on the subjugated (2003: 70). The legitimation of dispossession, and thus accumulation, has 'concealed the fact that they were born of the contingency and injustice of battles' (2003: 72). Its exemplary instance is evidenced in more recent times in the Atlantic Slave Trade and the seizure of indigenous lands under the cover of *terra nullius* following the conquest of the Americas (amongst a large literature addressed in Chapter 3: Galeano, 1971; Jalée, 1981; Braudel, 1986 [1979]; Todorov, 1992; Gilroy, 1993; Arrighi, 1994; Venn, 2000).

   The correlation between power, accumulation, dispossession and property is similarly exposed by Roberto Esposito, in *Persons and Things*, who argues in his account of the reduction of persons to the category of things that,

   > (I)t is the possession of things, or their loss, that marks the real distinction between winners and losers after war. Nevertheless, in peacetime too, possession signals the power relations between various persons and their varying degrees of personhood ... To possess a patrimony meant not only to have things ... but also to exert dominion over those who had less, ... and who were therefore forced to place themselves in the hands of the possessors. (2015: 24, 25)

David Graeber (2011) has provided ample evidence of the connection between war, dispossession and a lasting history of indebtedness. And I established earlier the machinery that relay the debt society to dispossession and the new 'war machine' of financial capitalism.
2. Another important feature is the specific property regime underpinning capitalist practices and values and the link with colonial expansion, a regime which from the 18th century has encompassed the progressive privatisation and commodification of land, labour, money, knowledge, and now the living in all its forms (Arrighi, 1994; Polanyi, 2001 [1944]; Shiva, 2002; Rajan, 2006; Venn, 2009a; Dardot and Laval, 2014). Again I have shown already that for capitalism commodification has been a necessary condition for the privatisation of value created by labour, and for financial capitalism to operate today. What is at stake here is not only the question of the (historically variable) conditions for a market to operate, but the deeper issue of the reduction of all collectively established social goods and all creatures to the order of things, and thus available for ownership by individuals and institutions, as Esposito (2015) indicates, and as I examine further on. Commodification is thus in alliance with the objectification and abstraction of persons and forms of life, a view consistent with, yet extending Marx's notion of the 'fetishism of the commodity' in his critique of value as determined within capitalist political economy (1970 [1867]: Ch. 1). This abstraction, which underwrites the treatment of humans and other creatures as things from which to extract value, authorises practices of slavery as well as the oppression of those considered 'other' or inferior at various points in history, for instance, the colonised, women, the subaltern, the working class, as a large literature has long exposed. Today, abstraction is instrumentalised in the form of metrics and accounting practices that universalises and prioritises market rationality and values, as Miranda Joseph (2014) has shown.

My argument is that it is generalised commodification, that is, the systematic conversion of common goods into private and tradeable property, that makes possible the reduction of everything to a calculus, abandoned to the cold heart of accountancy and information, cashed out in an audit culture that institutionalises the administration of humans and non-humans in terms of an all-inclusive administration of things. Importantly, it implies the abolition of the distinction between the calculable and the incalculable, the profane and the sacred, and thus the abolition of the values relating to finitude, and to the aesthetic and ethical dimension of being (Stiegler, 2006: 91; Venn, 2009a: 226). The point of view of co-constitution or compossibility inscribed in the standpoint of a politics of the common challenges this commodification of everything in neoliberal capitalism.
3. Capitalism itself can be seen as a specific form of a market economy characterised by this property regime and its prioritisation of possession as mark of power and autonomy. It is characterised equally by a

politico-economic discourse that privileges market rationality as the basis for a new 'reason of state' underlying the exercise of power in the form of a biopolitical governmentality working for capital (Foucault, 2007; Terranova, 2009; Lazzarato, 2015). The vital role of notions of rights to property and the question of what category of things can be privatised has been central in the emergence of this economic regime, as I discuss more fully in Chapters 4 and 5.

4. A central aspect of the apparatus of dispossession relates to crucial epistemological, ontological and ethical shifts that have reconstituted the imaginaries circumscribing economic behaviour, political action, social policy and people's conduct in contemporary times. They can be summarised in terms of the correlation of three forms of general equivalence that have coalesced in the emergence of financial capitalism. They relate to money, information, and the market, and thus to the processes of monetisation, informationalisation and marketisation that I have analysed above in terms of their central role in financial engineering and the consolidation of the power of capital. Let us start with the role of money as 'general equivalence' as summarised by Jean-Luc Nancy. In his extension of the Marxian analysis of money, he claims that nowadays,

> the complexity of interdependent systems (ecolo-nomic, socio-politico-ideo-logical, techno-scientifico-culturo-logical, etc.) depends on a general interconnection: that of money by means of which all these systems function, and to which, in the last instance, they return, since all operations relating to production, exchange, and distribution must lead to a profit. (Nancy, 2012: 15)

He adds that,

> henceforth the regime of general equivalence absorbs almost ... all the spheres of existence of humans as well as the ensemble of existing beings. This absorption passes through a close connection between capitalism and current technical development ... It is, to be precise, the connection of an equivalence and an unlimited interchangeability of forces, products, agents or actors, meanings or values. (2012: 16)

To the functioning of money as general equivalence, as condensed in Nancy's claim, one can add the general equivalence operated through informationalisation and the performativity of systems, whereby the process of accumulation has been deepened and generalised. This is explored in Lyotard's analysis in *The Postmodern Condition* (1984 [1979]) where he presciently alerted us to the role that the informationalisation and commodification of knowledge is playing in the process of the mobilisation of new communication and digital technologies by capital to generate more capital directly, and to recruit minds. His important point is that, through cybernetic-derived systems and the logic of equivalence determined by translatability into computer language, the performativity and efficiency of economic, social, political and administrative agencies and practices are all brought within the scope of a particular instrumental set of prescriptions (translatable and codable into algorithms), whereby they can all be measured and judged (1984 [1979]: 1–6, 13, 14ff.). These transformations by-pass the principles upon which modernity as a (problematic) project of emancipation was founded (problematic because of the rationalistic and Eurocentric tendencies in its foundation, as I explored elsewhere – Venn, 2000 and 2002); yet they complete the instrumental and calculative rationality that was the counterpart of the project. At the same time, these same transformations now provide the technological tools for the totalising project of neoliberalism (or 'cosmo-capitalism' as Dardot and Laval describe it, 2014: 12). Furthermore, by erasing the values inscribed in these principles, they contribute to the delegitimisation of struggles for radical alternatives whilst announcing new despotisms (Lyotard, 1984 [1979]).

A third system of equivalence comes into view in the light of Lyotard and Nancy's arguments, namely, the equivalence whereby the capitalist market has come to function as a conceptual relay and technical 'affordance' – extending Gibson's (1977) concept of affordances – to enable several key epistemic and ontological parameters of the modern imaginary to be reconstituted in terms of a regime of truth and a view of human beings that are congruent with (neo)liberal political economy and social policy. The effect is to make it possible for the ideas and tropes of rationality, efficiency, modernity, progress and the goal of unlimited growth to implicate or substitute for each other because of their mutual relation to the market as theorised in liberal political economy. One effect is that the self-referential character of this doubling is thereby veiled. Whilst this link has come to be regarded as self-evident, its logic needs a brief unpacking. This is because important epistemological presuppositions and political implications are embedded in the evolution of the capitalist form of the market as an instrument of general equivalence that go to the heart of the search for postcapitalist alternatives.

Historically, the conditions of possibility for growth to become a measure of progress and prosperity relate to the co-emergence and co-constitution of several developments that define modern times: the idea of modernity as a grand project to be accomplished incrementally over time and across territories (Lyotard, 1984 [1979]); capitalism as I have defined it, that is, as characterised by a specific property regime and by commodity as a universal, determining and all-encompassing category; the elaboration of liberal political economy as a technique of government and a technology of the social inscribing a biopolitics of populations (Foucault, 1979); and the structural dependence between capitalism and colonial regimes, operated through the apparatuses of an imperial governmentality (Foucault, 2008; Venn, 2000, 2002, 2006a, elaborated in Chapter 3). I will highlight three phases in this evolution, for they punctuate the genealogy of neoliberalism and thus supplement the historico-political narrative of capitalism which I am constructing, particularly in making sense of the functioning of the market as a third form of general equivalence, binding and being bound by the other two.

The phases inscribe three perspectives corresponding to shifts in the conceptual framework being elaborated in the period from around 1750 to 1850 during which liberal political economy gradually becomes determinant. The starting point for a genealogy of these shifts is the emergence of the view encapsulated in Enlightenment thought according to which the goal of emancipation is to be thought not in terms of the idea of salvation founded in theological or religious beliefs, but in terms of a project guided by the progress of reason, and instrumentalised in the form of the process of modernisation. The essential agency for accomplishing the project was posited to be a critical, objective and free 'Reason', exercised by autonomous subjects, unfettered by the hold of power, such that the progress of reason could be aligned to the linear progress of society. Its classical expression is in Kant's 1784 essay 'What is Enlightenment?' It is important to bear in mind the exclusions and 'otherings' entailed by the logocentric, ethnocentric and phallocentric thrust of the concept of reason in the Kantian problematic and also its compatibility with anthropocentrism (see Derrida, 1982 [1972]; Foucault, 1991; Henriques et al., 1998 [1984]; and Venn, 2002 and 2010 for a decolonial critique). At stake in the project was the emancipation of society and human subjects from bondage and 'immaturity', an emancipation that for Kant required the autonomous, unitary rational subject critical of power to function as regulative idea (Kant, op cit).[2] Thus, the shift in conceptual framework needs to be located in the context of both a departure from the 'classical episteme' (Foucault, 1970)[3] and struggles against forms of oppression at the time, exemplified in the American, French and Haitian revolutions. These were the circumstances when the principles and values advocated by radical thinkers such as Thomas Paine were transcribed into the idea of fundamental human rights and political demands consistent with these rights, notably, universal suffrage, the equality of all, the idea of a providential state, a cosmopolitics that cuts across differences of class, race, gender. It is this emancipatory thrust in the more radical side of Enlightenment thought that spurred struggles against all forms of oppressive power from the 18th century.

This context of ongoing political and theoretical struggles is necessary as background against which to make sense of what radical Enlightenment as project was meant to break with, namely, the *'ancien regime'*, the established hierarchies of power and subjugations sustaining inequalities, a *'raison d'etat'* founded in the sovereignty of the Prince or the King, and in imperial right or might, supported by an onto-theology founded in religion. Incidentally, as we know, the substitution of autonomous reason for religion as foundation for the project of emancipation, and the occidentalist framing of this notion, has provoked its own serious and much debated problems regarding the categorisation of the vast majority of people as less rational, and thus subject to exclusions that applied to Europe's 'others' and women.

In the next phase, and in the context of the consolidation of liberalism and colonial and industrial capitalism, a post-Enlightenment outlook or imaginary emerged in which concepts of progress, modernisation, freedom of the market, property, growth and prosperity became linked in a metonymic chain such that they relay each other. In this phase, the market and its regime of truth and claim to rationality functioned as the crucial hinge or node whereby the terms were co-articulated, facilitated by generalised commodification. As I will show in Chapter 4, this was theorised differently in the discourse of political economy, notably in Adam Smith, Adam Ferguson, Thomas Malthus, Jeremy Bentham, David Ricardo, John Locke, though significant conflicts in terms of a moral economy and the role of the state differentiated their positions. Crucially, the political struggles throughout the 19th century were animated by the problem of how to conceptualise the motor of 'progress', and the ethical stakes inscribed in the different solutions proposed at the time. In particular, the conflicts centred on two approaches, namely, the (utilitarian) arguments which claimed that the free market and exchange operated as this motor, with the market doubling as the model of rationality informing governmentality and biopolitics, versus an idea of the common good grounded in the imperatives of an ethics of responsibility for the vulnerable and disadvantaged that should guide intervention by the state as the mark of the progress of society. It is a lasting conflict that still divides the 'left' from the 'right' today, though inconsistent attempts to find a 'middle way' between market interest and the common interest and public good in varieties of social democracy have occasionally shaped political economy and social policy in many countries. From my account of finance capitalism, it is clear also that neoliberal political economy abandons the principle of collective responsibility for the vulnerable and the poor.

It could be argued that the totalising thrust signalled in both Lyotard's and Nancy's analyses of contemporary modes of equivalence is consolidated by the harnessing of the model of 'progress' – conceptualised as linear 'development' through 'modernisation' and competition – to the model of unlimited growth and its accumulative machine epitomised by 'The Market'. The market, it must be said, is often invoked in fundamentalist rhetoric as a kind of transcendental force, a *deus ex machina*, thus a metaphysical entity, metonymically aligned with money. It explains why those afflicted with neoliberalism require a *gestalt* switch to break the fixation induced by this doctrine. The iconic force of the market and of the growth imperative in modern times has its basis in this conceptual reconfiguration, instantiated in the current phase of market capitalism framed by neoliberal political economy. Thus, instead of relays or mediations, operated by way of the process of exchange as theorised in classical political economy, or by values underlying the general or common good, one finds the logic of identities, that is to say, the concepts have merged along a chain of identities facilitated by informationalisation and performativity – as Lyotard intimated – such that progress has become synonymous with modernisation and development, and so on. We could represent the chain thus: progress/modernisation/development = technical advancement/performativity/efficiency = prosperity/growth = commodity culture = the market.

The mindset or imaginary grounded in this circuit of equivalences and its epistemic supports has been disseminated through international regulatory bodies, NGOs, think-tanks, and the stratagems of 'soft power', affecting social and economic policy across the world. With the dominance of this scheme, the functioning of the capitalist market as enabling mechanism and as governing idea is now secured through a technicised management guided by a machinic logic as Deleuze and Guattari explain (1988: 456–460), rather than by reference, notably, to the 'invisible hand' and the process of exchange, as in the Smithian political economy. It could be argued that with these shifts, neoliberal political economy inaugurates a counter-emancipatory project involving a definite break with the older conceptual framework, yet eliminating in the process the foundational narratives that guided the politics of emancipation (Venn, 2006b). What is eliminated are the ethical goals of government, signalled both in liberal political philosophy and classical political economy's idea of a moral economy, as the Scottish Enlightenment thinkers Adam Smith and Adam Ferguson (2007 [1767]) well understood (e.g in Smith's *Theory of Moral Sentiments*, 2009 [1759], discussed by Amartya Sen, 2009; also Dardot and Laval in *Commun*, 2014). The abandonment of the idea of a moral economy in neoliberal discourse is encapsulated by the shift from the concept of exchange (and 'fair price') in Smith, or in neo-classical theory of marginal utility and rational choice theory, to the standpoint of generalised competition as the essential mechanism driving 'progress' and growth (see Foucault, 2008: 147; and Chapter 3). It should be noted however that the technocratic and utilitarian impulse in neoliberalism was incipient in liberal capitalism and the rationalistic and scientistic side of Enlightenment, as will become clear in Chapter 4. It could be said that for the neoliberal way of life, emancipation = possessing/shopping, that is, an egocentric project driven by the economy of desire and 'lack', that itself feeds into the debt society (and which is besides consistent with a politically divisive 'politics of identity').

Several important conclusions follow from my analysis of the neoliberal discursive and practical reconstitution of the inter-relationship binding the economy, the state and the social. First, the co-articulation of information, money and the market operated by way of their digitisation has enabled the three modes of general equivalence to become integrated at the heart of financial capitalism. This is clearly evident in the form of the computerised algorithmic trading of derivatives or 'virtual' or intangible capital on the financial market that performatively and exponentially leverages the value of money-capital, creating in the same process the superrich at one end and dire poverty and inequalities at the other end. In effect, the derivative market, as the key ingredient of 'shadow banking', and as an abstract calculus framed by the equivalences I have described, has automated the process of dispossession; as I argued, this machinic character of financial capitalism represents the exemplary instance of the debt society.

Secondly, the ongoing instrumentalisation of these modes of general equivalence through the processes of informationalisation, monetisation and marketisation has provided the techniques for enabling the administration of the domain of the social and the administration of things to be undertaken according to the same technology of management and accounting practice and the dehumanised values and interests invested in them, as Lyotard (1984 [1979]) foreshadowed. This instrumentalisation, as I have noted, is facilitated and legitimated by generalised competition as governing idea and value, and as currency in political rhetoric. Besides, what this whole manoeuvre tries to abolish or delegitimise is the space of contestation and dissident politics. Taken together, these two conclusions enable us to grasp why the mindset and regime of truth corresponding to the totalising thrust in neoliberalism requires that the 'losers' and the indebted – whether individuals, particular groups or nations – must be sacrificed, that is, that they be the target of precarisation, soft terror and/or a thanato-politics. The temptation of neo-fascism for many whose lives have become precarious or impoverished as a consequence of these developments is a worrying development.

Thirdly, the abandonment of the prioritisation of the common good and its underlying ethics of responsibility for others brings to light two features which one needs to make explicit in order, on the one hand, to locate neoliberalism as a counter-emancipatory and amoral project, and, on the other hand, to detect in Enlightenment thought a major flaw that has undermined its goal of an emancipation grounded in the principles of universal fundamental rights. They both relate to how to theorise the interconnections that bind together the relation to oneself as an ethical subject, the relation to others, and the relation to the world.[4] The conventional approach locates a religion as the framework that assigns their place to the dynamics connecting the modalities of these relations constitutive of subjectivity and establishing their coherence. Thus, until the emergence of the Enlightenment, the inter-relations were understood within an onto-theology such that religion provided the principles and the norms of conduct circumscribing the three forms of relations that shape subjectivity. Enlightenment thought, by shifting the foundation onto the autonomous rational subject and an epistemology privileging the sciences to the exclusion of other 'regimes of truth', breaks with both an 'hermeneutics of desire' (Foucault, 1984; Venn, 1985) and an ethics grounded in the transindividual dimension of becoming (Henriques et al., 1998 [1984]; Venn, 2010). This shift opened the way for a technologisation of the process of formation of subjects, alongside the technologisation of the question of value, which has culminated, via biopolitical governmentality in the 19th century, in the neoliberal idea of reconstituting the subject or the self according to the model of the 'enterprise' and its regime of truth as Foucault has argued (Foucault, 2008; McNay, 2009).

Fourthly, a fundamental decentring is now required to counter this shift, implicating the elaboration of different ontological, epistemological and ethical foundations for relocating the place of humans in the order of things and for a politics of the common. It suggests the idea of a 'strategic universalism' (Gilroy, 2005), based on responsibility for both the other and for the world which humans and other living creatures inhabit in common. It implies a definite break with subject-centred philosophies, and the logocentric, phallocentric, ethnocentric and anthropocentric privileges associated with such philosophies. It is clearly a break with the idea of the autonomous, self-centred, self-interested individual as the epitome of the (neoliberal) agent whose actions are shaped by a neo-utilitarian perspective modelled on market transactions and its cold rationality. It proposes instead post-anthropocentric principles, and a standpoint that dethrones the idea of the self-sufficient egocentric sovereign subject which supports the model of 'possessive individualism' (McPherson, 1962), a concept ultimately grounded in the 'metaphysics of individualism' (Barad, 2007: 23). Besides, the conceptual framework I am outlining makes visible both the transindividual dimension of being, that is, the material and socio-cultural world that exceeds yet operates as conditions and dwelling for the constitution of the individual, as well as the question of singularity understood in terms of the (Arendtian) 'who' of action and intention, that is, the one who is answerable as agent, and the one who is called to responsibility for the other (as developed in Levinas, 1984 as I examined in Venn, 2000, and in Chapter 6).

Fifthly, the shift from liberalism to ordo- and neoliberalism, when relocated against this background of epistemological and ethical mutations, makes visible the stakes with regard to the values and principles underlying effective, non-procedural democracy, that is to say, the practice of liberty, the defence of fundamental rights, the principle of safeguarding the general interest and common good through the principle of the redistribution of wealth, capabilities and risks in the interest and for the welfare of all, and the problematisation of the role of a centralised sovereign state as organising mechanism.

In modern times the developments outlined above were inherent to, or incorporated into capitalism and liberal political economy, in spite of the political, ethical and economic conflicts within liberalism as a political philosophy seeking a balance between the common good of society and the interest of a market economy. My analysis in Chapter 4 of these tensions or contradictions – strikingly inscribed in the thought of John Stuart Mill as I will show – will highlight the conflicts opposing 'radical liberals' – who were no revolutionaries – to utilitarians in the 19th century and reveal the different ontologies and systems of value that informed their different assumptions about the nature of human beings and thus their different visions of the good society. This genealogical approach to the ethico-political grounds of varieties of liberalism will enable me to foreground the terrain of conflict in which these differences were inscribed, and thus to better expose what neoliberalism breaks with and stands for (Foucault, 2008; Venn, 2009a; Ashurst and Venn, 2014).

One can point out also that, with the (supposed) ending of the Cold War and the collapse or defeats of socialist projects across the world, the current dominance of neoliberalism has ensured that growth has taken the place of the general interest or common good in political rhetoric. Foucault's genealogy of neoliberalism makes this clear when he shows that the process of privatisation and 'generalised capitalisation' promoted by neoliberals cashes out their view that 'there is only one true and fundamental social policy: economic growth ... only economic growth should enable all individuals to achieve a level of income that will allow them the individual insurance, access to private property, and individual or familial capitalisation with which to absorb risks' (2008: 144). This equivalence of growth and the general interest, inherent in liberal capitalism, is prevalent in political as well as in (mainstream) economic discourse, whilst now only serving the process of accumulation by hoarders and holders of property and capital.

Another side of this equivalence is the fact that the principle of collective responsibility for the welfare of all underlying socialism as a political idea, partly instituted in the 20th century in the form of a welfare or providential state, has been abandoned in many countries, replaced by the claim that (liberalised/liberated) capitalism works for the benefit of all, namely, by way of the mythical 'trickle down'(see Chang, 2010: 137ff., and Stiglitz, 2013: 8 on trickle down as myth). In its place, one finds a discourse of capitalist relations that prioritises the mutation of the self-interested individual into the 'resilient', 'enterprising' or 'corporate' subject driving the new social order founded on competition and its neo-utilitarian, amoral worldview, as Foucault (2008), Ashurst and Venn (2014), Dardot and Laval (2010), and many others have argued.

Much is at stake here, since the abandonment of the idea of collective responsibility for the general interest or general good undermines the very basis of democracy. This is because liberal democracy is founded on the people's explicit consent to the authority of the state, yet this authority is granted only on the understanding that consent be cashed out on the expectation that the rewards, opportunities and risks arising from the creation of wealth by the productive and collective activity of all citizens will be equitably shared. The classic arguments are developed notably in Locke's *Two Treatises of Government* (1963 [1690–1780]), though his view of consent is undermined by the double-think inscribed in his toxic notion of tacit consent. The expectation of equitable distribution has historically been at the heart of the idea of a 'social contract' between state and citizen underlying democracy (e.g. in Rousseau's *The Social Contract*, 1998 [1762]), at least in theory, for the state is far from being a neutral force in such settlements, since it tends to be the instrument of dominant power, thus enabling asymmetrical relations of power to be institutionalised (Lazzarato, 2015).

The idea of collective responsibility is inscribed, besides, in the notion of the social bond and its affiliation with the idea of the common good, the argument being that the social bond, much deployed in political rhetoric, refers (or should refer) to the active, collective, inventive and renewed constitution of social, cultural and environmental goods or wealth. From this viewpoint, this collaborative activity is what constitutes the building blocks sustaining a sense of belonging through common ownership, as well as through the sharing and the conviviality of life in common; solidarity is born through this active and collective constitution of political constituencies. The moral economy underlying such a view of the relation between the state and the citizen and the question of consent is evident in the discourse of socialism, and even in some aspects of the political economy of thinkers such as Adam Smith, Adam Ferguson, and J.S. Mill. One should bear in mind here the argument that, in order to avoid the despotism of the majority, the idea of the general will underlying consent must be limited by the priority accorded to the ideal of collective responsibility for the protection of the weaker members of a community, and by the proviso that the protection of universal rights and liberties be paramount (argued in J.S. Mill and others, as I discuss in Chapter 4). It is precisely these protective provisos that are swept aside by the new relation of power between capital and labour, signalling the emergence of a new despotism (see also Brown, 2003, 2015; Negri, 2015). Equally, these apparatuses exemplify trade contracts in which all the risks and costs are stacked up on the side of less powerful states and their pauperised populations (Monbiot, 2013). Viewed in terms of the shifts I have described, neoliberal corporate capitalism is revealed as the culmination of a series of political, social, economic, military, technological and legal strategies elaborated against a background of emancipatory struggles stretching across centuries and nations, involving class, race, ethnic and gender relations of power, with regimes of accumulation as stakes. Such struggles are evidently still going on.

Notes

1   Even heterodox analysis such as by André Orléans in *The Empire of Value* criticises the neglect of the 'social relations underlying market behavior' by neoclassical economists who privilege utility in the determination of value (2014: 26); he highlights instead the central role of money and of 'the mass of subjective reckonings and opinions' that go for example into the assigning of a value to a share (2014: 5), and, generally, the extent to which non-market calculations and transactions are part of 'socially created values' (2014: 322).
2   One should note Kant's ambivalence regarding the role of the state as agency with regard to the relation to power and to the question of freedom.
3   The episteme in Foucault's sense refers to the complex of concepts, theories and assumptions that circumscribe an historical period's worldview supported by and supporting the epistemological or conceptual framework that determines the production of knowledge considered valid in the context of the period.
4   There are several ways to examine these inter-relations describing the dynamics whereby subjectivity, the domains of the social and of material life, and specific discourses of being are entwined. Foucault notably, in his *History of Sexuality*, foregrounded the inter-relations of knowledge, power and subjectivity in his analysis of the 'forms and modalities of the relation to oneself whereby the individual constitutes itself and recognises itself as a subject' (1984: 12, discussed in Venn, 1985). They involved an 'hermeneutics of desire' correlated to 'plays of truth' invested in 'techniques of the self' tied to practices that enact the 'arts of existence' (Foucault, 1984). Politics enters into this dynamics, either implicitly or explicitly, because power is always-already invested in these relations. As I examine in Chapter 6, the perspective in Foucault's work has been significanty extended in contemporary thought regarding the standpoint of relationality as a principle guiding the conceptualisation of the self-other, human-animal, nature-culture and human-world in terms of compossibility, co-constitution and complex becoming.

2
In the Shadow of Tipping Points: The Political Economy of Climate Change

The state of the world: Stressors and conflicting pressures driving climate and environmental policy

Nothing captures the contradictions and stuckness at the heart of the tragedy of climate change as the decision by President Obama on 17 August 2015 to grant final permit to Royal Dutch Shell to drill the Arctic for oil in the Chukchi Sea yet doing so just a few days after he himself alerted the world about the dangers of global warming when he announced his administration's support for the US Clean Power Plan (now proposed for repeal, October 2017). This Plan was described as the way forward for reducing emissions in the USA by 32% by 2030 through investing in renewable forms of energy such as solar and wind; a further irony is that the Plan, though moving in the right direction, would have cut US emissions by only 6%, whilst the reality is that 'a cut of 80% is required to prevent dangerous global warming' (*New Scientist*, 2015a: 6). His argument for allowing drilling is that 'our economy still has to rely on oil and gas' (Goldenberg, 2015: 14).

What this statement implicitly recognises is the enduring dependence of all major economies on fossil fuels, not just for heating and electricity generation, but for transport, including military aircrafts, etc., and the myriad by-products of the petrochemical industries, particularly, plastics. So, although renewable forms of energy are making an increasing contribution (amounting to 55% of new capacity worldwide, though currently only 10% of electricity is generated from renewables – Brahic, 2017: 32), the pressures arising from a carbon-based economy are not just technological but economic since vast wealth is locked into fossil fuel companies, whilst social and cultural factors relating to patterns of consumption further encourage dependence on carbon. Calculations of greenhouse gas footprints from CO_2 and methane pick out cars, coal and cows as the main sources of emission (Holmes, 2017: 35); and I would add capitalism to these 3Cs. The Trump Administration's recent shifts in policies regarding energy and the environment simply pour oil on the troubled waters of climate change.

The contradictions are encapsulated in Naomi Klein's *This Changes Everything: Capitalism vs. the Climate* (2014) where the chasm between the interests of capital and the imperatives of arresting the damage to environments, ecologies and biomes is exposed in great detail. I shall address this crucial issue below to point to the dynamics underlying the fact that for the moment the interests of capital tend to prevail. The case of Shell illustrates the problem, since although they subsequently abandoned the drilling, it was only because their findings indicated that the Burger J well in the Chukchi Sea would not yield sufficient oil or gas to be commercially viable. Even so, the president of Shell USA, Marvin Odum, admits that the area continues to have 'important exploration potential' (Ahmed, 2015). We must assume that corporations and governments planning such hazardous drilling in the polar regions do know from the published scientific evidence that these areas have fragile ecosystems where many dangers await, notably, the risk that drilling could release part of the immense store of methane in the permafrost, a gas which is 86 times more damaging as a greenhouse gas than CO_2 over 20 years according to the IPCC (also Ananthaswamy, 2015: 38–41).

Shell's explanation for evading their responsibility points to another important feature of the impasse I have just noted, for their reasoning is that they 'do not see governments taking steps now that are consistent with 2°C scenario' (Evans, 2016: 6). This reasoning about inadequate governments' response to global warming appears more and more realistic in light of the difficulties in implementing the measures advocated at the Paris conference of 2016 (Conference of Parties, or COP 21). This should not be surprising since governments are subject to the same dynamics that account for the domination of short-term business interests trumping those of global warming. Indeed, Shell expects the rise in average global surface temperature to be 4°C by 2100, a calculation factored into its New Lens Scenario as part of its forward planning (Macalister, 2015: 12–13). This expectation may appear rather pessimistic, but it is completely in line with many scientific assessments shared by influential and well-informed bodies such as the World Bank, the CIA, and the International Energy Agency (IEA) (*Guardian*, 2015: 1); even projections from existing 'green' policies indicate that the world is on course for an increase of between 3.6 and 4.2°C (Pearce, 2014: 8–9), a figure confirmed by Climate Action Tracker in 2017 which indicates 3.6°C as likely (*New Scientist*, 2017: 30). The problem is that, as I noted in the Introduction, the increase in average global warming is already 1.1°C above pre-industrial temperatures, whilst the rate of increase is accelerating. It is estimated that the targets for reducing emissions agreed at the Paris summit (COP 21) in 2016, if acted upon, would still result in an increase of global average ocean temperature of over 3°C (Heffernan, 2017a: 30). This is well short of the 2°C which is the least worse situation for manageable warming, partly because such a rise is already locked in due to current greenhouse gas emissions. Reports of the concentration of greenhouse gas emission (GHG) indicate it had reached 400 ppm in 2015, whilst currently the world produces 41.9 gigatonnes of CO_2 emissions; such levels are likely to remain for generations (World Meteorological Organisation [WMO], 2016). A worrying possibility is that the methane in the permafrost in North America and Siberia will be released this century with further warming, thus accelerating all the effects of climate change. Sadly, the ascendency of deniers, together with the lack of real progress in sufficiently reducing emissions make the forebodings of irreversible tipping points all the more likely.

Yet, global warming and its anthropogenic cause have been a matter of global concern for decades, as the Brundtland Commission (1987) detailed quite some time ago. In spite of disputes about fluctuations in warming, an analysis by the National Oceanic and Atmospheric Administration (NOAA, 2015) confirmed steady increases in global temperature from 1880, in spite of fluctuations, adding to the earlier prognosis of the global warming scenario, though there exist variations in calculations of the extent and distribution of warming. Furthermore, NOAA's Annual Greenhouse Index shows that human activity has caused an increase of 37% from 1990 to 2015. As we know, IPCC reports have abundantly documented the facts and effects relating to climate change; their findings have been widely accepted by governments and NGOs and discussed at the many inter-governmental climate summits. The latest report of the IPCC (IPCC, 2014) is 'unequivocal' in confirming the earlier conclusions, particularly regarding human activity as the main source of climate change, even if some predictions, for example regarding the pattern of droughts, or the rate of increase in global surface temperature have been altered from earlier assessments.

To get a fuller picture, let us look at some of the main consequences of global warming that a mass of findings has confirmed and that are now in the public domain. Maps of the world, produced by many agencies, for instance the Met Office Handley Centre (using the HaD CM3 computer model) have illustrated the consequences of a 4°C increase in average global surface temperature above pre-industrial times by 2100. Though there is significant variation across the globe, the gradient of warming, from a typical 6–7°C to 14°C in the Arctic area with a global average of 5.5°C, shows that vast areas of the earth's surface will become uninhabitable or inhospitable for humans and a whole range of species. The effects extends to all the earth's systems. A summary of what to expect even if we do not experience the worst case scenario should include the following:

- Global warming will result in changes in the weather, in rainfall, and in the pattern of currents, the diminishing size of the ice caps, a rise in sea level, an increase in ocean acidity due to carbon dioxide absorption and the consequent destruction or bleaching of coral reefs, and loss of dissolved oxygen in the oceans, seriously affecting marine life (Schmidtko et al., 2017). Large areas of the planet will become unfit for humans and for agriculture, whilst the heating of the oceans will impact on earth systems like the Gulf Stream and monsoons in Asia and West Africa, further damaging habitations and food production for billions (Pearce, 2017a: 31).

- It will produce extreme weather such as frequent heatwaves, violent storms, floods, and droughts, depending on location, causing extensive damage to agricultural lands, buildings, natural habitats, etc.
- The melting of ice caps and glaciers will result in rises in sea level, perhaps by as much as 3 metres by 2100 (and eventually 20 metres – Le Page, 2017: 32), with consequent flooding of low-lying areas, coastal towns, and loss of fertile land, affecting food production and much else. Already the large Thwaites glacier in Antarctica is rapidly melting, as are the Zachariae and Jakobshavn glaciers in Greenland (Pearce, 2017a: 31). Earlier findings have highlighted the accelerating melting of the Larsen C ice shelf (6,600km^2 iceberg, much bigger than the already melting Larsen A and B) which will likely provoke further melting of the glaciers behind it, resulting in greater rises to the sea level in the future than previously calculated (Mathiesen, 2015: 17). The break off of a massive iceberg there in January 2017 (Davis, 2017), and evidence in July 2017 that Larsen C is likely to soon slide into the Weddell Sea in Antartica, confirms this finding (Amos, 2017). Indeed, improved modelling has indicated that previous models have underestimated the amount of melting, notably from the West Antarctic ice sheet (Payne, 2015).
- Furthermore global warming, by causing the permafrost in the Arctic region to melt, will release carbon in the form of carbon dioxide and methane, thus altering that region from acting as a carbon sink to a carbon emitter, resulting in a vicious circle of further warming.

We know too about all the other consequences that would follow when we add other sources of alterations to our biosphere due to chemical, plastic and biological pollution, leading one to conclude that the combined effects will cause calculable and incalculable irreversible damage to ecologies, biodiversity, biomes and so on, and negatively impacting the ability of humans and other forms of life to adapt. I noted in the Introduction the reference to the concept of 'plasticene' that some scientists are using to draw attention to the biophysical mutations due to the effects of plastics on the environment, particularly the oceans where an estimated 5.25 trillion pieces of plastic weighing over 260,000 tonnes float at sea. The evidence shows that they provide a new ecosystem – a 'plastisphere' – which passes into the food chain through fish, and can have pathogenic as well as epigenetic consequences (Reed, 2015: 28; see also the papers in Gabrys et al., 2013). The combined impact of all these new stressors is confirmed in a study by the UN Environment Programme (May 2016) which concluded that the level of degradation of natural resources by humans is already outstripping the planet's ability to cope. As resources such as arable land and usable water become scarcer due to the widespread damage as well as because of population increases, the pressures are likely eventually to produce water wars and land wars to add to ongoing conflicts triggered by the imperative for commodities security, notably, around mineral extraction (see for example, Shiva, 2002; Roy, 2015). The geopolitical consequences alone will be immense.

All this information has been in the public domain for some time, disseminated through the stream of media reports of ongoing findings and accounts of climate change summits and agreements, and many scientific analyses apart from IPCC reports (see also Hulme, 2009). The same findings have prompted Pope Francis to urge clear and effective intergovernmental action to deal with climate change, but motivated by the ethical imperative which regards humans as custodians of the earth who have a moral duty to safeguard it (Pope's Encyclical Letter, 2015). One would have thought that caution and enlightened self-interest would lead to the same objective.

There are of course many initiatives that aim to reduce emissions or limit the damage in some way. They fall into three categories, namely, green or renewable energy programmes in parallel with changes in behaviour to minimise both energy and environmental damage; technological fixes; and market fixes. The former is broadly informed by environmental and ecological politics united around campaigns for significant reductions in emissions through shifts away from cars and air travel as modes of transport, further cuts in coal and other fossil fuel production in favour of renewables, and changes in lifestyle including giving up beef. Such politics draws from a long history of struggles to protect the environment and 'nature' generally from the ravages wrought by the exploitative and the short-term interests of an uncaring capitalism. It opposes the ontology which supports mastery over non-human beings and natural resources. Yet, though individuals can contribute in many ways through their own behaviour, only structural transformations – in power generation, modes of transport, urban planning, location of food production and manufactures, shifts in eating habits, cultures, economies, technologies and so on – would make a difference.

Technological fixes, or plan B, range from the sensible to the outlandish, for example, from the idea of combining bioenergy with carbon capture and storage (BECCS), to adding particles to the stratosphere to deflect sunlight, or proposals such as increasing the production of algae to absorb CO_2 by fertilising the oceans (Klein, 2017: 34). Whilst carbon capture and storage or 'negative emissions' is a good idea in principle, the problem is that capturing a vast amount of CO_2 'requires large amounts of energy, land and money' (Le Page, 2015b: 11), and would impact negatively on biomes and a whole range of species because of loss of habitats. Using biomass for energy has the same problems of requiring vast amounts of land (about 500 million hectares – Heffernan, 2017b: 30), an already diminishing resource which is required for food production for a growing population, whilst climate change reduces available arable land. There are many more ideas, some of which would indeed help in the objective of limiting warming. The main problem with relying on technological fixes is that they keep intact the economic system and could delay the structural changes that the situation calls for.

The main pitfall concerning the geo-engineering and other purely technical measures to tackle climate change and related crises such as environment damage and food poverty is that it feeds the illusion that the capitalist market itself can find solutions to the underlying issues, thus making it unnecessary to make radical changes to the economy. In any case, most of the proposals are costly, untested, and are likely to result in adverse and unpredictable effects. Clearly, some of the proposed measures will help in the short term, such as encouraging the substitution of renewable sources for coal, oil and gas by fixing a carbon price that would price out fossil fuels and motivate investment in alternatives. However, much as carbon trading, price substitution by itself would not prevent a 2°C increase, which is now the base line (Le Page, 2015b: 11).

The key point is that capitalist market solutions for climate change leave unchanged the dynamics fuelling the burning of fossils, particularly the forces prioritising private and corporate accumulation over other factors and considerations. A brief look at some of the mechanisms driving the global economy reveals the vicious circles feeding resistance to change as well as exacerbating the risks stacking up. The overriding vector is the massive wealth already locked up in the form of assets tied to fossil fuel reserves, constituting a 'carbon bubble' ready to burst (Le Page, 2017: 33). Fossil fuel companies rely on the value of the reserves they already own to entice investments from pension funds, insurance firms, banks, etc. Hundreds of institutions would need to start a programme of disinvestment into other stocks to manage the possibility of financial stability as global warming becomes more urgent than it already is. Yet, as Pearce (2017b: 33) points out 'some in the fossil fuel industry dismiss the idea they are exposed to any risks'. Thus, the Independent Petroleum Association of America has claimed that 'pension funds would lose trillions if they all sold their shares in oil firms' (ibid.). Meanwhile fuel companies are borrowing about $100 billion a year from banks to invest in finding new sources of oil and gas on the assumption of continuing growth in demand. These are high-risk ventures, yet completely in keeping with the combination of faith in neverending economic growth and the resilience of the market. Initiatives from those who recognise the situation I have been describing, e.g. those who are promoting the idea of decoupling energy-based emissions from growth (Brahic, 2017: 32), or the policy advocated by the European Systemic Risk Board, which has counselled a gradual transition to renewables to avoid a 'hard landing' for the economy, are moves in the right direction, but this effort is undermined by deniers and climate sceptics, encouraged by the fossil fuel lobbies (Le Page, 2017: 21). Unfortunately, financial capitalism runs the game, for now.

The sense that we are reaching a limit becomes even clearer when we look at a number of other developments that will intensify all the other stressors which are already provoking drastic alterations in the planet's life-support system. They illustrate the kind of dilemmas and conflicting pressures that are blocking the path to the more realistic and inventive programmes needed to slow down the relentless rush towards tipping points affecting environments, ecologies, resources and economies.

The problem is thus not simply about the extent of warming and its effects, but about the dilemmas I described at the start. My concern therefore is not only with discussing the consequences of global warming but equally with constructing a narrative that highlights the role of capitalism and the model of growth-as-development as the parameters aggravating the situation as well as impeding progress towards agreements binding all governments to reduce emissions sufficiently and to limit and prepare for the damage already built in. The examples I highlight below will widen the scope of analysis to demonstrate why it is necessary for analysis to uncover the underlying economic and political forces, the assumptions and values, and the conceptual frameworks sustaining the current situation.

Reports from the International Energy Agency (IEA) reveal that India, as part of its development plans, aims to double coal production by 2035 by building half of the world's proposed 1,200 new coal-fired power stations (Jose, 2015). But due to the falling costs of solar energy, India has cancelled 14 gigawatts of coal-fired power stations in May 2017 (Hill, 2017). This though must be set against the report by The Institute for Energy Research that reveals that India plans to invest $10 billion in new coal-fired stations over the next five years (IER, 24 July 2017). The Trump Administration is also supporting coal-fired and nuclear plants, in the process cancelling Obama's Clean Power Plan (Puko, 2017). Other countries, including China, have been cutting back on emissions of CO_2 to reduce pollution and expand renewables. So, although the picture is not very clear, the fact that, as The Institute for Energy Research (IER) also reported, many countries still have plans for constructing many more coal plants remains a cause for concern (IER, 24 July 2017, citing Urgewald's account). Overall, the situation adds weight to the findings that 'global CO_2 emissions are rising faster than ever', making a 4°C increase all the more likely (Le Page, 2015b: 11). The contribution to climate change of the combination of the so-called 'coal renaissance', fracking for gas – which releases methane – shale oil extraction, drilling in the Arctic and elsewhere, when added to already entrenched features of the carbon economy, particularly our reliance on the petrochemical industry to provide products for the plastic world, makes the forecast of serious irreversible damage beyond dispute.

To the continuing reliance on a carbon economy, I want to add the destruction of environments and ecosystems due to the scale of transformations being undertaken as part of the scramble for more mineral resources to feed growing demand, led by conglomerates in the extractive industries. It concerns the $60–70 trillion plan for infrastructure proposed for 'developing' countries over the next 15 years in order to access these minerals and other resources essential for growth. This is a staggering amount when it is juxtaposed against the fact that the value of all currently existing infrastructure globally is estimated to be around $50 trillion (Laurance, 2015: 26–27).

The plans include developments in the Amazon and adjoining Andes mountains for mining and fossil fuel that are creating a whole range of unforeseen destructive consequences. For example, the 12 projects for the Tapajos river will result in the loss of 10,000 km^2 of forest by 2032, clearly adversely affecting carbon dioxide capture by forests. As part of the developments, 53,000 mining leases have been granted for exploration and extraction in the Amazon (Laurance, 2015), thus adding to the ecological footprint of these industries supporting contemporary technology, notably, the scramble for lithium for batteries used in digital and other appliances. Already, effluents from mining are polluting rivers and causing ecocide.

The same scale of transformation of the ecosystem concerns the plans to set up 29 mega 'development corridors' spread across Africa, requiring huge investments, for example, $100 billion from China, and a little less from India, Brazil, Canada, the USA, for the construction of infrastructure such as road networks, dams, ports, and power-lines that will alter the ecology of vast areas. The scale of the changes and collateral damage which such anthropogenic activity will have on the earth's environment is not difficult to imagine. A sad example of unintended consequences concerns the 50,000 kilometres of road carved up in rainforests in equatorial Africa, mainly by loggers in the last 10 years, which has led to the slaughter of two-thirds of the world's forest elephants, as the roads have enabled poachers to reach previously inaccessible forests (Laurance, 2015: 26).

The examples above, and countless others across the world, confirm the view that the competition for resources and for growth, in GDP as much as in corporate profits, every time trumps the forebodings regarding the impending disasters associated with the converging crises I have highlighted in Chapter 1 (see also Naomi Klein's arguments about 'disaster capitalism' in *The Shock Doctrine*, 2008). Indeed, the kinds of corporate 'development' such as the search for oil in the Arctic or the 'coal renaissance' have a self-fulfilling effect in terms of global warming and climate change, since they ensure that, through feed-back loops in the system, the prognostics of 4°C will turn out to be accurate. The sense that we are stuck between the rock of a feral capitalism unable to help itself and the hard place of planetary destruction, has become inescapable. And there is as yet no credible plan B in sight that would at least try to achieve a steady state sustainability (Daly, 1997; Jackson, 2009). As noted, solutions proposed based on market and/or technological fixes alone have their own limitations, since ideas such as using biomass to feed power stations as part of 'negative emissions' programmes would need to be scaled up considerably to be effective; and in any case relying on biomass will use up land for growing food, making it unviable by itself (Pearce, 2015: 8, 9). Indeed, to achieve the 1.5°C target agreed at COP 21 in Paris in 2015, there would need to be zero emissions after 2050 as well as a programme of carbon capture, or 'negative emissions', amounting to 500 giga tons by 2100, requiring massive investments in developing the appropriate technologies and industries (Pearce, 2016: 30–33).

Towards longer-term solutions

We can begin to see that the stuckness to which I am referring is not due to a lack of information but is instead anchored in the very material, institutional, discursive, technological and historical constituents of a world economy driven by ceaseless growth, accumulation on a global scale, destructive technologies, and assumptions about the way of the world that block alternative forms of life. To make matters worse, the processes we are dealing with are very complex and interlocking, the amount of information in the public domain is mind-boggling (though poorly accessed by most people, who can therefore be prey to disinformation), much of the scientific data comes with degrees of probability, and the models depicting the effects and patterns over time are still evolving (Hulme, 2009). Nevertheless, the fact remains that enough reliable knowledge has been produced over the past few decades to make us confident about the key dimensions of the problem. Let us look at this.

First of all, since the overriding conclusion to be drawn from the above is that the problem of climate change relates to wider structural problems beyond what the conglomerates associated with fossil fuels and the extractive industries are doing, and beyond finding technical 'solutions' like geo-engineering that would, as noted, simply limit the damage whilst avoiding the need for radical change. The recognition that geo-politico-economic interests and anthropogenic activities lie behind global warming and environmental degradation leads us to consider long-term responses that directly address the difficult task of altering the parameters that have underlied the transformation of the world over the last two centuries. These relate to ideas of 'development', 'progress', private accumulation, property, governance, the common good and so on that I discuss by reference to liberal political economy and governmentality in Chapters 1 and 4.

For a perspective on this task, we could look at key features of contemporary times that go to the heart of the limits that now oblige us to change course. They concern key measures of 'consumer capitalism' and 'development' that link the question of limit to not only incessant economic growth as condition and goal but also the correlation of modernisation and 'progress-as-development' with increasing energy requirement and consumption. In terms of climate change, it is worth pointing out that the latter interconnection is widely assumed, for instance, in the UN Development Report (2015) which asserts a correlation between per capital energy consumption and Human Development Index (HDI is a measure of levels of 'development' in terms of life expectancy, education, literacy, standard of living). That same analytical framework has led various reports by the UN Commission on Sustainable Development to conclude that reduced energy consumption to reduce emission has a greater impact for 'developed' rather than 'developing' countries.

Whether the link between energy consumption and 'development' is established in terms of HDI or in terms of GDP – that 'mismeasurement' of the quality of life, as Joseph Stiglitz, Amartya Sen and Jean-Paul Fitoussi (2011) have argued (see also Clark and Yusoff, 2014 on 'combustion and society', and Urry, 2014b, on 'fossil fuel societies') – the language takes for granted the model of progress and development which correlates it to growth and prosperity. The iterations of growth across many parameters – GDP, output and sales by firms, levels of consumption, incomes, the size of profit and thus shareholder value, private wealth accumulation, population, etc. – is so prevalent that one forgets that it is the combination of a capitalist economy and the discourse of liberal political economy allied to it that had provided the basis for this model (the arguments are presented in Chapter 4). As I argued in Chapter 1, this conjuncture has validated the conversion of the project of emancipation and social justice into a vocabulary whereby prosperity and 'wellbeing' could neatly slip under the sign of growth whilst serving the imperatives central to capitalism as an expansionary system based on the exploitation of people and resources.

A wider picture of these linkages, sometimes encapsulated by a 'hockey stick' diagram to emphasise the exponential growth in key parameters in contemporary times, will enable me to draw out other features relating to the contemporary situation. The diagram charts the long historical span or *longue durée* studies of key factors affecting the confluence of crises today shows slow growth or a near steady situation from industrial times until we reach the post-Second World War period. From around the 1950s, we witness dramatic growth in GDP, carbon dioxide concentration, water consumption, motor vehicles produced and sold, paper consumption, global investments, fisheries exploited, population, loss of tropical rainforest, species extinction, average surface temperature, correlated to measures of 'development' or 'prosperity'.

The acceleration in rates of increase coincide with key developments that have defined the post-war period, namely, the Marshall Plan for redevelopment, the Keynesian and Fordist politico-economic settlement which established the basis for a boom in consumer spending built on the security of employment and access to services encapsulated by the welfare state. It is worth recalling that the settlement between capital and labour was motivated by the context of the conflict between capitalism and socialism fought out through the Cold War. It rested on the redistribution of wealth through taxation and social security based on full employment and a welfare or insurantial system, both of which had put a premium on economic growth, as I explained in Chapter 1. Besides, social democratic solutions in terms of promoting a consumer society added to the sense that the state and capital could work for the betterment of all. Since then, for both the 'left' and the 'right', and in spite of the renewed chasm between the rich and the rest, and in spite of the forebodings of limits to the planet's capacity to keep on feeding growth, the latter has become the panacea for curing all social ills from 'underdevelopment' to inequality.

But the model of incessant growth comes up against the natural limits which diagrams of 'peak oil' – and peak everything – unmistakably illustrate (Hubbert, 1956, updated by Deffeyes in *Beyond Oil*, 2006; see also, Heinberg, 2007). The details do not matter, for they change with new information. What is important and will not change significantly is the shape itself in the form of a Bell curve representing a normal curve distribution, that is, showing gradual increases followed by inevitable decline after a 'tipping point'. Adding new discoveries and new sources such as oil from shale and gas from fracking makes only minor differences without affecting the overall prognostic of tipping points, as studies of the depletion curve have shown (World's Oil and Natural Gas Scenario, 2004).

Indeed, when assessing the overall impact of converging tipping points involving other critical factors such as resources, industrial output, food production, and so on, we can build a rough picture of the likelihood of crashes, including of human populations, as the World3 model, originally developed by Meadows and colleagues in 1972, updated in 2004 illustrates (Meadows and Randers, 2004). These modellings of course make assumptions about patterns that may not all hold over the long term. Nevertheless, in the light of the findings about global warming, climate change, resource depletion, and so on, and the resistances to radical change which I have been underlining, the forecasts signal a period of intense crisis well before the end of 2100. The point of view of sustainability and steady state have recognised this reality as a starting point for some time (Daly, 1991 [1977]; Jackson, 2009 amongst many analysts).

The problem is not just about the extent of global warming and its effects, but with the conflicting pressures and the feed-back loops affecting all the parameters I have been examining so far. The worry is that it is not just environmentalists and scientists who can anticipate these events; governments, corporations, and NGOs like the World Bank and the United Nations recognise what is in store, at least in terms of warming, as the Royal Dutch Shell assumption of a 4°C rise in their forward planning demonstrates. Yet, as I noted earlier, such information seems to have no effect in halting plans by some countries to either increase the production of coal, or embark on fracking for gas in shale deposits, drill in the Arctic region for oil, and promote massive investments in the extractive industries. Even modest proposals for limiting greenhouse gas emissions, and efforts to develop renewable technologies are threatened by the development plans underway from corporations and by the 'modernising' programmes announced by many countries, as I summarised above.

I think we need to understand the current intensification in the scale of these developments as well as the resistance to change by reference to the effects of financial and corporate capitalism, for they reflect the interests hard-wired in neoliberal and new right strategies and in the shift in the balance of power towards owners of capital. Financial capitalism as an accumulation machine has incited competition for the ownership of assets in the form of raw material, land, 'real estate' especially in urban areas, communications networks, social services, etc., to generate growth in profit. The hyper-inflation of money-capital generated by new financial instruments and rent-seeking devices is now the new driver for growth, as I explained in Chapter 1. A vicious circle has set in as the different pressures combine to accelerate growth across the board compelled by inflation in money-capital. Indeed, the same pressures have triggered wars and conflicts for the control of critical raw materials in the Middle East, Central Africa, the Amazonian basin, the South China Sea, etc., and has contributed to the establishment of despotic regimes, widespread corruption and the curtailment of liberties in many parts of the world.

It is this situation that has prompted many analysts to foreground the question of the structural forces, existing economic and social models, and the vested interests preventing or impeding effective or radical programmes of action, such as, at the very least, a 'Marshall Plan' to tackle climate change. These structural forces include the spatial/territorial, temporal and scalar disjunctures due to the conflict of interests dividing nations and transnational corporations for they reduce or curtail the scope of individual states to develop alternative and sustainable ways of living. These are the same vested interests that have transposed the question of the anthropogenic source of climate change into a problem that the market itself is supposed to be able to fix through appropriate shifts towards renewable energy capture without radically challenging the capitalist framework. The political and economic stakes involved in radical transformations, such as a move away from the dominance of a carbon economy, explain why resistance to change has been so vehement, especially on the part of those who benefit most from the way things are, a resistance organised around a managed scepticism towards climate change and the promotion of technological fixes. The issue of what is to be done is thus already shackled by the politico-economic realities, precluding more radical measures, since those would require a break with neoliberal capitalism and side-line powerful players in the global economy (Urry, 2011, 2014b).

These are the reasons why I and many others have been arguing that the problems of climate change, the depletion of resources, the destruction of habitats and damage to ecosystems are inter-related events, driven by the political and geo-economic forces bound up with global capitalism and its inherent compulsion for unlimited growth to feed the machinery of accumulation (e.g. Klein, 2014; Moore, 2015). It is chiefly this implication regarding capitalism and its underlying values and assumptions that obliges us to search for postcapitalist solutions. The latter require that we take the long view into desirable and possible futures as well as undertake an interrogation of the past to make visible the political, social and cultural dynamics in which our present is caught up, as I go on to do in the next three chapters.

3
Colonialism, Dispossession and Capitalist Accumulation: A Decolonial History of the Present

Locating the postcolony: Growth, accumulation and connected crises

I have been arguing in previous chapters that there are crucial features to the developments underlying the merging of the crises I have been examining which are decisive from the point of view of understanding why they have happened and what can be done to avert the spread of despotic regimes as social and environmental conditions become unmanageable. Following many analyses, I have emphasised the perspective that this merging, far from being a matter of unfortunate coincidence, relates to the fact that the crises are both dynamically interconnected and are anthropogenic, implying that we can interrogate human activity and institutions and existing ways of life and values for the likely causal links. Besides acknowledging the constructed and contingent character of the key parameters affecting the likelihood of a tipping point – i.e. a point when a previously stable state of a system reaches a point of collapse or transition – the approach I am developing argues that the systemic character of the processes at work obliges us to recognise that they operate according to the dynamics of complexity, or 'second order' systems.[1]

The upshot is that we need to connect the simultaneity of the crises to the fact that economies, natures, technologies and cultures form co-variant, co-constituting and mobile systems. Sadly, the prevalent approach to the current predicament amongst policy-makers is circumscribed instead by a mechanistic and instrumental mindset that prevents the formulation of coherent programmes to tackle the interconnected problems we face (Venn, 2000; Stiegler, 2008). It is hampered by a reluctance to think geopolitically, not just about the environment, but other key parameters such as the economy, resources, regional conflicts and their repercussions across nations. Radical analyses of capitalism do highlight important features of the wider dynamics, for example, that developed by Lazzarato (2015), who foregrounds the power of capital and money to shape state policy, locating this power by reference to the longer history of the relationship between state and capital in terms of what he calls 'state capitalism' and its failings.

Yet, in both orthodox and many radical analyses one dimension tends to be neglected as part of the wider context affecting crisis, namely, that of what the co-articulation of capitalism, colonialism and modernity (Venn, 2000) means in terms of the forces operating today to uphold the matrix of dominant power. This chapter focuses on this dimension to show the extent to which key mechanisms and values that we associate with capitalism and its consequences have their roots in colonialism as a general process of dispossession, and in terms of abiding infrastructural and cultural legacies that reinscribe older relations of power and capital across the world. In particular it will become clear that we can detect mutations of the older assemblages of dispossession in the apparatuses that today link global financial capitalism, neo-imperialism and modernisation, cashed out in the process of the commodification and privatisation of everything, and in strategies that couple 'liberalisation' (Stiglitz, 2001) with new forms of subjugation or servitude, and with the project of 'development-as-progress'. An obvious illustration of these dynamics is the flows and circuits that we associate with the practice of offshoring (Urry, 2014a) which I signalled in Chapter 1.

The broad outlines of the deconstruction of the apparatuses or dispositifs of coloniality have been established in postcolonial studies and now from a decolonial perspective (for example, in Mignolo, 2011; Mbembe, 2001; Quijano, 2000). The latter recognises that coloniality has its effects not only through the economic, political, geographical, spatial, environmental and administrative dimensions operating in the 'postcolonial' present, but also through colonial and subaltern imaginaries that lie deep in the psyche. So, whilst as a project it aims to make visible the material and discursive structures of the apparatuses supporting exploitation and subjection, it equally seeks to undo the structures and imaginaries that support coloniality; this 'delinking' thus connects with analyses that interrogate the broader interconnections underlying convergent crises.

A further dimension shaping the genealogy of crises points to the argument that in contemporary capitalism, the interconnections are facilitated by three 'general equivalences', as I explained in Chapter 1 by reference to Nancy (2012) regarding money, Lyotard (1984 [1979]) on the role of information and cybernetic systems, and financial capitalism's restructurising of the market to serve as general equivalence via informationalisation and monetisation. This new logic operates on a global scale and circumscribes geo-economico-political systems affecting all manner of transactions. Besides, monetisation not only enables the coordination of the other two forms of equivalence, as I argued, but functions to reduce all values to the monetary form that suits business accounting practice and financialisation, thus marginalising or overwhelming all other values and epistemologies and forcing conformity to the global interest of capital, with negative impacts everywhere: on environments, resources, inequalities, social policy, and so on. The postcolony is already captured within these orbits and power dynamics.

The perspective of 'intertwined histories' (Said, 1993) which I have been indicating also implies that the problems cannot be dealt with as separable and distinct events, since change in any part of the interlocking and heterogenous systems has effects, sometimes unpredictable, in other parts of the complex whole, which means that solutions proposed for any one of them, for instance, environmental destruction and climate change, or tackling widening inequalities, will directly affect the other spheres such as the global economy, including in so-called 'developing' economies. The implications for effective change add to the sense that we may well be witnessing the passing of a whole period that started with the Industrial Revolution and saw the global ascendency of liberal capitalism and what I have analysed as 'occidentalism', i.e. the co-emergence of modernity, capitalism, colonialism and the constitution of the 'West' as a world-making composition of powers (Venn, 2000). At stake are the very foundations of the kind of world which these forces have constituted over the last two centuries to suit the interests of dispossession and domination.

A third feature of the historical conjuncture defining contemporary times, as I outlined in previous chapters, is that with the emergence of industrial-cum-liberal capitalism some two centuries ago, the project of 'progress' that we find in the discourse of classical political economy and modernity has become bound to a model that requires unlimited growth and 'enrichment'. The co-articulation of capitalism, 'enrichment' and the necessity of growth has been the foundation upon which a particular idea of prosperity has been built – though obviously a degree of growth is necessary in order to meet essential needs and to supply the vital necessities of an increasing world population. This conceptual framework is invested in both material infrastructures and institutions securing production and in an imaginary which has been globalised, as I explained in Chapter 1. It is a feature that I will interrogate further on by reference to the production of inequalities through wealth transfer that pauperises specific populations in the postcolony and everywhere. So, whilst the interconnection of crises has forced the recognition amongst a growing number of dissenters of the folly of an economy founded on a property regime which is dependent on accumulation through dispossession, privatisation and neverending growth, the basic premise and assumptions have not been sufficiently challenged in public debates.

It can be argued therefore that although the crash of 2008 has helped to concentrate minds on the urgency of the problems the world faces, the self-referential character of the concepts and categories of liberal and neoliberal political economy has produced a kind of politico-economic unconscious in which these concepts and market capitalism have coalesced in the minds of many policy-makers across the world; this mindset now underpins a common sense that blocks the imagination of postcapitalist alternatives.[2] An implication concerns the problem of decoupling the model of growth from ideas of prosperity or wellbeing, a problem analysed in recent critiques of growth, such as, amongst others, Foucault (2004a, 2004b, 2007, 2008), Jackson (2009), Latouche (2009), Stengers (2009), Harvey (2010), Wilkinson and Pickett (2010) and Urry (2011, 2014b). My argument is that this decoupling implicates the establishment of a different ontology and ethics and alternative technologies and ways of living when considering new foundations for postcapitalist societies, as I will show in Chapter 6.

However, this task comes up against the systematic denunciation of counter-discourse opposing capitalism and 'business as usual' as subversive or naive or damaging. The intensity of struggles in which existing relations of power and wealth are the stakes is exemplarily illustrated in the use of military force in many 'postcolonies', notably, in Latin America in the 1970s and 1980s to destabilise left-leaning regimes, and against decolonial struggles across the world as part of the Cold War. This background of ruthless and murderous wars in which socialist alternatives were the stake and had to be destroyed needs to be borne in mind, since the dire legacy of the Cold War survives in the form of despotic regimes, 'failed' states, civil wars and apparatuses of soft power in the postcolony that assist in the capture of resources by global corporations and dominant states. Indeed, the process of pauperisation across the world relies on carceral regimes and militaristic agencies for their effectiveness; such mechanisms have now become an integral part of the geopolitical landscape (Mbembe, 2001; Venn, 2006a).

Colonial expansion, dispossession, markets and the emergence of capitalism

Underlying the tendencies which now bring the world to the tipping points foreboded by convergent crises, one finds a determining feature, namely, a long history of accumulation, developing over a number of cumulative stages or phases, driven by historical, technological and political forces which require careful elaboration to avoid simplification. An extensive literature exists which calls attention to what Harvey, developing Marx's analysis of capital, calls 'accumulation by dispossession', a process that for Harvey 'takes a seemingly infinite variety of forms in different places and times' (Harvey, 2010: 244; also Harvey, 2003; Marx, 1970 [1867]). My analysis in Chapter 1 already highlighted key aspects of this historical process by relocating the present state of the world by reference to the correlations linking forms of accumulation/dispossession to regimes of property, to systems of circulation and distribution of resources and knowledges, forms of commodification, and of course to underlying regimes of power, including by reference to those inscribed in histories of colonial and class dispossession, the effects of which can be uncovered across all these systems.

In making these claims about the longevity of forms of dispossession, I shall juxtapose two series of studies. First, the *longue durée* or long-term periodisation of economic and social development analysed particularly in Fernand Braudel's (1984) three volumes opus, *Civilization & Capitalism*, Giovanni Arrighi's (1994) *The Long Twentieth Century*, and Karl Polanyi's (2001 [1944]) *The Great Transformation*; and secondly, the genealogy of neoliberalism and biopolitcs established by Michel Foucault in his lectures from 1975 to 1979, edited and translated as Foucault, (2003), (2007) and (2008). This is because, on the one hand, the first series helps to support the argument that liberal capitalism is a special case of a market economy and makes clear the role of colonialism in its consolidation; whilst, on the other hand, Foucault's work makes visible the exercise of power in shaping the apparatuses or dispositifs of governmentality that emerged in conjunction with capitalism and liberal political economy, and that put into place, in both colonised and colonisers' territories, the institutional, legal, disciplinary, political and subjective mechanisms that underpinned their efficacious functioning. Both series enable us to explore the wider socio-political and historical developments leading up to the present conjuncture, and the role of liberal and now neoliberal capitalism in this process.

By foregrounding the constitutive role of colonialism in the history of capitalism up to the present, the chapter throws light on a whole history of systematic appropriation and pauperisation that alters one's perspective regarding our current predicament. It is worth noting that the poor, and so-called 'developing' and poorer economies increasingly occupy an important place in many dissident accounts of inequality, notably Wilkinson and Pickett (2010), Stiglitz (2010), Piketty (2014), or Chang (2010), thus echoing the arguments of those like Harvey (2010) who locate dispossession as a key parameter in the critique of capitalism. Yet, as I have been arguing, interrogations of the economic crisis generally tend to neglect the existing literature in 'decolonial' studies which demonstrates the continuity between today's geo-politico-economic conjuncture and the older colonial period when the success of capitalism, measured in terms of its ability to deliver growth for 'Western' centres and prosperity for elites, depended upon the transfer of wealth from those pauperised in the process, as I have shown in Venn, (2006a) and (2009a). A more trenchant and historically informed examination of the present global economy is therefore needed to show these continuities, particularly in terms of growing inequality, built-in and institutionalised disadvantages, ecological destruction, climate change and resource depletion.

In order to do this, we could start with the proposition that the evidence in the history of European colonialism, and mounting evidence in our 'neoliberal' times, shows that capitalism is an intrinsically zero-sum game, which means that it necessarily produces poverty and inequality at the levels of both nations and globally (Venn, 2009a). In what follows, I will link this reality to an analysis of the colonial roots of liberal capitalism and to mechanisms such as offshoring and new forms of enclosure whereby today neoliberalism has extended the inequalities and the destruction and plunder of the planet to 'postcolonial' period. I will then strategically use Foucault's genealogy of liberal and neoliberal political economy and governmentality (2003, 2007, 2008) in order to underline two important features of this logic of destruction and exploitation, namely, the relationship connecting unequal accumulation and the emergence of 'consumer culture' to the model of 'progress' and 'development' and to growth-as-prosperity, and secondly, the role of what Foucault calls the 'discourse of race war' as an integral dimension of the processes involved.

The connection between colonialism and unequal accumulation has long been demonstrated in a large literature, indicatively, in Eric Williams (1964), Arghiri Emmanuel (1972), Immanuel Wallerstein (1974), Samir Amin (1977), Pierre Jalée (1981), Fernand Braudel (1986 [1979]), Tzvetan Todorov (1992), Giovanni Arrighi (1994), a corpus which I have analysed previously (Venn, 2006a, 2009a). I will summarise some of the salient issues because they have become invisible in many current accounts of connected crises, and because the historical dimension of colonialism supplements Foucault's analysis of the relationship between political economy, governmentality and power. Additionally, a decolonial account of the means whereby unequal exchange and the extraction of 'surplus' value were secured reveals the fact that such forms of exploitation or domination do not happen by themselves but depends on mechanisms set up precisely to disadvantage the subjugated, including through discourses that legitimate differences by claiming they reflect 'backwardness' or deficiencies in terms of 'rationality', productive capabilities or progressive values. Decolonial interrogation targets these mechanisms to show the conflicting interests, and thus the question of politics and power inscribed in exploitative regimes.

Ironically, the iniquity of colonial dispossession is acknowledged in Adam Smith who highlights the great benefits for Europe of the 'discovery of America' contrasted to the 'savage injustices of the Europeans' that made colonisation 'ruinous and destructive to several of those unfortunate countries' (1812 [1776]: 348). Smith was speaking about the transformation in trade and the fortunes of Europe that the New World made possible, thus recognising that the conquest of the Americas has been a key factor conditioning the emergence of mercantilism. One can extend this wider view of economic transformation to link liberal so-called 'laissez-faire' capitalism with the opening up of the 'East' for colonial empires and the increase in trade with Asia from around the middle of the 18th century, after the end of Portuguese monopoly in the region (India and S.E. Asia, then later China and Japan). Arrighi (1994), Braudel (1986 [1979]) and Polanyi (2001 [1944]), who have differently explored this episode in the genealogy of capitalism, are all in agreement about the crucial role played by this European expansion in the triumph of liberal capitalism.

Braudel for example notes the fundamental importance of 'free "primitive accumulation" that the plundering of Bengal meant to the English' after 1757 (1986 [1979]: 222), whilst Arrighi has shown that the 'liberalization of the Indian trade' (referring to the abolition of the East India Company's monopoly in 1813) 'helped the import-substitution efforts of European and American governments and businesses and resulted in widespread losses of foreign markets for the British cotton weaving and finishing industries' (1994: 262). This was when 'political control over large, captive, unprotected economic spaces became the main source of external economies for British business. The Indian subcontinent, with its huge textile industry and commercialised agriculture, was by far the most important of these captive and unprotected economic spaces' (Arrighi, 1994: 262). Ruthless exploitation followed the imposition of 'free trade', supported by the most brutal military means (Colley, 2002; Galeano, 1971; Semmel, 2004; Newsinger, 2006), whilst,

> Railroads, steamships, and the opening of the Suez Canal in 1869 transformed India into a major source of cheap food and raw materials for Europe ... In the late nineteenth and early twentieth centuries, the large surplus in the Indian balance of payments became the pivot of the enlarged reproduction of Britain's world-scale processes of capital accumulation and of the City's mastery of world finance. (Arrighi, 1994: 263)

The fortunes made directly helped to consolidate and ground the politico-economic hegemony that Britain exercised in Europe during what he calls the 'Long Twentieth Century', starting with the defeat of the French by Britain in 1814 – a war financed by the loot from India as he shows – and inaugurating what is referred to as 'Pax Britannica' (Polanyi, 2001 [1944]: 14).

This background to the emergence of capitalism needs to include as condition the extensive development in pre-colonial times of market economies in India, China and other parts of the world. The contrast between this period of relatively more advanced economies outside Europe and the poverty and 'underdevelopment' to which these regions were reduced after colonisation adds to the argument against capitalism as an avenue for collective prosperity. Braudel (1986 [1979]) – undoing the more Eurocentric analysis of the economy in his earlier work (1974 [1967]) – points to the following conditions for the epochal shifts that announced the birth of capitalism and modernity: the rise of the merchant class and mercantilism in Europe in the previous two centuries or so; the role of banking and monopolies controlling the network of commercial exchanges linking Western Europe to the more developed market economies of India and China via Arab states (Arrighi, 1994: 40; Braudel, 1986 [1979]: Chs 1, 2, 3); the importance of the great economic cycles in Europe, particularly the shifts in financial power from Genoa and Venice (15th to early 17th century) to the Dutch and Amsterdam from the late 16th century. Braudel singles out the central role of trade networks and sites of economic activity, mainly cities, fairs, trading compounds, already established as economic and cultural hubs before industrialisation in Europe, linking Europe with India, China, Japan, the Muslim world, and after the Conquest in 1492, the Americas.

What the historical accounts I'm outlining show is the complexity and sophistication of the trading networks and products that European colonisers took over and reconstituted to serve their interests. An exemplary case is that of the circulation of silver that shows the correlation of its production, extracted from the huge mines at Potosi in Bolivia and other mining centres in South America from the 16th century, with export, then the minting of coins in different parts of the world, and their circulation in the form of currency in Europe, India, China and Japan. Thus, in 1614, about 400 different currencies circulated in the Netherlands (Braudel, 1986 [1979]: 196, 197), whilst up to 'half the silver mined in America between 1527 and 1821 found its way to China', which already had an extensive market and money economy, and widely used silver currency in internal and external trade (Braudel, 1986 [1979]: 198). Indeed, as Braudel demonstrates: 'For long ages – centuries before the Europeans sailed round the Cape of Good Hope – there had been immense networks of trade covering the Indian Ocean and the seas bordering the Pacific' (1986 [1979]: 219).

Describing the system of networks within networks, of relays linking all parts of the world, especially after 1492, he says: 'The Portuguese, Dutch, English, and French traders borrowed from Muslims, from Banyans (in India) or from the moneylenders of Kyoto, the silver without which no transaction was possible from Nagasaki to Surat' (1986 [1979]: 220, 221). In short, 'The networks of trade encircled the world', notes Braudel (1986 [1979]: 148). Equally he points out that 'Equal and unequal exchange, balance and imbalance of trade, domination and subjugation serve to draw a map of the commercial world' (1986 [1979]: 204). In this new phase of market economies, with Europe deriving enormous wealth from the pillage and exploitation of the resources of the Americas, it was the merchants who reaped the greatest benefit, whilst 'The rich became excessively rich, and the poor wretched' (1986 [1979]: 211). A familiar story nowadays.

This correlation of accumulation and pauperisation is emphasised also in Arrighi's (1994) analysis of the colonisation of India with regard to the emergence of capitalism when he details how the wealth extracted had served to finance the extension of the British Empire through conquests elsewhere and wars in Europe (I summarise this argument in Venn, 2009a: 209–211). Their analyses support the claim of a continuity in the process of European accumulation through different phases of global colonial expansion from the conquest of the Americas to the present via notably the 'Scramble for Africa' and the 'Middle-East' in the 1880s, and now a new phase of globalisation characterised by financial capitalism and new 'looting machines' (Burgis, 2015). Decolonial counter-history foregrounds the intimate connection between the emergence of industrial capitalism and the products and wealth associated with the Atlantic Slave Trade, notably silver, sugar, cotton, spices, tobacco, a wide variety of plants from the Americas (Williams, 1964; Fryer, 1984); it supplements the conventional narrative that points to technological innovations such as steam power, the railways, factory production as key drivers of industrialisation.

The next phase of global expansion brings into view the role of oil, aluminium and other raw materials essential for the emergent electrical, chemical, petrochemical and car industries that were the basis for the second industrial revolution, again built on colonial loot, notably, in the wake of the

'Scramble for Africa' in the 1880s. Finally, in addition to these older resources and their intensified extraction today, we now see the capture of new materials such as coltan and cobalt (mainly in Central Africa) and lithium (mainly in South America), essential in the manufacture of digital and electronic devices, that feed into what some writers call the 'third industrial revolution' grounded in information technologies and in the expanded and rapid flows of goods, people, money, cultures. Concerning this current phase of global capital, we need to bear in mind also the consequences for producing inequalities of the new forms of rent-seeking devices dominated by financialisation and its universal and borderless scope as I described in Chapter 1 (further details in Venn, 2009a: 210, and Venn, 2006a). The analyses of the colonial period which writers like Braudel, Arrighi and Polanyi have produced echo the effects of current phases of privatisation and 'liberalisation' in terms of the intensification of dispossession and the production of inequalities across nations and continents, established in works I have cited, for example, Townsend (2000), Stiglitz (2001), Wilkinson and Pickett (2009) and Atkinson (2015).

What I am trying to establish is both the sense of a continuity in terms of the logic of dispossession and private accumulation, as well as in terms of some of the apparatuses put in place to effect the transfer of wealth. Yet, one needs to recognise the heterogenous, mobile and pragmatic character of these apparatuses. To illustrate the kind of complex dynamics and geography of these developments and the contribution of colonialism to the genealogy of capitalism, one could look at the Triangular Trade system linking the slave trade, plantation economy and industrialisation through circuits and the circulation of goods, raw material, people, and wealth between Europe, Africa, the Americas/the West Indies (Fryer, 1984). Two aspects are worth considering, concerning, first, the assemblages or dispositifs themselves, including the authorising discourses examined below and what they reveal about the process of appropriation; secondly, the link between the exercise of power over the subjugated and the management of captured territories and wealth. Both have legacies that we need to factor in when we address the contemporary situation.

The Triangular Trade[3] amply illustrates the international yet embedded character of many of the mechanisms supporting the process of generating and appropriating wealth, especially the economic instruments such as letters of credit, international loans, the commission system, the circulation of currency operating through specific relays such as merchant families, trade hubs, banking practices, trade routes, etc. (Braudel, 1986 [1979]; Arrighi, 1994). Braudel, speaking about plantation economy, says:

> More straightforward than the regions of second serfdom, these were capitalist creations par excellence: money, credit, trade, exchange tied them to the east side of the Atlantic. Everything was remote controlled from Seville, Cadiz, Bordeaux, Rouen, Amsterdam, Bristol and Liverpool. To create the

plantations, everything had to be brought over from the old continents: the masters ... black Africans ... the plants themselves, except for tobacco ... the techniques of sugar production. (1986 [1979]: 272–273)

The Triangular Trade is but one amongst a host of other examples which demonstrate that, underlying the process of accumulation, we find the deliberate and planned establishment of the means to ensure wealth transfer to the rich and powerful. Generally, these are discursive (say, liberalism, classical political economy, tropes of savagery), institutional/administrative/legal (namely, colonial governors and administration, the system of taxation, property laws, systems of security and militarisation), economic (banking, the joint-stock company, currencies, tariffs, sugar plantations) and technological (mining, sugar refining, navigational instruments, slave ships, military technology, etc.). As an example regarding colonial economic regimes, we can signal the following: In India the introduction of free trade as well as a whole series of laws such as about land ownership – which introduced a new basis for new, often crippling, taxes and tariffs (Prakash, 1990; Arrighi, 1994; Merefield, 2004; Birla, 2009). In Ireland, similarly, laws such as the 1660 Navigation Act which prohibited all Irish export to the colonies, or the Cattle Acts of 1663 and 1667 that restricted cattle production, or the Staple Acts of 1671 that ended the flow of sugar and tobacco into the colony (Armitage, 2000: 148–151); they all ensured that the Irish economy could not compete on equal terms and could only become a dependent economy serving British interests alone. Today, the global machinery of extraction and transfer of wealth put into place in the period of European colonialism and imperialism has grown in sophistication, operating through arrangements that perpetuate unequal terms of trade and unequal exchange.

These mechanisms include 'structural adjustments' forced on the post-colony or ex-colonies, land and mineral grabs or enclosures, debt financing, tariffs on exported goods, the conditions of technology transfer and 'intellectual property' trading, the influence of 'advisers', and conditionalities that are usually attached to soft power including 'aid' packages, the sale of military hardware, infrastructure building, and so on. One should add the policing role of surviving Bretton Woods institutions like the IMF, the workings of the WTO and inter-governmental cartels like G7 and G20, which reinforce the rules of the game that support unequal exchange. Kleptocracies or the vulture class in many supposedly 'postcolonial' countries complicitly facilitate the process of dispossession, and embezzle what's left. The case of the activities of 1MDB (1 Malaysia Development Berhad) is a classic example, for it shows the interpenetration of global finance, the economic and political power of local elites, 'development' used as a vehicle for the appropriation of the nation's wealth, and the role of offshoring through the network of enabling and unregulated mechanisms operating in the interest of private accumulation (Ramesh, 2016).

Equally, these measures and activities demonstrate the centrality of the colonial enterprise in the emergence of some of the elements which Foucault highlights in his concept of governmentality, namely, the new economic rationality centred on the market, the problem of security in Europe and in the colonies, and the governmentalisation of subjugated populations as elements of biopower. In his genealogy of biopolitics and neoliberalism, Foucault makes the important point that in the discourse of classical political economy the possibility of collective enrichment and progress in Europe depended on the extension of the market to cover the totality of possible goods, that is, provided that there be 'a globalisation of the market' such that through competition 'the entire world becomes its market' (2008: 55). It must be said, as Braudel and others establish, that from the 17th century, Europe as an economic subject, and as a plurality of states seeking a balance of force, had already taken the world as its economic domain, for 'the game is in Europe, but the stake is the world' (Foucault, 2008: 56). In *Security, Territory, Population,* he has linked the relationship of Europe with the rest of the world in terms of colonial domination when he said 'its relationship with the whole world marks the very specificity of Europe in relation to the world, since the only type of relationship that Europe must have and begins to have with the rest of the world is that of economic domination or colonization, or at least commercial utilization' (2007: 298). This attitude has a long and complex history, explored by many, for example, Gilroy (1993) and Pagden (1993) (details in Venn, 2000, 2006a).

The key issue from the point of view of the implication for the contemporary phase of globalisation is the systematic reliance, then and now, of the prosperity of the 'West' upon the profit derived from activities in the colonies and now the 'postcolony' (Emmanuel, 1972; Polanyi, 2001 [1944]; Joxe, 2002; Newsinger, 2006). Many of the instruments may not be the same, but the attitudes remain the same, and many key institutions and infrastructures set up in the colonial period continue to provide support for the new mechanisms of private and corporate accumulation. Here one could highlight the role of 'treasure inlands' (Shaxson, 2012) such as the British Virgin Islands or the Cayman Islands and the wide range of practices to do with 'offshoring' regarding banking, financial capitalism, commercial transactions, the secreting of wealth from tax regimes, and so on which John Urry has explored as part of his critique of neoliberal capitalism (Urry, 2014a, and in Chapter 1).

Another essential element in the genealogy of liberal capitalism that I am sketching is the effect of the commodification of land, labour and money, that is, what Polanyi called 'fictitious commodities', on the grounds that they were not produced for sale on the market (2001 [1944]: 75, 76, 204), and have often not been thought of as things that could be privately owned. The case of land is typical, for in Europe land became 're-territorialised' and thus available as a commodity for the market after the Enclosures, whilst land grabs in Australia and the Americas under cover of *terra nullius*, and in India and Africa through forcible 'legalised' privatisation (Prakash, 1990) enabled the capture of wealth through property tax, etc. Interestingly, land is still in theory not privatised in China, as Wang Hui has pointed out

(2009: xxvii). Indeed, the history of colonisation is marked by the privatisation and commodification of land previously regarded as inalienable common wealth and subject to customary rights, say, amongst indigenous Americans and Australians, and in parts of India and Africa before colonial occupation. It is worth recalling that the idea of common land in Europe before the Enclosures retained the crucial distinction between wealth and property upon which Arendt (2000) insisted, and that capitalism abolishes. Increases in the velocity and volume of circulation of these new 'commodities' correlated with the rate of profit (as the Physiocrats amongst political economists knew, see Braudel, 1986 [1979]); the process contributed to wealth creation for owners of capital, whilst also unsettling equilibria, thus adding to the pressures to rethink the economy in terms of a 'free market' and 'free trade'.

The *longue durée* history of the relation of colonialism to capitalism and economic discourse enables one to highlight the fact that the neglect of the legacy of colonialism in analyses of the current economic crisis results in an incomplete and flawed view of the economic landscape whilst obscuring the function of pauperisation or wealth transfer in the consolidation of liberal capitalism and political economy in the 19th and 20th centuries. Equally, it obscures the pre-existing material and discursive conditions that have supported the intensification of inequalities which has occurred with the predominance of neoliberalism in the last 30 years.

The picture I am drawing shows that inequality within and between nations is not simply about 'relations of productions', but rather about the apparatuses (and the subjectivities) put into place for the purpose, working in a pragmatic manner, and thus subject to constant tactical and strategic modifications. Today, as I noted, the global machinery of extraction and transfer of 'surplus' set up in the period of European colonialism and imperialism has grown in sophistication, whilst a new scramble is currently taking place whereby arable land in 'developing countries' is being bought up by sovereign funds and transnationals, and mineral rights secured, with China and India joining the fray. A genealogy of capitalism, and its constitutive relation to dispossession, colonial and otherwise, needs to take account of these politico-economico-technical networks and assemblages if it is to have a purchase on the events leading up to the emergence of liberal and now neoliberal political economy and the socialities they sustain.

The 'discourse of race war': Subjugating, 'othering', taking

The point of view emphasising the material, institutional and discursive conditions and apparatuses that constitute economies, and their associated socialities and regimes of power leads us on to my second theme as part of reframing the genealogy of neoliberalism. Foucault's interrogation of the discourses that authorise these regimes of power, and thus systems of oppression and exploitation, points the way. The perspective I have developed above concerning the colonialism/capitalism nexus provides the wider vista for relocating the genealogy of power from classical sovereignty to governmentality and biopolitics. A key text that adds to my analysis is *Society Must be Defended* (Foucault, 2003) which introduces the idea of the 'discourse of race war' as part of theorising the relationship between colonialism and dispossession. In his analysis, the 'discourse of race war' is understood by reference to the form of power over life, or biopower, that he associates with the classical theory of sovereignty characterised by the power of the sovereign to kill or to let live (Foucault, 2003: 240). This is contrasted to a biopolitics centred on a technology of power that takes 'man-as-living-being' and 'man-as-species' as targets for a management whose principal aim is the maximisation of a population's capacities (2003: 242) in line with 'the power to "make live" and "let" die' (2003: 241). Its field of intervention is public hygiene, health, reproduction, education and training, and the environment or milieu (2003: 244, 245); one of its aims is to minimise the effects of the accidental, for example through a system of insurance and techniques that have subsequently developed in the form of the apparatuses of social security.

The difference with respect to biopower is that the latter is a 'political technology' (Foucault, 2000: 417) that operates a radical division of a population into

> them and us, the unjust and the just, the masters and those who must obey them, the rich and the poor, the mighty and those who have to work in order to live, those who invade lands and those who tremble before them, the despots and the groaning people, the men of today's law and those of the homeland of the future. (Foucault, 2003: 74)

Biopolitics, on the other hand, is focused on the question of the development of 'technologies of the social' (Foucault, 1979) that deploy practices of normalisation and disciplining guided by normative discourses to condition the formation of subjects and specific groups or populations as an intrinsic component of the exercise of power as a positive force aiding the productive process (Foucault, 1975, 1979; Henriques et al., 1998 [1984]). In the period of liberal capitalism, increases in the productive capacity of populations clearly served the economic interests of owners of capital.

The process is more complicated than might appear because power is at once diffused and centred, located in agonistic spaces of the social, whilst knowledge of relevant factors and their effects is imperfect, allowing for undecidability as well as spaces of dissidence. There are crucial differences too regarding the exercise of power over the subjugated in the colonies where one encounters a hybrid of the two technologies of power – biopower and biopolitics – in the form of imperial governmentality. This form of power exercised over a colonised or subjugated population was characterised by the military strategy framed by the 'us versus them' mentality, thus devoid of a sense of responsibility for those categorised as 'other' or as recalcitrant subjects. As we know, the subjugative thrust intrinsic to imperial governmentality was sanitised through the doctrine of a

Christianising and 'civilising mission' that provided cover for colonial expansion whilst masquerading as moral duty.

The key point is that, for Foucault, subjugation and the 'discourse of race war' form a mutually reinforcing couple: 'Racism first developed with colonization, in other words, with colonizing genocide' (Foucault, 2003: 257). Racism thus has similarities with the relationship of war which prescribes that 'in order to live, you must destroy your enemies' (2003: 255). Yet he says that in its functioning, 'racism does make the relationship of war ... compatible with the exercise of biopower', for, 'The death of the other, the death of the bad race, the inferior race (or the degenerate, or the abnormal) is something that will make life in general healthier: healthier and purer ... In a normalizing society, race or racism is the precondition that makes killing acceptable' (2003: 255, 256). Clearly we encounter such sentiments at the root of fascism and fundamentalist rule. It can be argued that all systems of exclusion and all unequal relations of power put into play one or more elements of the binary matrix that authorises 'killing' the other as an expression of sovereign might and right, a view qualified by Foucault when he points out that 'killing' includes 'the fact of exposing someone to death, increasing the risk of death for some people, or, quite simply, political death, expulsion, rejection, and so on' (Foucault, 2003: 256).

We have seen many examples of this kind of political liquidation and exclusion in recent times, from the treatment of migrants, 'asylum seekers', and those escaping postcolonial wars and neo-colonial enclosures, to the hounding of specific groups of people on the basis of race, ethnicity/caste, religion, gender, sexuality, class, political allegiance and so on; at the limit, the 'discourse of race war' provokes genocide, that is, a 'thanatopolitics' (Foucault, 2000: 416; see also Mbembe's [2008], related notion of necropolitics evident in the deployment of terror, colonial and otherwise). These forms of the othering of the other as inferior, as dangerous, or as the contaminating outsider, or as those who must be sacrificed (Agamben, 1998), are part of a system of security that aims to cast the 'other' as a threat, that is, viewed as the source of division or pollution or risk. It is a strategy that lends legitimacy to the discursive move which locates them outside the sphere of concern or responsibility of those positioned as the 'masters', the 'betters', the 'pure', the legitimate, the hard-working, the righteous, the 'true' believer.

To highlight the longevity of forms of dispossession, and to foreground war and conquest as its originary instance, one could note Graeber's (2011) reference to the interesting case of landless 'low castes' people in a region of the Himalayas referred to as 'the vanquished ones', and who continue to be in a situation of being permanently indebted to the landlord caste descended from the original conquerors. These subjugated people are still paying back the 'debt' incurred at the point of dispossession through shocking forms of repayment imposed by the 'superior' caste, yet to which they submit simply because they regard the situation as 'just the way things worked' (2011: 9). Similar examples of a fateful resignation hard-wired into a culture exist in many parts of the world, relating to forced bondage and conquest as the origin of a 'debt' still being repaid by the descendants of the vanquished (see Mark, 2012 regarding Mauritania). One can cite also the tragic case of Haiti, forced to pay a vast fortune to the French for the costs the latter incurred during the Haitians' war of independence in 1825, a 'debt' only repaid in 1947, whilst the crippling effects endure still.

The important element which I want to keep visible is that, tied to the 'discourse of race war', or rather tied to what is at stake in the dividing strategy which that discourse operates amongst a population, is the fact that the underlying motivation is the need to legitimise dispossession and appropriation by appeal to the moral authority of some discourse or other. This is typically to be found in a religion or the myth of racial destiny that underwrites the naturalisation and essentialisation of differences. Equally, the process of othering is often grounded in the claim of natural necessity, as in varieties of evolutionism recruited in support of racialisation. Today, the standpoint of natural necessity is transmuted into the idea of the superior efficiency and rationality of capitalism and its technological supports, determined by (often simplistic) cost/benefit accounting, and equated to, or packaged as progressive modernisation and development. Such arguments function as rhetorical moves in the play of power, and provide a vocabulary framing socio-economic policy.

The search for moral authority has a venerable pedigree, inasmuch as the discourse of political economy in modern times such as in Adam Smith ultimately appeals to the idea of the general good as legitimating basis – though as we know, he argued that this end is unknowingly served by the aggregate of individual self-interest (examined in Chapter 4). In neoliberalism, by contrast, the discourse of legitimation relies on claims to greater efficiency in the use of scarce resources and the maximisation of value secured by what it posits as 'unimpeded' market mechanisms, particularly 'competition'. However, the claim that the system ultimately benefits the needy flounders in the light of the fact of growing inequality and destitution even in rich countries over the past decades, as I have already noted by reference to studies such as those of Wilkinson and Pickett (2010), or Stiglitz (2013). Evidence for their arguments regularly appears in countless reports, e.g. recently, by the International Labour Organisation report 'World Employment and Social Outlook 2015', that underlines the link between precarisation of work and inequality and poverty (Torres, 2015).

Thus, underneath the discourses that posit essential differences, or the proper order of society as basis for inequalities, one uncovers a political economy of race and class and gender exploitation (Venn, 2011). Mechanisms of disavowal are often at work in such discourses whereby dispossession or relations of subservience are made invisible by being displaced onto the language of naturalism, superior reason, good order, benevolence, or else parsed in terms of the catch-all concept of progress and its metonymies, such as in the claim of a 'civilising mission' (Derrida, 1997b: 27; Said, 1978; Venn, 2000: 56). Revisionist historians even today dress up colonial exploitation in terms of the benefits the subjugated derived in one way or another. As ever, the poor and the down-trodden are supposed to be grateful, or consider themselves lucky that it isn't worse.

The point of charting the shift which Foucault examines is that one could argue that the discourse of neoliberalism combines elements of a racialisation of populations with a management of capacities to constitute a neo-biopolitics, thus prompting analysis to see in this shift similarities with imperial governmentality, that is, a form of governance that necessarily splits a population into antagonistic couples: the docile and the insurgent, the productive and the unproductive, the victors and the vanquished, us/them. And, since neoliberalism abnegates state or collective responsibility for the general or common good anyway (as I noted in Chapter 1 and will show in Chapter 4), its discourse in principle legitimises the othering of the other that not only provides ideological cover for exploitation, but easily slips into 'a new racism modeled on war' (Foucault, 2003: 258). Today, incited by the pressures arising from crises, the othering of the excluded other intensifies the tendency to criminalise or demonise all those who are not 'like us': the immigrant, the refugee, the 'abnormal', the 'outsiders'.

It is clear then that the bigger picture that I am outlining makes visible not only the constitutive role of colonialism in European and global redistribution of wealth from 1492, but binds the genealogy of capitalism not just with mercantilism at one end and neoliberalism at the other, as Foucault (2007, 2008) for example does, but also with the genealogy of Western modernity, the development of the Industrial Revolution, phases of globalisation, and with the normalisation of military power (Venn, 2006a). By adding the historical context beyond Europe, one can begin to construct an analytical framework that integrates the economic, the political, the technical and the discursive in a more complex and revealing way than appears in conventional analyses. It uncovers too what the 'invisible hand' of 'free' market or 'laissez-faire' capitalism hides from view, that is, not only the pauperisation which is intrinsic to it, but also the fact that '(T)here is nothing natural about laissez-faire; free markets could not have come into being merely by allowing things to take their course. Just as cotton manufactures – the leading free trade industry – were created by the help of protective tariffs, export bounties, and indirect wage subsidies, laissez-faire itself was enforced by the state' (Polanyi, 2001 [1944]: 145).

The question for today is about the ways in which the shift to financial capitalism as I described it in Chapter 1 has altered the location of the poorer or weaker economies within global relations of power. I shall explore this by reference to the functioning of generalised competition in the discourse of neoliberalism as understood in Foucault's analysis, my aim being to correlate financial capitalism's drive for the domination of markets worldwide with the 'normalisation' of 'societies of control' (Deleuze, 1990) tied to the increasing militarisation of societies. This view resonates with Foucault's point regarding the relation of domination or colonisation which, according to the discourse of political economy, Europe needed to have with the rest of the world if the globalisation of the market from the middle of the 18th century was to advance the enrichment and 'progress' of Europe, as I noted above.

Universalising competition, neoliberal governance and the structural dominance of global capital

In this concluding section, I want to show the extent to which neoliberal determination of the framework for economic transaction globally, and corporate strategies for the appropriation of critical resources and 'surplus value' from the 'postcolony' dovetail each other. The logics underlying the two processes are correlated by way of the concept of competition as operator, particularly in its generalised form that, equally, correlates with 'the generalization of the economic form of the market' (Foucault, 2008: 243). To analyse this conjuncture, we can return to Foucault's (2007) genealogy of governmentality, and that of biopolitics and ordo- and neoliberalism (2008), elements of which I summarised above by reference to coloniality as a general process of domination and dispossession (see page 65). I picked out the central role of competition in the earlier phase of the emergence of governmentality from the operation of 'police' in the 17th century as a 'technological assemblage' (2007: 312) that enabled the establishment of 'a mobile, yet stable and controllable relationship between the state's internal order and the development of its forces' (2007: 313), to that of the emergence from the 18th century of a state rationality drawn on the market as model. In the earlier phase, following the Treaty of Westphalia in 1648, competition was driven by the shift from competition for territory inside Europe amongst the dominant powers to competition in the search for wealth creation and extraction extended to the whole world. It was a 'transition from the rivalry of princes to the competition of states' that was 'one of the most funadamental mutations in both the form of Western political life and the form of Western history' (2007: 294). I indicated earlier how this mutation required that the world be the stake and domain for Europe, and my account of colonial expansion and appropriation in the previous section described the state-sponsored strategies and apparatuses put into place to achieve this goal.

In more recent times, competition has acquired the status of a superior rationality in the discourse of neoliberalism, replacing exchange as in classical political economy. It is foregrounded in Foucault's analysis of post-liberal discourse when he charts the shift from classical political economy to German ordoliberal's 'vital politics' and American neoliberalism. He points to the ordoliberals' arguments promoting the role of competition as 'a principle of formalization ... (C)ompetition as an essential economic logic will appear and produce its effects under certain conditions which have to be carefully and artificially constructed' (2008: 120). The ordoliberals thus reject the 'naive naturalism' of classical political economy that assumes that competition is a natural phenomenon inscribing 'natural' forces and propensities rather than being the result of calculations and planning. Their critique of 'naive naturalism' targets the assumption that, through the mechanism of exchange the market works to establish the 'true price' of commodities (2008: 31, 46, 120). In Foucault's account, ordoliberals' significant departure from classical liberalism is announced in the arguments of people like Walter Euken and Wilhelm Ropke, who, recognising the constructed and contingent character of economies, concluded that,

> the market, or rather pure competition, which is the very essence of the market, cannot appear unless it is produced, and unless it is produced by an active governmentality. There will thus be a sort of complete superposition (recouvrement) of market mechanisms, indexed to competition, and governmental policy. Government must accompany the market from start to finish … One must govern for the market, rather than because of the market. (Foucault, 2008: 121, 122–125; [Foucault, 2004b: 125]; see also my analysis in Venn, 2009a)

Neoliberalism in its 'more radical' American form goes further, for it 'still involves, in fact, the generalization of the economic form of the market. It involves generalizing it throughout the social body and including the whole of the social system not usually conducted through or sanctioned by monetary exchanges' (2008: 243). Furthermore, 'the generalization of the market beyond monetary exchanges functions … as a principle of intelligibility and a principle of decipherment of social relationships and individual behaviour' (2008: 243). When we juxtapose and extend this grid of intelligibility in the context of competition on a world scale, that is, in terms of its effect in determining economic and geopolitical strategies affecting all states, and in terms of determining the framework that enables capital to operate as smoothly as possible globally, we begin to recognise the extent to which the rules of the game constrain 'postcolonies' and weak states in an iron grip that yoke them to dominant economies and the interests of transnational corporations. Furthermore, the structural dominance of the global economy by financial capitalism is absolutely consistent with the promotion of competition as a central feature of neoliberalism. These are the reasons for claiming that the neoliberal determination of the framework and corporate instruments for extracting wealth globally dovetail each other by way of the discourse promoting competition. Today the logics underlying this situation interpenetrate in the operation of globalised and virtualised or intangible capital working in tandem with the capture of assets in the form of land, mineral rights, infrastructure, sovereign debt, and so on.

The consequences have been clear for some time, for, state intervention to favour competition has become the ubiquitous reality, including by opening up the apparatuses of social welfare and resources such as water, minerals and land in the 'postcolony' and elsewhere, for private acquisition in the interest of the market, that is, of capital. Besides, neoliberal governmentality premised on the universalisation and globalisation of competition necessitates the standardisation of systems of management across all these areas, operating through the laws, the regulatory apparatuses, the property regimes, the fiscal and monetary policy, accounting practices, etc., to ensure that comparison of 'efficiency' and 'value for money' can be aligned with an audit culture. Indeed, competition has become the universal motto, functioning as a regulative idea determining calculation across all sectors of the global economy and all aspects of society and individual behaviour, as Foucault (2008) and Dardot and Laval (2010) show, with clear effects for the 'postcolony'.

Furthermore, it has become evident also that claims about the role of generalised competition as the mechanism which is supposed to enable the 'private sector' to deliver better efficiency and 'value-for-money' in public services and businesses alike rely on a number of mythical assumptions, since the evidence shows failures and cost-inflation in many cases where an industry, say, energy production, or a service such as public transport or health has been privatised. As Andrew Glyn argues, 'It is hard to find robust evidence of the effects on productivity of a switch in ownership to the private sector' (2007: 39). In his analysis of the case of the privatisation of public utilities in the UK, what is clear is that the new owners and managers gained most as profits increased whilst the wages bill fell: 'The big gainers from privatization were those that "stagged" the issues of shares (selling them for a quick profit), the firms in the City which earned large fees from arranging privatizations and management ... (whilst) the main losers were those workers who lost relatively well-paid, unionized jobs' (Glyn, 2007: 40). More recently, the many cases studied by Mariana Mazzucato (2013) amply debunk the myth of the private sector as more risk-taking and innovative than the public sector which is claimed to be risk-averse by mainstream economists. Paradoxically, the reframing of the global economy according to the principle of competition for market share and higher returns has also stimulated the formation of global monopolies and oligopolies by conglomerates seeking to increase their market power and by-pass arcane or porous state regulations to give themselves an edge. The underlying motivation is share value maximisation, as I underlined in Chapter 1 by reference to the effects of financial capitalism for all companies quoted on the stock exchange.

The 'postcolony' has not been spared in that process of reorganisation of the framework to suit the enterprise economy and corporate capitalism in their global drive for accumulation and growth. As we know, 'postcolonies' have become the sites for outsourced production as corporations restructured their operations to maximise profit or increase market share, building upon institutions, regulatory frameworks and other mechanisms of control that had been set up during the period of colonialism or that have been reconstituted in the light of transformations in global capitalism especially from the 1970s. These mutations include the extent to which global capital has become geographically more dispersed and diverse, operating across manufactures, the communication industry, finance, with many key players being located in the so-called 'global south' – for example, Mukesh Ambani, Carlos Slim, Jack Ma, Wang Jianlin. Furthermore, geopolitical power relations have helped to shape this world, particularly through organisations such as the IMF, the World Bank, forums such as G7 and G20, and many NGOs.

In the light of these transformations in corporate capitalism, one can regard the process of 'offshoring' (Urry, 2014a), as a response to, and a vehicle assisting 'accelerated accumulation' and 'accelerated poverty' (discussed in Chapter 1). Amongst other effects for the 'postcolony', one can highlight the perpetuation of unequal exchange and the increased precarisation of already cheap and captive labour, often experiencing new forms of servitude. Other consequences of corporate and geopolitical strategies for market share and profit maximisation include mass migration from mostly ex-colonies, the global traffic of people, neo-slavery conditions in many sectors of the global economy, the interpenetration of mafia and licit or regulated capitalism, the legacies of the Cold War in the form of client states, and the normalisation of corruption, for example, regarding the activities of local 'kleptocracies' (Appiah, 1992) that have intensified destitution in the 'postcolony' and everywhere.

My analysis supports the view that it is the pressures associated with the new mechanisms of wealth accumulation that have encouraged disregard for the damage which the savage exploitation of the earth's resources to feed growth is causing and that we are experiencing in the form of climate change and the exhaustion of the planet. It could be argued therefore that the result of an economy founded on the primacy of competition has extended the logic of war to encompass the planet itself and all that dwells or exists in it; the anthropogenic transformations threaten the equilibrium of planetary systems and the existence of many species, possibly including the human.

The consequences are far-reaching, for apart from the economic, environmental and geopolitical effects I have noted, the new order fundamentally unsettles the relationship between the state, the economy and the polity, signalling the failure of capitalism to deliver the goods as well as foreboding political instability and ultimately the failure of democratic institutions across the world (Brown, 2015). The deterioration of the relation between the state and the polity can thus be linked to the logic of war that underlies capitalist competition (see also Deleuze and Guattari, 1988: 421). It sanctions brutal employee/management relations that are reiterated across many other sectors of the economy and society, increasingly in the form of the militarisation and robotisation of bodies and minds, from the treatment of workers in outsourced manufacturing in countries where a cheap supply of labour is available, to neoliberal schooling. Furthermore, the pressures inherent in corporate strategies of domination and survival have motivated the formation of cartels, oligopolies, 'small-world networks' of the powerful, and the disabling of employee opposition, the stakes being the reduction of risks and the defence of territory for owners of capital.

The logic of war inherent in capitalism as a zero-sum game, reiterated in generalised competition and in imperial strategies of power reflected in the 'discourse of race war', is reproduced in another important arena of struggle. It concerns the extent to which the conflicts arising from pauperisation and dispossession have put a premium on ubiquitous surveillance in what Deleuze has called 'societies of control' (Deleuze, 1990). My argument is that what we are witnessing is the repatriation as well as the globalisation of colonial strategies of power that took the form of imperial governmentality (Venn, 2006a), encapsulated in terms of the 'us versus them' perspective that increasingly shape the relation between the subjugative state and its polity, whereby power operates through practices of the disruption, destabilisation and division of the polity. Democracy cannot survive in such circumstances.

Resistance to this state of affairs is taking many forms, from decolonial critiques of the fundamental values and assumptions that underlie pauperisation and the plunder of the earth to initiatives countering the politics of austerity and reasserting a politics of commons, as I noted in the Introduction. Privatisation, incidentally, has been successfully overturned in some places, notably in Bolivia in 2000 where the Cochacamba rebellion against the privatisation of water resulted in it being returned to the people as part of common or collective goods (see Parance and Saint Victor, 2014 for an analysis of the question of rights to common goods).

To develop further what is at stake and to locate the forces of resistance in a history of struggle, I shall turn in the next chapter to a genealogy of liberal and neoliberal thought to uncover the ontological, ethical and epistemological issues inscribed in the conflicts that marked the birth of modern capitalism, and that a politics of commons opens up for discussion.

Notes

1   Such systems are characterised by inter-dependencies, feed-back loops, co-constitution, relationality, non-linearity, metastability, far-from-equilibrium, self-organisation and poiesis (Bateson, 1980; also Latour, 2005; Simondon, 2005; Venn, 2010; Wolfe, 2010).
2   A related issue for the question of alternatives is that the discourse of liberal political economy which emerged from the 18th century, particularly after Adam Smith's *The Wealth of Nations* (1812 [1776]), and the ascendency of a utilitarian biopolitical governmentality, has gradually succeeded in constituting an outlook amongst experts and 'development' advisers which is founded in faith in the 'market' and its particular rationality, despite variations within liberalism – particularly, the later J.S. Mill and J.M. Keynes (see Chapter 4) – and despite opposition from anti-capitalist struggles. Its success has been built on two correlated strategies, namely, the establishment of the institutional, legal, financial, geopolitical and military assemblages to delimit conduct and suppress dissent, and the dissemination of doctrines promoting liberal and, later, neoliberal capitalism. With regard to the latter, one should point to the major influence of a host of 'right-wing' think-tanks and pressure groups in shaping both public and expert opinion, notably, the Mont Pelerin Society (Mirowski and Plehwe, 2009; Peck, 2010) and the agencies that sway economic and social policies such as The Adam Smith Institute, The

Heritage Foundation, the American Enterprise Institute, the (now gone but not forgotten) Atlantic Bridge, and so on; they are backed by corporations, business syndicates and media conglomerates, behaving as a 'small-world network' in terms of decision-making and agenda setting supporting corporate capitalism, as I explained in Chapter 1 (Coghlan and MacKenzie, 2011).

3   The Triangular Trade linked English (and European) commerce and manufacturing to the slave trade and to plantation economy in the Americas and West Indies, growing in importance from the 18th century at the time of the emergence of liberal political economy and industrial capitalism (see Gilroy, 1993). The architecture of the Trade has the following components: ships left English ports (London, Bristol, Liverpool) laden with textiles, weapons, cutlery, copper and brass rods, beer, manufactured in all parts of England; these were sold or bartered on the African coast to buy slaves who were shipped as cargo in the dreadful 'middle passage' to the West Indies and sold there; the ships were loaded with produce from the colonies (sugar, rum, spices, molasses, tobacco) and carried back to England to be sold. Profit was made on each leg of this triangular circulation of goods, people, money. The largest share was amassed by merchants and shareholders rather than planters themselves, as detailed by Fryer (1984) and as Braudel shows (1986 [1979]: 197, 198, 272 ff.), although many small investors also benefited, since many shopkeepers, etc. regularly bought shares in each trip. Banking and insurance gained an enormous boost, e.g. the Barclay brothers, whilst Lloyds became the principal underwriters for many trips.

4
From Liberalism to Neoliberalism: A Dissident Genealogy

On the emergence of liberalism

I argued in the previous chapter that the addition of colonialism as a general process of dispossession and subjugation to the history of the present provides a more productive and realistic historical context for challenging the rules of the game and so opens the way for alternatives to varieties of capitalism. The search for alternatives concerns the reassessment of the grounds upon which to constitute resistance to forms of oppressive power, and it relates to the principles that should inform the political, economic, technological and ethical practices consistent with postcapitalist societies. I now explore these issues by turning to the struggles going on in the period of liberal governmentality regarding the discourse of political economy and political philosophy, struggles that were concretised around the issue of the general or common good and the role of the state in advancing this goal. The aim of the analysis is to show the extent to which conflicts today put into play similar concerns around issues of liberty, rights, autonomy, democratic representation, and so on; it thus provides a background against which to try and clarify the stakes involved for a politics of commons. The question of the principles that can constitute the conceptual foundation for postcapitalist, post-individualistic, post-anthropocentric ways of being and doing can then be addressed in the final chapter where I will draw out the implications of this alternative perspective for formulating possible solutions to the problem of convergent crises.

In my analysis so far, I have underlined the historical importance of the alignment of state rationality with market rationality as understood by political economy to constitute a biopolitical governmentality, for it has strengthened the hold of liberal capitalism (Foucault, 2008; Terranova, 2009; Venn, 2009a). This new composition of the relation of the state to the economy has, amongst other things, institutionalised the property regime authorising the progressive commodification of everything which has itself become a key component of the growth model and the intensification of accumulation, with the kind of consequences I have reviewed in previous chapters. In more recent times, the underlying forces behind such shifts have enabled money, the market and informationalisation to operate a general equivalence that has intensified inequalities through mechanisms such as those supporting the debt society and the 'society of control', as I argued previously.

A major feature of these recent developments that I would associate with neoliberalism is the intensification of the conflicts between the general or common good and the interests of transnational corporations and individual self-interest. It is one of the consequences of the reconstitution of the relation between the state and capital in line with the neoliberal prioritisation of 'free enterprise', competition and the rhetorically 'free' market, with troubling implications for social cohesion and the foundations of a democratic polity, as I will explain in relation to the question of the role of the state in ensuring a balance between public and private interest. As we know, the welfare or providential state institutionalised the balance in terms of a system for a more equitable redistribution of wealth and power through progressive taxation and the protection of workers' rights. It is this post-war political settlement, and the ethical and political principles underlying it, which are threatened by the new rules of the game framed by neoliberalism and the new machinery of wealth transfer that I examined in Chapters 1 and 3. But the problems I am addressing in the book require approaches that do not simply aim to restore previous settlements, since the conflicts would remain around the process of extracting a 'surplus' from the working class and the oppressed everywhere, as discussed in Chapter 3. Equally, it would leave in place models which have shaped social and economic policy for a long time, including about growth. An abiding issue is that the conflicts prowl around the question of what was at stake in the idea of a moral economy in liberalism, tied to the issue of the legitimacy of (non-despotic, non-totalising) state power. It is one of the questions which this chapter explores as part of the objective of establishing the alternative foundations for postcapitalist and postliberal forms of sociality, drawing from Ashurst and Venn (2014).

The analysis below begins this task by first providing a counter-history and counter-narrative of our predicament as a step towards formulating alternatives to capitalism. This critical genealogy of the present[1] is necessary because in the conventional narrative of the 'progress' of nations that capitalism is supposed to have facilitated, the mechanisms of inequality are made invisible as a result of the stratagem whereby the dispossession intrinsic to most economies has come to be 'the buried knowledge' hidden by the 'juridico-political' discourse of power that has normalised the power and privilege of the mighty as legitimate and rightful, underwritten either by politico-theological discourse or by the discourse of political economy (Foucault, 2003: 8–11; see Venn, 2006a, and Ashurst and Venn, 2014). As I have pointed out in Chapters 1 and 3, historically, the authority of these discourses, and the economic and ideological success of liberal capitalism in particular, have benefited from the degree of redistribution in the 'developed' world made possible on the basis of the extraction of a 'surplus' through the machinery of wealth transfer from the colonies (see also Samir Amin, 1974 and Rosa Luxemburg, 1968, amongst a host of works that detail this machinery, examined in Venn, 2006a). A 'surplus' was of course extracted not only from the subjugated and slaves in the colonies but from the industrial working class in Europe as well, as has been extensively established in studies ranging from Friedrich Engels' (1969 [1887]) research on the conditions of the working class in 19th century England to Piketty's (2014) wide-ranging historical account of the production of inequality in capitalist societies.

Above all, what critical genealogical analysis demonstrates is the importance of locating struggles for social justice and an equitable distribution of wealth and life chances as a central component in any understanding of societies founded on the normalisation of inequalities of one kind or another. In terms of discourses of legimation, these struggles took on a different complexion from the 18th century in the context of the Enlightenment (and its contradictions) and the co-emergence of liberal political economy, industrial capitalism and biopolitical governmentality, as I have underlined. Liberalism was marked by this historic conjuncture, including the consequences for politics of the French, Haitian and American revolutions and struggles throughout the 19th century around projects of emancipation in search of political, social and economic transformations. Apart from radical thinkers and activists such as Tom Paine or Mary Wollstonecraft, the more perceptive liberal theoreticians of reform were concerned with the form of governance and the laws that would protect the liberty, autonomy and rights of individual citizens whilst also insisting that the market must be free from undue state interference or restrictions. The contradictions and political stakes inscribed in these events remain at the forefront of political and philosophical reflection today; they are ambivalently and differently reiterated in debates both in terms of resistance to fundamental change as well as in 'postliberal' discourses around democracies to come. Both positions put into play the stakes that animated Enlightenment philosophy particularly regarding the possibility of an emancipation for humanity as a whole. The radical tendency in this project, as opposed to its instrumental and conservative dilution as I explained in Chapter 1, has supported a cosmopolitical standpoint (Derrida, 1997a; see also Venn, 2002) that I am recasting in the form of a politics of enlarged commons. The point of a return to the period of emergence of liberalism and commodity capitalism is to demonstrate important continuities and absences or 'forgettings' that impede the task of rethinking the goals of emancipatory politics today, especially in the light of the erosion of these goals in sectarian identity politics.

The problems and legacies of liberalisms

It could be argued that the classic example in which all these contradictions or disjunctures are played out is John Stuart Mill, in whose work the dilemma of self-interest and the general interest try to co-habit, expressed in the conflicting pulls inherent in the thorny problem of trying to balance the freedom of the market with the idea that the (democratic) state has a duty to operate for the common good in the name of equity and in order to guarantee the protection of individual liberty and rights. Interestingly, starting out as a proponent of market freedom and utilitarianism (though qualified) he gradually moved towards the 'left' as the question of ethics came to occupy a larger place in his thinking, at least in the eyes of Ludvig von Mises and Friedrich Hayek, those early theoreticians of neoliberalism and co-founders of the Mont Pelerin Society. Nick Gane's analysis of neoliberalism points out that this shift in Mill's position was denounced by von Mises as the corruption of classical liberalism by 'socialist ideals under the influence of his wife, Harriet Taylor' (Mises, 2005: 153–154, in Gane, 2015: 137). The political, economic and ethical stakes could not be clearer. Indeed, we can detect the ambivalence of Mill's position in his arguments defending the principle of utility whilst recognising problems that arise for the issue of safeguarding the common good, since the market is driven by self-interest. His solution, or way out, was to appeal to an 'ethics of utility' guided by the injunction that such an ethics should motivate one 'to do as one would be done by', and to 'love one's neighbour as oneself' to ensure that 'laws and social arrangements should place the happiness, or (as speaking practically it may be called) the interest, of every individual, as nearly as possible in harmony with the interest of the whole' (Mill, 1991 [1859]: 148). The clearly Christian underpinnings of Mill's ethics (or deontology) echo the universal Unitarian principles advocated by Harriet Taylor and many other reformists in the 19th century motivated by Dissenter Christian beliefs. This is a dimension in the genealogy of liberalism and neoliberalism which is unfortunately neglected in accounts of the principles promoting the idea of the welfare state, leading many analyses of social and political change to underestimate the contribution of Dissenter beliefs and ethical considerations in motivating the many reforms and movements of resistance in the 18th and 19th centuries (the historical details are developed in Ashurst and Venn, 2014).

Furthermore, Mill's thinking shows his clear recognition that conflicts of interests and unequal power relations exist in the real world when he argues that the question of liberty must imply placing limits on the power of rulers through the guarantee of 'political liberties or rights' and 'the establishment of constitutional checks' to ensure 'the consent of the community' by way of a body representing the interest of the community (Mill, 1991 [1859]: 60). The reason was that these 'modes of limitation' of sovereignty were necessary in order to guard against the abuses that ensue when the interests of rulers could be assumed to be against those of the governed – an interesting implication for democracy when one juxtaposes Joseph Stiglitz's view that the politico-economic complex today operates in the interest 'of the 1%, for the 1%, by the 1%' (2013: xxxix; see also Lazzarato, 2015).

Regarding the question of the abuse of power, Mill goes on to establish that what is needed is a situation in which the interests of the rulers were not 'habitually opposed to those of the people', but 'that the rulers should be identified with the people; that their interest and will should be the interest and will of the nation' (1991 [1859]: 61). This condition was slowly and partially instituted with the enlargement of suffrage which he firmly supported and which was very much integral to the political standpoint supported by liberal reformers. The key parameters of liberal political and moral philosophy identified by Mill, namely, the necessity of limits to the power of rulers, the guarantee of liberties and rights, the principle of consent, and political arrangements that safeguard the interest of the people as a whole (or the general interest) have long been and continue to be at the heart of debates and struggles about effective democracy. In terms of a genealogy of neoliberalism, the issue concerns the extent to which the neoliberal doctrine fundamentally subverts democracy, with the help of media conglomerates which endeavour to manufacture consent, particularly in line with a populism of the 'Radical Right' (see Nancy MacLean's [2017] investigation of the funding of such activities).

Three concerns stand out when we examine the shift from liberalism to neoliberalism: they relate to the question of the essential conflict that divides general interest from private interests together with the question of the rights and ethical principles implicated in them, such as the idea of equity (Arendt, 2000; Venn, 2006a); they relate also to the problem of the form of rationality that should inform government, and, as I have been arguing, they pertain to the critique of the model of neverending growth as basis for 'progress'. Liberal political philosophy reconciles this matter of opposing interests and the consequences for rights and liberties in two ways: first, in terms of the institution of a political system based on 'elective and temporary rulers' operating as representatives delegated by the people to act in their interest (Mill, 1991 [1859]: 60), and secondly, by equating the aggregate of private interests with the general interest and establishing the state as arbiter and legislator of the general interest.

In the classical political economy of Smith, this is achieved by way of the mysteries of the 'invisible hand', his argument being that since every individual, seeking his own self-interest, 'neither intends to promote the public interest, nor knows how much he is promoting it ... he intends only his own gain ... [yet he is] led by an invisible hand to promote an end which is no part of his intention' (Smith, 1812 [1776]: 354, also p. 352). His reasoning is that the system works because in spite of the fact that every individual seeks to obtain the greatest benefit from his or her own investment of capital or labour, this desire leads to 'improvements in the productive power of labour' and an 'increase in the quantity of useful labour' and thus results in increases in the prosperity of the country as a whole, the net consequence of which benefits the 'three different orders of people': those who live by rent, those who live by wages, and those who live by profit (Smith, 1812 [1776]: 212–214). Good governments would be those that establish the conditions for this process to proceed unimpeded, implying also limits to the power of the state. And so, the injunction that governments, in order to be thought democratic and just, and thus be able to claim moral authority, must operate in the general interest to benefit all citizens, is thereby satisfied – at least in theory and in political rhetoric, for in practice state policies depend on relations of power.

Nevertheless, the Smithian argument is precisely the kind of reasoning which has ensured that growth has come to occupy a determining role in the process of securing consent to the state, that is, the argument that growth is supposed to produce the necessary aggregate wealth and means for improvements in the condition of all the people. Though explicitly expressed in the discourse of political economy, conditions for the premium placed on growth were prepared by the antecedent shifts in the 'art of government' towards 'pastoral power' and the 'science of police' that had already put on the agenda the question of new technologies for the advancement of 'public utility' and the pursuit of 'the common welfare and salvation of all' as Foucault highlighted in his genealogy of governmentality (1979: 12ff.). However, with the coupling of capitalism, biopolitics and governmentaliy in the emergence of liberalism and political economy, economic growth became synonymous with a win–win situation, at any rate in Europe, provided one assumed the mythical 'trickle down', and provided one 'forgot' the massive wealth that had accrued directly or indirectly to holders of capital from colonial, plantation and slave economies as I have shown in Chapter 3 (see also Arrighi, 1994; Venn, 2000 and 2006a). Today, the mechanisms of wealth transfer from the poor and 'middle' class to the very rich, as organised within the scope of the dominance of financial capitalism, serves the same purpose of legitimation through the abracadabra of growth, rather than by reference to the general interest or a redistributive justice ensuring the welfare of all – though conservative political spin deploys the rhetoric of common good or greater prosperity to hide the fact of pauperisation and precarisation.

So, a telling ambivalence fractures the utilitarian version of the liberal and neoliberal solution to the question of distribution, since the implication is that it is precisely because the aggregate of private interests 'naturally' works for the benefit of the (Benthamite) 'greatest happiness' of the greatest number that it should be preferred to state intervention in the economy to effect a degree of equitable distribution of wealth. The latter option, so the argument goes, is at the cost of distortion in the price mechanism and undue interference in individual liberty. In other words, it is the claim to an underlying moral objective – though inoperative at the individual level – that saves the system from the objection that, when freed from state intervention to equalise the interest of all, an economy founded on the pursuit of self-interest (or greed) alone necessarily produces inequality (as established in previous chapters) and is therefore iniquitous.

Smith, it must be said, was motivated by the search for a moral economy, as evidenced in his reflections in the *Theory of Moral Sentiments* (2009 [1759]), where in search of 'the practical rules of morality' or a deontology he examined issues of virtue through an analysis of sympathy, benevolence, prudence, justice, duty, selfishness and the passions. The principles or rules developed found expression in his recognition of the destructive effects of the colonisation of America that, instead of benefiting the colonised through growth in trade, was 'ruinous and destructive to several of those unfortunate countries' because of the 'savage injustice of the Europeans' (Smith, 1812 [1776]: 348 and Book IV, Ch. 7). The priority of moral goals is clear too when he argues that the duties of the sovereign should include 'that of protecting, as far as possible, every member of the society from the injustice or oppression of every other member of it' (Smith, 1812 [1776]: 560), a view one can juxtapose with his claim that 'Whenever there is great property, there is great inequality' (1812 [1776]: 561), as it enables us to infer that the kind of protection he speaks of implies redressing, through redistribution of some kind, the balance of gains from an economy geared to the maximisation of private interests.

The Smithian position, as I have highlighted it, is crucial in helping to pinpoint the nature of the tensions at the heart of liberalism itself, evidenced in the disputes about social policy and reforms in the 19th century (Ashurst, 2010; Ashurst and Venn, 2014); it is this rift that neoliberalism consolidates by abandoning the idea of a moral economy and relocating the question of rights and liberty within the capitalist logic of individual choice and individual responsibility (Foucault, 2008). Dardot and Laval's (2010) insightful analysis in *La nouvelle raison du monde* charts this break in the discourse of political economy to show that it involved, amongst other departures, several crucial shifts away from the Smithian model of society. The key initial displacement principally involved the substitution of Nature for God as ultimate foundation of social order in the discourse of utilitarian liberalism, and as inscribed in that discourse's perverse interpretation of John Locke's foundation of natural rights, particularly regarding rights to property and life. The displacement has crucial implications for the question of limits to government because the utilitarians presupposed a fixed human nature endowed with innate propensities, particularly acquisitiveness, as foundation for the economy and social life, a nature which the 'free market' is supposed to incarnate and cash out.

It is worth summarising the main arguments in Dardot and Laval as they help to clarify what is at stake in neoliberal political economy with regard to its opposition to the principle of state intervention to compensate inequalities and protect fundamental rights, and in terms of the pursuit of non-economic, moral goals as ultimate ends of government. Their account of the relationship of political economy to government picks out three central parameters at work in the early formulations of both political economy and liberalism in the 18th and 19th centuries: 'the nature of the individual, the order of society, the progress of history', articulated in terms of 'three types of considerations, the anthropology of interest, the mechanism of the social and the progressivism of history' (2010: 27). They form heterogenous ensembles that further depend on whether their ultimate foundation refers to divine law or to the 'laws of nature' – though the two often overlap in the discourse of political philosophy. This foundation has major consequences, since the invocation of God's will, as in Adam Smith and Adam Ferguson, inaugurates a connection between political economy and a moral economy, a connection that, as I have been arguing, runs deep in the splits between the more 'radical' or moral side of liberalism and the amoral utilitarianism inscribed in Bentham and Malthus' position and in today's neoliberal political philosophy. I should add the Enlightenment as background, not only because Smith and Ferguson are part of the (Scottish) Enlightenment, but because the differences within liberal political economy in some important ways draw upon and accentuate the ambivalence in Enlightenment thought, articulated in the split dividing its emancipatory from its instrumental project (Lyotard, 1984 [1979]). It is a tension which is exemplarily embodied in the trajectory of J.S. Mill's work as I highlighted earlier, and in the disputes amongst ordo- and neoliberals later (see Venn, 2006b; Gilbert, 2014; Ashurst and Venn, 2014; Gane, 2015; as well as Peck's 2010 account of neoliberal reason).

Dardot and Laval's analysis adds a different dimension in showing how the matter of ultimate or transcendent foundation entailed different theorisations of both state rationality and human nature, with implications for politics, rights, sovereignty and social policy. The question which they investigate is the different conceptualisations of what was thought natural concerning 'human nature', conceptualisations that functioned as foundation for the conflicting views of civil society, the economy and the role of government. They show that Smith and Ferguson assumed that human nature was characterised by both a natural predisposition to empathise with fellow creatures as well as an equally natural drive for self-interest. It is this ontological standpoint that required solutions to the problem of the 'compatibility between the moral order produced by the impulse of sympathy and the economic order derived from the pursuit of interests' (Dardot and Laval, 2010: 32), that is, 'how benevolence, justice and interest may be combined' (ibid.). They point out that Ferguson, in his *Essay on the History of Civil Society* (2007 [1767]), opposed the idea that 'happiness consists in the possession of the greatest amount of wealth, goods and honours' (2010: 31), thus departing from the supposition that humans were incorrigibly selfish and motivated by a desire for accumulation; he argued instead that goodness, pity and benevolence were not cancelled by interest or self-love, since we also crave the approval of others and seek their sympathy, whilst 'the desire for gain is the great source of injustice' (Ferguson, cited in Dardot and Laval, 2010: 35; see also Jacquet, 2015, regarding cooperation and the desire for social approval). This desire for accumulation, as they remind us, was regarded as a vice by the Ancients – though we know that it has since been viewed as either proof of being an 'elect' in Weber's analysis of the spirit of capitalism, or as proof of success and enterprising acumen in Evangelical and neoliberal discourse. We shall see in Chapter 6, where the issues of a postcapitalist ethics and a politics of commons are further examined, that the question of altruism and empathy, as well as the problem of ownership, remain central to the matter of solidarity and social cohesion and do not depend on possession (Gallese, 2003; Virno, 2008; Venn, 2014).

For now, we can return to the Smithian solution to the problem of reconciling a moral order dedicated to the general interest and an economic order based on self-interest. As Dardot and Laval point out, Smith was aware of the discourses, particularly of the Physiocrats, which had proposed a solution that prioritised the economy and 'a despotism of the market' on the grounds that that was in accordance with natural order as originally willed by God, an order which the 'new science' of the economy was thought to uncover (Dardot and Laval, 2010: 45). Interference by the state in the economy was therefore considered to be against the 'natural' order; instead the aim of the state should be to ensure 'respect and knowledge of the divine law that had established a natural order' (ibid.). By contrast, Smith saw the aims of government as being to promote 'the quality of social relations, respect for others, civility, public discussion ... guided by the interest of society' (2010: 42). Smith is able to defend this position because the 'Smithian anthropology reduces all human motivations to two fundamental desires: the desire to better one's condition, which rests on self-love (which for him derived from the instinct for self-preservation), and the desire for approval by others which proceeds directly from sympathy' (2010: 60). The former leads to growth through productive activity geared to betterment, amplified also by the growth in population that creates shortages which incite further productive activity, whilst increased production holds out the promise of the peaceful progress of society. These twin impulses shape Smith's solution to the problem of finding the right balance or a just measure between economic and moral orders, granting a role for both the economy and the state, yet at the same time naturalising them, for, as I noted above by reference to his 'invisible hand' argument, an economy driven by the self-interest of individuals is supposed to quite 'naturally' promote growth and thus the general interest.

I think it is important to follow up the implication of this naturalism in Smith's arguments about the limits of government, especially Book V of *The Wealth of Nations* (1812 [1776]) where the following article headings make explicit his view that the state should confine its action to improving the conditions that promote unlimited growth, namely: the defence of the country; ensuring internal peace and security through the 'exact administration of justice'; the development of 'public works'; the 'education of the youth' and 'the instruction of the people'. Tellingly, these titles cover the issues of sovereignty and its limits, the scope of the law, and an idea of social administration, that is, issues at the heart of liberal political philosophy, with implications for the current neoliberal reconstitution of the social order through appropriate transformations of the 'framework' circumscribing social policy and the role of law, as Foucault (2008) has shown. The key functioning of the invisible hand in all this reveals the providentialist metaphysics that animates Smith's system (Foucault, 2008; Venn, 2009a; Dardot and Laval, 2010: 63). It prompts us to wonder about the implicit or disavowed metaphysics underlying neoliberalism, and its appeal for fundamentalists, which I examined in Chapter 1 in relation to the onto-theology of debt.

Ferguson, interestingly, deployed a more explicitly moral standpoint when he argued that the state should seek internal peace through encouraging strong 'affective bonds' amongst citizens, supported by laws that, in recognising that unconstrained self-interested passions can lead to injustices and the excessive accumulation of wealth by a few, would 'essentially aim to "contain" and "anticipate" the dire effects of these passions' (Dardot and Laval, 2010: 43). I would juxtapose as a condition enabling accumulation, the existence of specific property regimes legitimating appropriation, as I have been arguing, and the invention of money, a point Locke (1963 [1690–1780], 1959 [1896]) already made. Indeed, Dardot and Laval highlight the way in which Locke's arguments for a right to property, elaborated in the *Essay Concerning Human Understanding* and the *Second Treatise of Government*, have been both central to the emergence of liberalism as well as misused by political economists to justify appropriation. They summarise Locke's well-known ideas about rights to property, the implications for liberty and the role of government, and they point to the distortions or forgettings, especially about the provisos in Locke about the quality and quantity appropriated that imply limits to possession in his model.

Let us unpack this. Much depends on the premise that we are all creatures (and the property) of God, endowed with reason and the ownership of oneself. For Locke, specific duties follow from this, particularly regarding the preservation of oneself and the rest of humanity, the ability to understand the laws of nature, and the scope of natural rights (Dardot and Laval, 2010: 76). His theory of property and limits to government also follows from the same premise, since his argument is that humans are given the earth and its resources in common, such that we are co-owners of the fruits of the earth, but since the duty of self-preservation entails that we use our reason to make efficacious use of the earth, we can, in the pursuit of self-preservation, appropriate that to which we have 'mixed' our labour. Locke however sets limits to this 'natural right', namely, first, it is legitimate to do so only to the extent that we can make good use of all that we appropriate through labour, and thus not spoil or waste the goods of the earth – for they are the property of God – and, secondly and crucially, that enough and as good land is left for others so that they may exercise these same duties, which are in effect duties towards God (2010: 82, 83).

Dardot and Laval's point is to examine the implications of the break which utilitarians like Bentham make, in the wake of Hobbes and Grotius, with the Lockean theological foundation and the moral obligation bound up with it. The post-Lockean problematic of property involves the grounding of natural rights and rationality in 'natural law', reflected in 'man's' desires or passions in the here and now (2010: 87–90). The key shift is that individual rights are made 'independent of social or political authority', though subject to convention (2010: 88), yet seen as fundamental and absolute. In that respect, the argument is that a certain view of what is natural, including the passions, is substituted for a foundation in God's will. It implicates an instrumentalisation of the right to property that detaches it from the right to liberties and capabilities (see also Sen and Nussbaum, 1993 on the capabilities approach, and below regarding Locke's legitimation of colonial dispossession which I have discussed elsewhere [Venn, 2006a]). The important point is that in the course of this shift, Locke's provisos limiting the extent of property that an individual could own, namely, that 'enough and as good as' land (or resources for living) be left for others are conveniently 'forgotten' – though it must be said that Locke also recognised that the invention of money made possible accumulation without spoiling.

Dardot and Laval highlight an aspect of the various shifts that we can connect directly with neoliberalism: it is the claim that the right to property as absolute and unconditional is invoked as foundation for 'the condemnation of the principle of any form of "redistributive justice"', thus as basis for rejecting 'any attempt aiming to compensate inequalities in the distribution of "natural assets" through a levy on the revenues of those most advantaged' (2010: 89). Neoliberalism, and Bentham and Malthus and other utilitarians before that, as we know, are in one mind about this rejection of redistribution, and the naturalising of inequality on which anti-welfare state doctrine rests, in spite of the political rhetoric that parades a commitment to reduce inequality and improve social justice whilst promoting programmes that achieve the opposite.

There is another equally important point to be made here which clarifies the stakes in the process of privatisation central to capitalism and its accumulative thrust. It is the fact that the problem of quantity and quality emphasised in Locke's provisos was resolved for Europe by the conquest of the Americas that made available immense wealth – the land and all its resources – that the colonisers reclassified as *terra nullius* and thus conveniently 'free' for confiscation or appropriation as part of 'primitive accumulation'. Locke's coupling of reason and rational conduct to the right to property, when linked to the claim that the colonised and indigenous people were less rational than European colonisers, and so were not making effective use of the land, operated as a key pretext or assumption to legitimate dispossession. The colonisation of the Americas, and the transformation of the world it brought about, was thus an essential condition of possibility for liberal capitalism, as I have argued elsewhere (Venn, 2000; see also Anthony Pagden's [1993] groundbreaking analysis regarding the new worlding that the New World made possible). Equally, the excuse that native American lands could be confiscated because they supposedly made poor, inefficent or non-rational use of the land needs to be set against the background of enclosures legally enforced in Europe, a process of dispossession similar to the disinheritance and commodification of collective or common goods. In the light of the importance I have placed on a property regime based on commodification as a defining characteristic of capitalism, it is clear that Dardot and Laval's discussion of the discourses that naturalise the right to property adds another set of considerations that throw further light on the emergence of liberalism and the tensions that have beset it from the beginning; it also helps us to see that the ongoing neoliberal privatisation of commons is a politico-military as well as an economic strategy.

It is worth adding that, in terms of an ontology, the correlation or affinities between the concept of possessive individualism (McPherson, 1962) and that of the Cartesian subject, which the discourse of liberal capitalism and that of occidentalist colonialism assume (Venn, 2000: 174), inaugurates the association of property with rationality which is a central feature of the tropes of 'economic man' one finds in political economy from the Physiocrats in the 18th century to Ayn Rand in the 20th century. It underlies too the (logo- and phallocentric) classification of non-Western people and women as less rational, a view that supported their exclusion from basic rights. Equally, it is important to emphasise that the privileging of the self-interested autonomous individual, which we find in the discourse of both classical and neoliberal political economy, is consistent with the critique of the 'metaphysics of individualism' in Barad's argument that '(I)t would be wrong to simply assume that people are analogues of atoms and that societies are mere epiphenomena that can be explained in terms of collective behaviour of massive ensembles of individual entities (like little atoms each, or that sociology is reducible to biology' (2007: 24). The critique of neo/liberal capitalism thus involves basic and conflicting epistemological and ontological starting points, as I have been arguing concerning the neoliberal model of the 'enterprise man' (Rose, 2007; Foucault, 2008; McNay, 2009; Ashurst and Venn, 2014). Besides, the different, if overlapping, conceptualisations of nature and human nature at work in political economy in the 18th and 19th centuries resonate with current debates around neoliberalism and the stakes involved, especially the attempt to naturalise existing social relations by appeal to sociobiology's and geneticism's claim to ground human conduct and social order in the fixity of biological processes and genetics, a strategy cashed out in the pathologisation or medicalisation of those who fail to embody the new norms of the enterprising individual (Rose and Rose, 2012).

Dilemmas of liberalisms: Between the market and the state, private interest and the common good

What I have wanted to show is that the tensions and disputes within liberalisms and political economy do not merely reflect theoretical differences, but were the counterpart of clear conflicts in values and political philosophy, the legacy of which still shape political struggles and social policy today. A further brief detour via John Stuart Mill's work will help to better understand this contradiction between, on the one hand, the ethical basis of governmental action anchored to ideas of social justice and, on the other hand, the privilege of the instrumental thrust in liberal and neoliberal governmentality which results when the latter aligns itself to the interests of market capitalism. This detour is useful in that it could be argued that Mill's search for a middle way – or 'capitalism with a human face' in more recent reformulations – is somewhat closer to the German ordoliberals, as well as some social democratic strategies. As we saw earlier, Mill's account in his essay, *On Liberty*, is noteworthy for both defending the theory of utility, yet qualifying it in such a way in his discussion of the 'quality of pleasure' that it leaves the way open for an 'ethics of utility' that basically imports a (Dissenter) Christian deontology to inform conduct towards others (Mill, 1991 [1859]: 148). Crucially, he adds that a condition should be 'that education and opinion, which have so vast a power over human character, should so use that power as to establish in the mind of every individual an indissoluble association between his own happiness and the good of the whole; especially between his own happiness and the practice of such modes of conduct, negative and positive, as regard for the universal happiness prescribes' (1991 [1859]: 148). His prescription is clearly not that of a government of conduct aligned to an acquisitive 'economic man', yet nor is it in alliance with the more radical struggles around class, gender and race going on at the time, though his support for reforms such as the extension of suffrage and so on is well known, as is his colonial paternalistic views about India (Viswanathan, 1989: 149, 150).

Much debate and confusion has been generated to this day because of the ambivalence in Mill's liberalism, since his attempt to reconcile capitalism, colonialism, a free market and the privilege of private property with the requirements implied by the general interest founded in the principle of equity and social justice, obliges him to force an individualist self-interest and an ethical universalism to co-habit. The impossibility of this disjunction is encapsulated in the split between those thinkers who advocated policies grounded in utilitarian and instrumental principles within the framework of 'free market' capitalism (Malthus, Bentham, Ricardo, and followers), and those guided foremost by egalitarian principles within the framework of the pursuit of the common good, but who do not reduce or identify it with those of business or with the aggregate of private interests. Amongst the latter thinkers from the period of the Enlightenment one finds radical thinkers and Unitarians such as Tom Paine, Mary Wollstonecraft, Toussaint L'Ouverture, Harriet Taylor, Mary Carpenter, the later J.S. Mill, Harriet Martineau, and also Josiah Wedgewood, Thomas Jefferson, Benjamin Franklin, and many others inspired by Dissenter and non-Trinitarian faith and/or Enlightenment ideals. The Unitarian approach presents the clearest contrast, for it is guided by the theological conviction that God's spirit is indivisible and dwells in all creatures who thus partake equally in that spirit. For them, the implication supports equality and respect for all irrespective of differences, hence their opposition to slavery for instance.

I will draw from two striking cases in the UK which the archival research undertaken by Francesca Ashurst (2010) has reconstructed to highlight the conflict about ultimate ends and values that radically cleave the 'left' from the 'right', both at the time when the apparatuses (dispositifs) of liberal governmentality were being put into place, and in today's 'structural adjustments' or 'modernising' programmes targeting the privatisation of the providential state (details of these and other cases are in Ashurst and Venn, 2014). On the reformist 'left' one finds Mary Carpenter, motivated by her Unitarian principles, who devoted her life to rescuing and educating poor children, many living on the streets, and excluded from the National or British Schools. She set up schools in barns, old warehouses, under railway arches, included 'Ragged Schools', and advocated a child-centred approach that started with attending to the basic needs of pauper children for food, adequate clothing, shelter and security. Her research into the conditions of these children provided evidence she presented at many parliamentary Select Committees to advocate her project of reform through education. Although the reforms going on at the time were integral to the consolidation of governmentality as a 'technology of the social' (Foucault, 1979), many were generated by 'radical liberals' motivated by the principle that the political and the moral dimensions of social policy were irreducible to the economic, indications of which were ambivalently incipient in Smith and more clearly in Ferguson as I have noted, a principle which neoliberalism discards. Along with other likeminded activists, Carpenter played key roles in the National Association for the Promotion of Social Science, the proceedings of which, together with those of the Statistical Society, had a major impact on the ideas shaping social policy and the apparatuses of governmentality at the time (Goldman, 2002; Ashurst and Venn, 2014). As a member of associations and committees alongside Harriet Taylor, J.S. Mill, Harriet Martineau (translator of Auguste Comte and promoter of sociology as a positive science), syndicalists, and so on, she also campaigned for women's suffrage. The projects of reform did not of course encompass the radical transformations which motivated socialists and revolutionary struggles.

On the 'right' we encounter William A. Miles, a Malthusian 'moral entrepreneur' and collaborator of the utilitarian Edwin Chadwick who was the main architect of the New Poor Law Act of 1934 which established the framework for the new management of poverty in the the UK, a management that was in agreement with the viewpoints of Bentham, Malthus and Ricardo. Chadwick employed Miles in the latter's capacity as a claimed 'expert', as he had conducted fieldwork amongst street children, delinquents and in prisons, and because he shared Miles' conviction that poverty and delinquency were the outcome of inheritance and 'contamination', a 'disease' reproduced amongst the feckless, the lazy, the vicious, those who formed a 'criminal class' or 'race', refractory to existing punishment (Ashurst, 2010). In his writings and reports, Miles expressed views about the poor, the delinquent, and crime and punishment that were widely shared by the majority of those in power – and still find support today amongst the many policy-makers who regard the poor as a pervasive threat or constant drain to be contained through forms of exclusion and punishment. Though his proposals for the harshest of punishment rather than education were not taken up, and criticised by some for being anti-Christian, his attitude to poverty that blamed the poor for their conditions was reflected in the emergence of larger prisons, their grim conditions and the use of transportation as a solution. Indeed, a similar attitude underlies policies such as the Blair government's policy paper 'No More Excuses' (Home Office, 1997) addressing delinquency in England and Wales in contemporary times, or the 'great exclusion' of the precarious, the poor and the marginalised in France over the last two decades (Malabou and Emmanuelli, 2009), or resistance to Medicare in the USA. The values inscribed in these policies are consistent with the neoliberal abnegation of state responsibility or duty of care towards all citizens and its displacement onto individuals through the slogan of responsibilisation and 'privatized social policy' or 'social market economy' as part of the 'economisation of the state' (Foucault, 2008: 144, 145; Dardot and Laval, 2010: 460, 461; Ashurst and Venn, 2014: 168ff.).

And so, my genealogical account of the shift from liberalisms to neoliberalism brings to light two related things: it rectifies the often neglected history of the at once political, philosophical, economic, ethical and social conflicts as conditions determining the trajectory of the transformations in capitalism; and it underlines the significant shifts in the political system and in society as a whole that lead up to the present. And it restores the important role which struggles around egalitarian politics, projects of emancipation, and also Unitarian and Dissenter activism played in driving these transformations. Basically, it shows that the differences correlate with opposing views about ultimate ends and means, split between, on one side, the belief in the possible perfectibility of human beings through collaborative, convivial and collective endeavour spurred by a mix of enlightened self-interest and altruism, and, on the other side, the assertion that social formations are founded on the primacy of individualism, selfishness and competitiveness, allied to an instrumental reason.

Interestingly, politico-economic strategies on both the left and the right have historically been elaborated in conjunction with the development of social scientific knowledge, or 'sciences of the social' such as statistics, to provide knowledge of patterns, regularities, probabilities and correlations characterising the behaviour and social life of populations, knowledge that made available the 'scientific' or 'objective' data which informed policy and programmes of intervention and regulation (for the crucial role of statistics as 'social physics' in the development of the apparatuses of governmentality, see Foucault, 1979; Hacking, 1981; Goldman, 2002; Ashurst and Venn, 2014 for details). The epistemology and the calculus involved in this 'objective' approach to policy and intervention is reflected in today's appeal to 'evidence-based' practices, often framed by business accounting and management practices, and increasingly subject to the ascendency of 'big data' and the algorithmic extraction and management of information. One consequence is the reduction of quality and the incalculable to quantity, thereby eliminating a distinction that many earlier political philosophers were keen to maintain, for example, Locke regarding the availability of land, Smith regarding education and the 'quality of social relations' (Dardot and Laval, 2010: 42), J.S. Mill (1991 [1859]: 148), concerning moral education as I noted above, and Ferguson on the quality of the social bond corrupted by the prioritisation of the economic sphere and the love for profit (Dardot and Laval, 2010: 58). The perversion of education today to serve purely utilitarian and economic ends would be a telling case of the planned destitution of the spirit.

What I wish to underline is the fact that struggles throughout the world repeatedly fight over these opposing values, ontologies, epistemologies, worldviews and politics. These struggles have resulted in essential gains and settlements, notably the idea of universal rights, including the implied rejection of all forms of slavery, the recognition of workers' rights through syndicalism, the principle of universal suffrage, and the recognition of the need for redistributive programmes to redress inequalities produced by unequal relations of wealth and power. As I noted previously, the optimistic standpoint of writers like Ferguson is reflected in Jefferson's (1776) preamble to the American Declaration of Independence, inscribed also in the French Declaration of the Rights of Man and the Citizen (1789), and instituted in the 1948 Universal Declaration of Human Rights – though it must be said that their politicisation or instrumentalisation via state legislation, e.g. as evidenced in the American Constitution, allowed for racial and other exclusions, and included elements compatible with capitalism, e.g. regarding the right to property. That standpoint has been central in motivating the revolutions and the constitutional changes that underpin the basis of contemporary democracy, including the establishment of the welfare or providential state. By contrast, the cynical view of human beings which prioritises individual self-interest and an egocentric ontology is cashed out in neoliberalism's universalisation and privileging of the principle of competition that, amongst other things, feeds into the current promotion of the politics of austerity alongside the punishment or sacrifice of the 'losers' in capitalism's zero-sum game.

It's easy to see now why von Mises, one of the architects of neoliberalism and the Mont Pelerin Society as its think-tank, took J.S. Mill to task for his apparent dilution of classical liberalism, and what he saw as Mill's 'slip' into 'socialism' because of his 'thoughtless confounding of liberal and socialist ideas' (Mises, 2005: 153–154, cited in Gane, 2015). When we recall that the project pursued by the Mont Pelerin Society was the rejection of Keynesianism, the defence of private property, the promotion of competition and individual choice, and above all resolute opposition to the ideas that promoted socialism and the establishment of a providential state, the stakes in the two visions couldn't be clearer. It becomes clear too that neoliberalism resolves liberalism's quandary of hunting with the dogs of capitalism whilst running with the hare of equity, namely, by opting for full-blooded capitalism, with the poor, the vulnerable and politically weak as hapless quarry.

From Adam Smith to Milton Friedman: Alas poor Beveridge

Looking back over this long and continuing struggle for equality and liberty, in Euro-America and the rest of the world, recent politico-economic history points towards the reversal of many gains. The 'Great Moving Right Show' (Hall, 1979) has empowered Chicago Boys' type economics and altered the balance between public and private interest, and capital and labour. Indeed, the reversals have 'eroded the very foundations of liberal democracy itself' which had implied or supposed 'a particular form of the subordination of executive power over legislative power ... the pre-eminence of public right over private rights, or at least a keen sense of the necessary delimitation of their respective spheres ... (correlated to) a particular relation of the citizen with respect to the "common good" or "public good"' (Dardot and Laval, 2010: 459). Neoliberal discourse, as I have been arguing, is happy to recognise these distinctions at the level of political rhetoric and ideological coding, yet undermines completely their 'normative character'. This has taken the form of the

> (D)ilution of public rights for the benefit of private rights, the submission of public initiatives to the criteria of profit and productivity, the symbolic devaluation of the law as the proper concern of the legislative sphere, the reinforcement of the executive, ... the tendency of police power to be free of judicial control. (ibid.)

Such changes reflect the new relations of force favouring the interests of capital and clearly threaten the rights associated with democratic accountability. As I outlined earlier, this danger incipient in the idea of a balance of power was precisely why Mill amongst others argued for the need to guard against the monopolisation of power by any specific group, namely, by advocating the institutionalisation of forms of limitation to political power – though as we know the liberal solution was and is ever open to subversion by power elites, operating through covert networks of influence inscribing the relations of force at any particular time (MacLean, 2017).

It is important therefore to locate the shifts Dardot and Laval identified in a wider context of struggle encompassing two sets of considerations. On the one hand, the continuity of a conflict between providential and New Deal type social policy in contemporary times and the problem of how to characterise the ends of government that had occupied radical reform and activism in the 19th century around the question of a just balance between the competing demands of social responsibility and private interests. On the other hand, the context is underscored by the mutations in the 20th century in the struggles pitting varieties of socialism against capitalism fought out in the form of the Cold War and wars of independence taking place in former colonies. So, on the one side, one could note that key figures of the welfare state such as J.M. Keynes and W. Beveridge fit well in the line of reformers of the 19th century concerned about redressing poverty and inequality, for example Mary Carpenter, J.S. Mill or Charles Booth. As liberal thinkers, they shared the conviction that state intervention and participation could bring about more equitable distribution of wealth and opportunities. It is well to remember that the background to such activities then and in the 20th century was revolutions and the rumour of revolution.

Thus, concerning the emergence of the welfare state and Keynesian management of the economy, analysis should take into account the terrain of conflict or agonistic terrain that circumscribes government strategies aimed at reducing tensions arising from inequalities and discontent. As we know, in the post-Second World War period the new apparatuses of governmentality were integrated within capitalism in the form of a mixed-economy or 'middle way' – capitalism-plus or socialism-minus – that for a time, and along with Fordism, delivered economic stability and relative prosperity for a larger constituency whilst also further shifting infrastructural costs and 'externalites' onto the state, as I will discuss in Chapter 5. In effect, the providential state instituted an 'insurantial technology' (Donzelot, 1979) that rationalised provisions targeting the management of poverty and its causes and consequences as well as the reduction of risks – underemployed capital, low productivity due to skill shortages, rising discontent, etc. – through strategies of containment, capture or else suppression. This wider context shows that Keynesian and welfare or providential state solutions to the Great Depression and post-war reconstruction built on this idea of an insurantial technology through further rationalisations of the biopolitics of populations. They can thus be seen as a politico-economic solution within liberal governmentality that, however, retained the sense of a social contract or perhaps social conscience, as evident in New Deal discourse and in the Beveridge Report (1942) that tackled the five 'evils' of unemployment, ignorance, illness, squalor and poverty.

In terms of a genealogy of neoliberal capitalism, the mutations in economic and geopolitical conjuncture in the more recent period can be seen as an intensification and globalisation of the conflict of class interest prevailing in the 19th and early 20th centuries. Events such as the Russian Revolution of 1917 and the fact that colonial liberation movements were often informed by emancipatory discourse allied to socialism, and the rise of totalitarian and fascist regimes, all added an unprecedented dimension to what were at stake. For instance, the context of Stalinism and fascism provided people like Friedrich Hayek and Milton Friedman with the handy veneer of defending freedom against the central planning of the economy associated with socialism. In this respect, Friedrich Hayek, arguing against Beveridge when they were both at the LSE in the 1930s, defended 'freedom in economic affairs' and 'basic individualism' set against 'socialist' planning in Chapter 1 of *The Road to Serfdom*; yet, they both relied on the emergence of totalitarianism of the 'left' and the 'right' in Europe to leverage capitalism into the exemplar of a democratic, free and rational system. His reasons couldn't be clearer: 'Although we had been warned by some of the greatest political thinkers of the nineteenth century ... that socialism means slavery, we have steadily moved in the direction of socialism' (Hayek, 2010 [1944]: 13).

Friedman too riled against 'collectivism' and central planning: 'central planning is indeed The Road to Serfdom' (Friedman, 2002 [1962]: viii); he looked forward to 'future desocialization' and praised a 'market-oriented approach and a smaller role for government' (2002 [1962]: ix), basing his conviction on the claim that economic freedom, civil freedom and political freedom formed a 'trichotomy' (ibid.). His view of liberalism in the 18th and 19th centuries as the movement that 'emphasised freedom as the ultimate goal and the individual as the ultimate entity in the society', and that 'supported laissez-faire at home as a means of reducing the role of the state in economic affairs ...; it supported free trade abroad as a means of linking the nations of the world together peacefully and democratically' (2002 [1962]: 5) is quite a distortion, for, clearly, in the light of the genealogy I presented above, it is a simplification of Smith and ignores the liberal reformers, though clearly he would find support in Bentham and Malthus. And it promotes the myth of laissez-faire and the 'free market', on the basis of which he advocated his list of what governments should not do in a free society (2002 [1962]: 35, 36). Equally, it erases the violences involved in colonial and imperial exploitation and oppression, as well as the fact that the history of capitalism up to the present has been marked by perpetual war (Venn, 2000, 2006a).

I have highlighted Hayek's and Friedman's arguments because they continue to have currency amongst a wide public which has bought into the rhetoric of the 'radical right', and they cast a shadow on projects of redistribution, emancipation and the protection of the environment from predatory capitalism that have implications for the likelihood of steady state and liveable economies. The same views inform opposition to the political settlements of the post-war period that had seen the setting up of the welfare state as both a concession won out of sacrifice as well as a bulwark against further erosions of capitalism, thus helping to thwart socialist advances in the 'west' as well as in the colonies. Ironically, welfare economics and the subsidising of infrastructures in the post-war period has indeed dampened the effects of capitalism since the latter as a zero-sum game necessarily pauperises, and thus necessarily makes insecure and precarious large sections of the world's population. As German ordoliberals recognised, it is this situation and its effects for the poor/pauperised that social insurance and the 'social market' are meant to offset (Foucault, 2008: 142). The Keynesian deal thus had the double advantage of alleviating the worst effects of pauperisation, whilst its economic strategy of full employment, by enabling people to spend a larger part of their income on consumer goods and services, further benefited private enterprise through growth in production and consumption. In terms of relations of political power, the settlement had the effect of securing consent, minimising security risks and keeping the population quiescent, especially in the context of the Cold War in which the fate of capitalism was at stake.

It is clear therefore that these were complex struggles involving different compositions of ideas about the field of intervention, the appropriate techniques, and the ultimate goals of good government. At the level of policy, they relate also to the question of the enlargement of public assets and an 'environmental politics', which I noted in previous arguments in terms of commons and the classification of infrastructural components of production as 'externalities' by firms. Furthermore, as I have argued in previous chapters, the strategy of a degree of redistribution in line with the New Deal and the welfare state, when added to the pressure for continuing accumulation, necessitates an economy dedicated to growth. Indeed, the hockey stick graph I referred to in Chapter 2 shows that the exponential increase in the use of raw materials and fossil fuels to feed that growth coincides with the emergence of the post-war consumer culture in the 'developed' economies and amongst the affluent elsewhere.

Yet, these changes, when set against the background of the emergence of biopolitical governmentality from the 19th century can be seen to re-inscribe the tensions at the heart of liberal political discourse itself. The important point is that liberal political philosophy, at least for defenders of a more egalitarian society like J.S. Mill and more recently William Beveridge, had been committed to the recognition that the principle of equity in the distribution of wealth and opportunities lies at the heart of the idea of democratic rule. The familiar argument here is that in order for state power to claim legitimacy, it must be able to claim moral authority and invoke the people's consent: yet, the latter rests on the governed freely acknowledging the rightfulness and just character of government – at least in a democracy, for we know there have been and there exist other legitimating stratagems relying on theology, or on 'traditional authority'. And the process of legitimation is open to ideological and hegemonic capture by 'technologies of the social' including increasingly by the mass media. By establishing that the neoliberal privilege of private interest actually benefits the rich disproportionately, and that furthermore, far from enhancing democratic liberty and freedom, it curtails it (contra Friedrich Hayek's contentions in *The Road to Serfdom*), the genealogy presented in *After Capital* deprives the neoliberal edifice of any moral ground whilst capitalism itself is shorn of its moral veneer.

Thus, the longer history of the present brings to light political philosophies that have divided radicals and (political) liberals for a long time, centred, on the one hand, on politico-economic objectives that privilege either the question of 'a good ethico-political end' (Lyotard, 1984 [1979]: xxiv), and, on the other hand, prioritising the problem of economico-technical goals that foreground matters such as growth, the price mechanism, the freedom of the market, trade regulations, taxation, the supply of money, fiscal and monetary stability, and so on. The former implies the need for transformations in relations of power encompassing human and non-human life; the latter is a management of the framework by the state that sustains prevailing unequal relations of power and secures private wealth accumulation.

It is well known now that the arrangements which institutionalised the idea of the welfare state, differently composed in different countries, started to come unstuck in the wake of the crisis triggered by structural and geopolitical transformations in the 1970s, including the oil crisis provoked by the oil cartels. Their effects added to the (temporary, now reversed) fall in the share of the national wealth taken by the top 1% of income earners (from 16% to 8% in the USA), consequent upon the redistribution of wealth produced by Keynesianism and Fordism and the low growth of the 1970s, as Harvey has argued (2005: 15, 16). These changes and the failure of Keynesianism to deal with the consequent depression, when added to the economic effects of the arms war tied to the Cold War fought out in savage wars in ex-colonies across the worlds, and the global recomposition of capital, opened up spaces which neoliberal political economy had been carefully preparing to occupy for decades. It managed to do so through altering the economic paradigm away from Keynesianism and gaining a foothold on policy-making via think-tanks and the exercise of corporate power (Mirowski and Plehwe, 2009; Peck, 2010; Wilks, 2013), something it succeeded in doing from the late 1970s in most 'advanced' economies, notably in the form of Thatcherism and Reaganism (fed on Hayek and Friedman), and the imposition of its framework on weaker, 'postcolonial' economies.

Other factors contributed to the consolidation of the neoliberal grip, namely, the demise of the USSR, symbolically signposted by the fall of the Berlin Wall in 1989, the bureaucratisation of welfare state apparatuses helping to feed discontent, and the legacy of Stalinism that has affected or infected the socialist project. The location of China as a determining player in the recomposition of capital globally requires its own space for a proper analysis. Above all, as I have shown in Chapter 1, it is the emergence of a debt society as a central component of financial capitalism that has provided the neoliberal economy and neo-biopolitical governmentality with the hard structural, institutional, and socio-cultural supports to strengthen the unequal relations of power between capital and labour.

The guiding thread in the journey from Adam Smith to neoliberalism has been to show that the problems today are much wider than a narrowly economic one since it involves, on the one hand, co-related crises at the levels of resources, ecologies and geophysical environments occurring all at the same time, incited by the imperative for growth shared by parties of both the conventional 'left' and the 'right'; on the other hand, the problems reflect differences in values and forms of life that point to incommensurable political, ontological, epistemological and ethical stakes. Indeed, with the ascendancy of neoliberalism and impending disasters relating to climate, ecologies and resources, all the contradictions and tensions within capitalism and liberalisms have come to a head. Furthermore, because capitalism in tandem with technocratic modernity have transformed the whole world on the back of colonialism and imperialism, more than 200 years of a particular history also comes to a point of transition.

It should be clear now why it has been necessary to take the long view of the developments that have led to the present crossroad. The genealogical approach has made it possible to tease out the linkages, some of which are well established such as between capitalism and liberalisms, some that tend to be marginalised such as the constitutive part played by colonialism in the emergence and growth of both capitalism and modernity-as-development, and other linkages that only historical search uncovers, established in Chapter 3. But much more is at stake, evidenced in the fact that opposition to forms of oppression across the world today is invested in a whole range of new initiatives, movements and forms of struggles against oppressions centred on class, patriarchy, racism, sexism, ecological and environmental damage. The picture of convergent crises that I have sketched, when added to these other considerations, obliges us to rethink the future on a quite different basis. What is fundamentally at stake, is not just the fate of democracy, but eventually that of humanity and the planet as a whole.

Note

1   In Foucault's work, critical genealogy refers to the historical reconstitution of the conditions which have produced a state of affairs in the present. Methodologically, it proceeds in the form of a 'descent' from a problem in the present, motivated by the search for a counter-history and counter-narrative in opposition to dominant history – the history of the victors. It engages with the notion of knowledge/power, that is, the idea that power is invested in the production of knowledges that in turn help in its efficacious exercise. Thus, critical genealogy is in alliance with the politics of resistance and with the history from below which oppositional groups establish to nourish their political engagements.

5
Towards a World in Common

This chapter and the next concern the elaboration of the material and institutional grounds for imagining and constructing alternative durable and equitable economies and socialities consistent with projects of emancipation and the reality of a small planet endowed with finite resources. They are in line with the underlying objective running in the different chapters, namely, that of challenging the long-standing economic, structural, epistemological, ontological and subjective practices and assumptions that have produced the convergent crises I have been examining. This chapter begins this task by clearing the ground for the post-anthropocentric and post-individualistic perspective elaborated in the next chapter, a perspective that draws from the work of authors whose research takes co-constitution, co-implication and compossibility to be fundamental features of life processes. It will accordingly emphasise the entanglement of humans with a world of objects, technics, other minds and living things, implying an essential symbiotic dynamics sustaining all life.

One of the arguments in support of the conceptual framework I am signalling is that knowledges embodied in ideas of how to live and in techniques and know-hows cumulate over generations and come to be hard-wired into the material and social worlds in which we exist as one amongst the host of other objects and beings, forming complex systems made up of co-constituting socio-cultural environments, ecologies, discursive formations, subjectivities, technics, objects, that is, as interconnected or looped networks of 'associated milieux', as I have explained elsewhere following Simondon's work and Oyama's (2000 [1985]) analysis of the 'constructive interactionism' characterising such systems (Venn, 2010).[1] This recognition is one of the starting points for arguing that what is described as infrastructure and externalities in economic discourse are in fact integral elements of the material and social world and have constitutive and supportive functions beyond the economic.

An implication is that projects of transformation must recognise that they all have historically specific material and discursive conditions of possibility, and that existing regimes of power/knowledge and of property, and existing interlocking environments, technologies, lifestyles and subjectivities too often act as obstacles blocking alternatives. The recognition that we are all locked into and invested in such milieux means that radical change requires a willingness to transform not only the material and environmental world but, crucially, minds. It is an issue well understood by neoliberals as evidenced in their (so far largely successful) effort to transform both world and minds over several decades, as I have shown in previous chapters (see also Dardot and Laval, 2010, especially in Chapter 13: 'The fabrication of the neoliberal subject').

It is clear also that all these approaches explicitly or implicitly emphasise the fact that it has taken millennia for the environments and the forms of life and cultures that now exist to have emerged from the complex, slow and indeterminate processes of co-constitution that bind all life in terms of interlocking systems.[2] Yet when set against the long time of human history, what is striking in terms of the political, economic and technological developments that are hastening the conjuncture of tipping points is the realisation that they have taken shape over a relatively very brief period of time. So, in a way, the shifts which I am proposing attempt to constitute a new balance, one that could avoid the repetition of the violences inherent in the systems and regimes of truth I have been dissecting.

Infrastructure or new commons? Incommensurable interests

Why new or postcapitalist commons? My aim here is to locate the concept of the common within the framework of the long periodisation which I have been developing and thus foreground another layer in the interconnections linking political economy, capitalism, liberalism, neoliberalism, environmental crises, and regimes of power and property. The arguments involve an understanding of the role which the emergence of what can be regarded as new commons played in sustaining capitalism, and the functionning of the state in the processes involved. In earlier chapters I have noted the existence of vast commons (land, forests, rivers, lakes, seas, etc.) that functioned as an integral part of productive capacity and life in common in many parts of the world before colonial dispossession, Enclosures in Europe and other forms of dispossession. As we know, what remains are the target of ongoing land and resource grabs everywhere. Here I'd like to extend the analysis by bringing into the equation the systematic enlargement of common goods or wealth, including the so-called social, cultural, and cognitive 'capital', and technical and environmental goods, that we can associate with the emergence of liberal governmentality.

As I discussed in previous chapters, Foucault's genealogy of liberal political economy shows that this form of governmentality, particularly from the 19th century, amplified the role of the state as the key agency for financing and putting into place infrastructural components as part of the policy of establishing the conditions for improving the creation of wealth. In his analysis, the aim of this investment had been to put into place technological, environmental, legal, educational and administrative institutions and practices as part of a biopolitics targeting the productivity of resources such as land and labour, and speed up and make more secure the circulation of goods and raw materials (Foucault, 1979, 2007; Venn, 2009a). I indicated also that the need for this phase in the development of capacity and productivity through improvement in infrastructure was well understood by political economists, for example, Adam Smith, but my point is elsewhere, namely, that it required the contribution of all citizens through their labour, general taxation, and effort to make possible the establishment of such common goods. Infrastructural improvements in colonial conditions, as in plantation economy, was motivated by more straightforwardly exploitative objectives within the framework of an imperial governmentality as I examined in Chapter 3.

Examples in the 19th century of the explosion in public works include urban development, land reclamation, better transport networks, the supply of potable water and other water works essential for both health and production, systems for improving hygiene, sanitation, education and training, measures to tackle poverty and delinquency, laws to protect and stimulate trade. Such policies enlisted the systematic application of statistics and findings from the nascent social sciences to aid the disciplinary techniques of 'rational' government (Goldman, 2002; Ashurst and Venn, 2014). It is an active biopolitical strategy, constituting a new concept of life and of the economy, requiring long-term planning and commitment of resources, informed by the discourse of political economy that itself emerged as part of the effort to develop a different rationality for state intervention, a new *raison d'etat* harnessed to the goal of wealth creation. The innovations besides were part of disciplinary strategies and 'technologies of the social' aiming to reconstitute the norms of the normal and the formation of subjectivities adequate for the needs of capital (Pasquino, 1978; Foucault, 1979, 2007; Henriques et al., 1998 [1984]; Terranova, 2009).

The political problem, however, is about the ownership and accessibility of the new public wealth or goods, since in liberal discourse everyone is supposed to benefit. The context, as I have emphasised, is the long-standing struggles for social justice and an equitable distribution of wealth and opportunities and their effects for discourses of legitimation and power; the question of a balance between private and the general interest was and remains central to this political goal. Some elements of this struggle appear to have marked the ideals of 'pastoral power', if we take the latter to refer to an 'art of government' centred on advancing 'the common welfare of all' by 'wise sovereigns' (Foucault, 1979: 10 ff.), a goal arguably affiliated in Europe to both the ideal of a Christian social order and to the notion of a social contract as basis for the legitimate exercise of power (as developed notably in Rousseau's *The Social Contract*, 1998 [1762]). All these parameters have had constitutive effects on the emergence of governmentality as a form of power that takes population, territory and security as central targets within the scope of an economy, as Foucault (2007) has established. I indicated in Chapter 4 with regard to liberal capitalism, that the Smithian political economy in the 19th century was at pains to justify market mechanisms on the basis of moral principles associated with the idea of 'common welfare', and I identified lasting contradictions and fractures within (varieties of) liberalism because of these claims. As I argued in Chapter 3, an important feature was the role of colonial capitalism as a condition for the kinds of solution that emerged.

I have frequently returned to the Smithian political economy because *The Wealth of Nations* is the exemplar of the new way of thinking informing biopolitical governmentality, including about the necessity of improvements in infrastructural components of productive capacity. Equally, his arguments in favour of incessant growth have been canonical for both political economy and liberalism as a political philosophy. Interestingly, Smith argued that public works that are necessary and advantageous for commerce, such as the construction of bridges, could pay for themselves through tolls and so on, though he optimistically or naively believed that, thanks to the working of the market, the cheaper cost for traders arising from these improvements in infrastructure would be passed on to the consumer through the lower pricing of goods, thus benefitting all (Smith (1812) [1776]: Book V, Part III, Article 1). And so, for governmentality and for Smith, and for political economy generally, the chief motivation in investing in infrastructure, that is to say, in common goods, was the goal of advancing economic growth, and consequently the 'progress' of nations and the general interest.

Quite crucial issues that arise from these arguments form the background for the critique of neoliberalism, for, as I have shown in Chapter 4, liberalism as a political philosophy, particularly in some of its more radical or reformist formulations, attempts to find a balance between political and economic principles, between on the one hand a moral economy relating to ideas of the common good and, on the other hand, the instrumental goals of the economy. Growth as I noted was seen as simply a means to further the objective of advancing the common good. Indeed, as I argued in Chapter 4, the historical evidence of conflicts within liberalism at the level of policy and politics testifies to the problems arising from the search for an efficacious balance between social and economic objectives in which an idea of commons and the protection of the general interest were at stake (Ashurst, 2010; Ashurst and Venn, 2014). I have also argued that the economic and ethical dilemmas created by this situation for liberalism are eliminated in the discourse of neoliberal political economy along with the ethical concerns involved, namely, by privileging the economic and the instrumental objectives grounded in a neo-utilitarian or neo-Malthusian politics that targets private appropriation, including the harvesting of commons, on the grounds that it would allow capitalism to deliver growth and prosperity more efficiently than competing systems, particularly socialism. In practice what this politics has achieved has been increased pauperisation and the reconstitution of the relationship between owners and non-owners of capital in favour of the former. So, amongst other things, neoliberalism privatises or monetises the ethical, converting it into what could be called 'ethical capital' – cashed out in slogans such as 'wellbeing' and 'happiness', etc.

Furthermore, the identity between prosperity and growth first elaborated in Smith's arguments has made it possible for growth to stand in for the general interest, an approach that has since become paradigmatic for economic policy, and endlessly and mindlessly repeated in political rhetoric by both the right and the conventional left. However, the focus on growth as principal measure of prosperity, or 'happiness' in utilitarian discourse, reduces the general interest to measures of income and productivity, cashed out in the obsession with GDP as the index of how well an economy is doing. Indeed, as Tim Jackson argues in *Prosperity without Growth*, 'The modern economy is structurally reliant on economic growth for its stability' (2009: 14). It is a model which is increasingly challenged, as I have signalled.

Equally, as I have argued, the equivalence between growth and the general interest relies additionally on arguments such as the 'trickle down' effect which claims that the bigger size of wealth produced supposedly benefits all citizens. Yet, this effect has repeatedly been shown to be a mythical fig leaf for capitalism, for instance in research by groups such as Oxfam (2012) examining increased inequality in G20 countries from 1990–2010. Stiglitz too has argued that 'inequality is the result of market distortions, with incentives directed not at creating new wealth but at taking it from others ...What America has been experiencing in recent years is the opposite of trickle-down economics: the riches accruing to the top have come at the expense of those below' (2013: 7, 8). He rejects as incorrect global corporation's arguments that its strategies for growth such as free capital mobility produces wealth for all (2013: 77–80).

The point to stress is that investments in infrastructure and social and cultural goods, or so-called 'capital', within the framework of biopolitical governmentality has over time combined smoothly with the myth of trickle down to uphold the model of growth-as-well-as-being and provide capitalism with political legitimacy. I emphasised in previous chapters that the historical diversion of wealth from the colonies to the 'centres', and now from the so-called 'developing' economies to the 'developed' or 'advanced' economies, has greatly helped in lending credibility to the capitalist narrative, though this dimension is an aspect of 'prosperity' which is conveniently erased in conventional economic discourse. The fact is that the inequality gap did not begin to close until after the introduction of reforms which led to Keynesian and New Deal type economic management within capitalism and the redistributive goals of the welfare state. Common ownership through nationalisation is of course a central plank of the socialist welfare state project.

Inequality has markedly increased from the 1980s with the 'rolling back of the welfare state', including the privatisations of its services and the common goods it administers, in contrast to the fact that the gap between social stratas had been reducing in the wake of programmes of redistribution (Harvey, 2005). The longitudinal studies of inequality and income distribution by Anthony B. Atkinson confirm the findings, as does the research in inequality established by Piketty (2014) (Atkinson, 1999, 2013). In short, there is simply no automatic correlation between growth and reduction in inequality or increases in the general prosperity of a population. So, whilst critics of trickle down advocate policies of state redistribution, the new orthodoxy vigorously rejects it; in this it remains faithful to the master thinkers of neoliberalism such as Hayek (in his *The Mirage of Social Justice* [1976]; see also Neal Curtis' critique of neoliberalism, 2013).

Redistributive social policy, it is worth remembering, is consistent with the foregrounding of the question of contract binding the state and all the people, a view shared amongst reformers in the 19th century, including J.S. Mill, who campaigned on ethical and political grounds for reforms that would benefit all, specifically through policies for which they fought long struggles, often against Malthusians and Benthamites, namely, schooling to benefit the poor, the extension of suffrage, the recognition of trade union rights, support for the destitute, and the extension of commons such as public libraries and amenities (details in Ashurst and Venn, 2014). It should be pointed out however that the notion of contract, in spite of its historical purchase for dissident politics, besides masking unequal relations of power, tends to reduce the plurality of 'the people' and the diffused assemblage of 'the state' to homogenous entities that can be recruited in political rhetoric for populisms of the 'left' or the 'right'. The main issue for contemporary politics remains the implications for legitimacy and radical democracy as a consequence of neoliberalism's elimination of the principle of the general or common interest and its ethical basis. Before I address this, I would like to extend the analysis of 'infrastructure' and 'environmental politics' by reframing them in terms of commons, and so provide further grounds for challenging corporate and financial capitalism.

From GDP to commons

One of the important reasons for seeking postcapitalist solutions to the problems I have identified relates to the neglect of the costs of what Tim Jackson (2009) highlights in his argument for an 'ecological macro-economics'. These costs include the value of 'household work, caring and voluntary work ... ecological or social damage from economic activities ... the health or environmental costs of pollution or the depletion of natural resources' (2009: 125). These are precisely the costs relating to changes to the asset base, changes that are ignored or skewed in conventional measures of wealth in terms of GDP because GDP narrowly focuses on aggregate demand, aggregate supply, and input and output ratios as indices of productivity. The convention, institutionalised in official or government statistics, is to cite nominal GDP, leaving out purchasing power parity (PPP) as measure of GDP that produces a different index for real wealth. Besides, as Jackson points out, labour productivity is a neat way of making invisible the fact that it depends 'on capital, on technological efficiency, and on resources' (2009: 127), compounding the fact that the accounting basis of GDP leaves unaccounted essential aspects of a country's economic capability or potential such as 'depreciation of capital stocks ... level of indebtedness ... the depreciation of natural capital (finite resources and ecosystem services)' (Jackson, 2009: 125). GDP is thus only a partial and inaccurate evaluation of a nation's wealth and its economic activity and potential since it neglects the essential role of commons – amongst other things – and it does not provide an indicator of the degree of inequality or the level of 'prosperity', that is, the dimensions of the quality of life which more closely express the general interest or common good.

Variations that provide more transparent indices of 'prosperity' are equally inadequate, such as the United Nations Human Development Index (HDI) – which includes factors such as life expectancy, education and income, factors which GDP neglects when 'counting only the monetary value of things exchanged in the economy' and assuming that 'these monetary values are equivalent' (Jackson, 2009: 125). A slightly better though still inadequate method is the GINI coefficient which is a scale for the frequency distribution or degree of dispersion of income and wealth in a given population. These indices along with the Atkinson Index – which shows up variability in income distribution especially at the lower end of the spectrum – point to the problems, but one would have to shift the framework altogether, for instance towards approaches such as in the idea of capabilities developed in Amartya Sen's (2010) rejection of GDP in the context of inequality and sustainability, or the broader issues discussed by Stiglitz and colleagues (2011) in *Mismeasuring Our Lives*. By contrast, my analysis has been developing a framework grounded in an idea of enlarged or postcapitalist commons for judging the general interest, and thus, for addressing issues of equity and justice that challenge the unequal relations of power between 'races', genders and class that correlate with capitalist property regimes. Here I will summarise the steps in the line of argument that opens towards this different postcapitalist standpoint, essential for imagining quite radical solutions to the crises I have been examining.

To continue with the genealogical approach, let us add a different layer to the role of biopolitical governmentality in the development of infrastructure and improvements in environmental resources and capabilities as part of the effort to enhance the productive capacity of the population, highlighted above. These improvements, for example, a healthy and educated population or an efficient transport network, are inputs also, but unaccounted for in firms' calculation of costs. The adoption of a business model for (mis)measuring value, and the accounting practice associated with it, distorts this picture of the aggregate cost of economic activity, whilst also reducing all activities to its monetary value alone. In any case, business accounting practice and conventional macro-economic accounts, shared today by both the state and orthodox economics, do not account for all those components of the quality of life such as free broad education, the availability of civic amenities such as public libraries, playgrounds, public parks and beaches, aesthetically pleasing and secure living spaces, good health, the strength of the social bond, a whole range of other social and cultural goods or wealth, and the guarantee of liberties and rights which would be inoperative without such public provisions.

A key point is that the model reduces the incalculable to the calculable, as in the case of education, or in the case of ecological damage such as, for example, the effects of chemical and biological pollution harming ecologies and habitats causing, amongst other things, the 'depreciation of natural capital', that is to say, the store of common goods. What is neglected at the level of the firm, as well as mismeasured by macro-economic calculations of value, are not only the kinds of qualitative or intangible wealth noted above, but also all the natural resources like the quality of the environment, biodiversity, non-renewable and scarce natural resources like minerals, coal, oil, and so on. Above all, what is neglected is all the immense store of know-hows and dispositions, that is, resources for living accumulated over generations, that equip a population to sustain a particular lifestyle, invested in knowledges of how to live and how to be (Stiegler, 2007). They are all vital ingredients in the process both of production and in sustaining particular ways of being or forms of life as examined in Agamben (2013), embedded in the everyday and the environment – the latter already worked upon by humans and so existing as part of 'naturecultures' (Haraway, 2003; Latimer and Miele, 2013, amongst a growing literature). These knowledges, capabilities and resources are either depleted or damaged or altered through the productive and cultural activity of humans, and thus, in one way or another, entail a cost to society.

Yet, such wealth and capabilities, when aggregated as infrastructure, are mostly regarded as 'externalities' by firms and thus as resources and 'services' that are mostly 'free' at the point of production or use. The point is that private firms do not directly defray the costs of either the depreciation of these factors of production, say, concerning the quality of the environment and infrastructure, or the increasing scarcity of critical raw materials which are used up, as with water and a whole range of minerals, though some costs are passed on and appear in the price for some inputs such as energy or water which firms also use.[3] The same can be said concerning the cost of the reproduction of a capability such as an educated and trained workforce. So, whilst these costs do not figure in individual firms' statement of accounts, they are instead 'externalised' onto public accounts, thus paid for through general taxation, that in principle includes tax on profits made by corporations, though as we all know, many transnationals now avoid paying through using tax havens and loopholes. Furthermore, with the establishment of neoliberal 'individual social policy' within the scope of generalised competition (Chapter 3 and Foucault, 2008: 144), the cost of providing inputs and factors of production benefiting firms, such as a skilled and healthy labour force, is increasingly being transferred directly onto individual citizens. In short, the state's intervention to improve productive capacity in accordance with neo-biopolitical strategies as well as the activities it undertakes to maintain good social order – for example, by means of ordoliberalism's idea of the 'social market' – ultimately plays into the hands, that is to say, the coffers, of companies' profits via the externalisation of the costs of commons and capabilities onto those who produce the wealth.

By contrast, what I have been foregrounding is the important and growing literature which regards much of the resources included in externalities to be properly part of commons, if one understands commons to refer, on the one hand, to the store of natural resources such as mineral deposits and land which should be, and in some places used to be, held in common as a collective wealth for a people. One could recall too Polanyi's arguments in *The Great Tramsformation* (2001 [1944]: 75) about the central role which the commodification of labour, land and money – those 'fictitious' commodities – played in the consolidation of capitalism. Increasingly, even 'resources' such as species are being monetised, that is, converted into 'capital assets' or 'commodities' ready for acquisition by corporations (as I noted in earlier chapters).

On the other hand, commons include the cognitive and affective capabilities collectively and cumulatively acquired or shared by a community, produced and reproduced over time as an integral part of a society's make-up. The latter, as intellectual 'stock', or 'general intellect', or (Heidegger's) 'standing reserve', includes knowledges of all kinds – theoretical, craft, artistic, customary, nurturing, as well as knowledge of how to live, and their inscription in ways of life, amounting to a great wealth of know-hows, capabilities, technics, and affective energies: it is this too which is made available for productive activity as part of what ecological economists include in 'throughput', yet is considered as 'free' resource or 'externalities' by private capital.

Until their relatively recent commodification, such 'wealth' had often been regarded as a common inheritance for the common good and for use in the general interest (Arrighi, 1994). Of course one must recognise that some elements of commons, for instance land, have historically appeared as sovereign wealth, serving the power of the elites who had appropriated it, that is, operating as basis sustaining the wealth and power of rulers 'born of the contingency of battles' (Foucault, 2003: 72) – and not yet as a 'free' resource for private ownership and profit. Indeed, in many cultures such as amongst indigenous people in the Americas and Australia before colonisation, and many indigenous communities still, common-pool resources (CPRs – Ostrom, 1990) such as land were and are not thought of as things that can be owned as property by anyone – an attitude to the earth as mother that made it possible for European colonisers to classify the land they confiscated in the New World and elsewhere as *terra nullius* (or nobody's land) and thus magically freed up for appropriation by the conquerors and the rich. One recent example typical of many other such cases concerns the Awajun of Peru who are resisting the concession of their territories to corporations with interest in oil, timber and hydroelectricity. The significant issue in these struggles is that incommensurable ontologies and cosmologies are at stake since the Awajun regard the river on which they live as a brother (Blaser, 2013). Such an attitude to other species and natural habitats opens towards a transcolonial ecology which refuses the categories and classifications dictated by 'conventional' epistemologies (see also Povinelli, 2016; Haraway, 2016; Tsing, 2015 for a wider analysis relating ecologies to capitalism, ethnography and the kind of co-habitance I explore later).

The issue for a political economy of commons is that the externalisation of costs has become the default position for financial capitalism, seen as an integral element of the search for minimising costs and expenditure and thus maximising profits – though corporations in many countries now both own privatised utilities and social services yet still expect the state to subsidise the cost of infrastructure and its upkeep at the public's expense, effectively shifting the cost to individual workers and to suppliers. Transnationals in particular, with their ability to shift costs and revenues across state borders, simply piggy-back on these assets provided at the expense of individual states. Admittedly, knock-on effects for prices can result, though increases are usually passed on to consumers and thus directly or indirectly add to inflationary pressures. In effect, the public is made to pay twice over – through general taxation and levies and through price increases – for the cost of 'improvements' in the conditions and factors creating wealth. So, the privatisation and liberalisation of what used to be considered as public or common assets, along with the hidden subsidy private enterprises receive through the externalisation of the cost of infrastructure and other factors of wealth creation, enables corporations to benefit doubly at the expense of the people as a whole.

An important issue arises also which is often lost sight of in economic analysis: it is the fact that the maintainance or up-grading of the range of material, technical and socio-cultural goods that I have noted requires the long-term planning, costing and allocation of a nation's resources, whilst conglomerates and financial capitalism operate at a global level according to the short-term objective of maximising profit heedless of the longer-term interests of national governments and their citizens, and indeed of the planet. The disjunctures of scale and interest result in distortions concerning the calculations circumscribing policy at the national level aiming to develop the 'infrastructure': health and education systems, the supply of energy, water, the maintainance of forests and woodlands, the protection of the range of common goods I have noted above. Clearly, these disjunctures impinge directly on programmes to tackle climate change and environmental degradation, since such programmes require long-term solutions and co-operation amongst all nations, whilst transnational corporations and those governments shackled to enterprise culture or to short-sighted nationalism are ruled either by short-termism or prioritise their own narrow interests. A case in point is India's plan to build hundreds of new coal-fired power stations to fuel growth, although it already is the single biggest consumer of coal (Chapter 2; Jose, 2015). So is any return to coal anywhere, as President Trump wants to do; fracking for gas in the UK is another example of short-sighted national policy that downplays environmental costs and sustainability (Le Page, 2016).[4]

It is clear therefore that the interconnected temporal and spatial disjunctures associated with finance capitalism and the interests of global capital have created additional conditions which induce governments to abnegate responsibility for safeguarding common resources and protecting the needy and vulnerable, which in effect means the abandonment of the ethical principles that had informed the setting up of many of the provisions and institutions which I have described as part of commons and that provided intangible benefits to people in terms of the quality of life, a dimension irreducible to business accounts. These shifts confirm core aspects of the political economy of neoliberalism, particularly the break with the political and economic principles underlying welfare state social policy. Values and interests, including ethical, spiritual and the long-term sustainability of life on earth are reclassified as optional extras, if not erased by this infernal machine. It is worth recalling that these values are meant to be consistent with the idea that common goods and interest are the responsibility of the state, the discharge of which cashes out a state's claim or duty to represent the interest of all citizens, a proviso underlying democratic legitimacy.

It is clear also that anti-state rhetoric is a move in a game in which the stakes are the goal of capital achieving more effective control over the framework for setting the rules of the game, namely through shaping the regulatory and decision-making apparatuses, and pressurising for the laws that are favourable to capital, for example, about taxation, or labour relations and labour law, or the ownership of property. We know from Foucault's genealogy of neoliberal thought that the various (often pragmatic) shifts in the application of political economy to generate social and economic policy have had for quite some time this objective of the reconstruction of the framework to better support capitalism and the market. The discourse of ordoliberalism is explicit enough about this, as Foucault explains: '... the main and constant concern of governmental intervention ... must be the conditions of existence of the market, that is to say, what the ordoliberals call the "framework"' (Foucault, 2008: 140). These include 'population, technology, training and education, the legal system, the availability of land' (2008: 141), that is, elements which are part of their idea of a 'social market' as supplement to the operation of the market, and which largely pass for externalities from the point of view of companies' costs.

As we saw, an added advantage for capitalism is that the process of accumulation by means of dispossessing nations and communities of their common wealth, and that nowadays is routed through apparatuses of financialisation, conscripts all citizens into the neoliberal social order in their role as consumers, savers and debtors (Chapter 1, referencing Foucault, 2008;

Lazzarato, 2009; Venn, 2009a; Marazzi, 2010). The liberalisation and privatisation of common wealth in effect impoverish us all both directly and indirectly, as well as diminish the human, since the privilege of self-interested individualism and the profit motive against collective welfare and security destroys the basis of solidarity. The role of a centralising state as relay, as mediating agency, and as the political instrument that legitimises the whole system needs to be stressed, especially as neoliberal doublespeak presents the state as a hindrance for business whilst relying on the state for authorising their business activities, including to relentlessly milk state apparatuses that deliver common goods. What we are seeing is the emergence of a neo-biopolitics in which technologies of the social serve owners of capital through all that is 'cold, callous, calculating, rational, mechanical in the play of properly economic competition' as Foucault argued when outlining ordoliberals' arguments for 'socialising' 'collective' elements of consumption (2004b: 247–248).

And so, the genealogy of commons brings into view the long struggles over dispossession and accumulation, in Europe and elsewhere – for example, over the Enclosures of land from the 12th century, accelerating after Westphalia, 1648, for reasons detailed in Chapter 4, or the elimination of centuries-old co-operative practices like the open field system in England (an old and long-lasting form of common pool resource management). It is this process of progressive dispossession which has resulted in the now taken-for-granted capitalist property regimes whereby everything is seen as property, as Hardt and Negri note in their excursus on commons in *Empire* (2000: 300–303) and their elaboration in *Commonwealth* (2011).

Equally, the distinction between common goods and property-as-commodity shows up the essentially collaborative and co-produced character of all the social or public, cultural and natural forms of wealth like libraries, museums, public galleries, parks, playgrounds, woodlands, rivers, beaches, shores, forests, and so on, that neoliberalism, pursuing its policy of the commodification and privatisation of everything, is already misappropriating (amongst a large literature, see Arendt, 2000; Venn, 2006a, 2006b on the distinction between wealth and property; Jeremy Gilbert's discussion of commons, 2014; Terranova, 2015; Amin and Howell, 2016; Vercellone, 2015, and many accounts of debates around the place of commons in thinking through alternative property regimes and forms of ownership). Yet, as I noted, these 'fruits of the earth' and these collective forms of social and cultural goods, developed or maintained and made available equally through public expenditure, constitute a common treasury to enrich the quality of life of all irrespective of personal means, creating a sense of belonging to a common space, and sustaining social cohesion and solidarity. Free access to such common goods, exemplarily libraries, in part offsets the inequities and deprivations of inequality, enriching the lives of those who have little. An enlarged view of commons should therefore include, besides the range of resources I have highlighted, all those amenities, provisions, institutions, services and capabilities that are part of what is often today described as social, cultural, and intellectual or cognitive so-called 'capital', but that are in truth a common inheritance.[5]

At the practical level, questions surface about the economics of commons and common pool resources (CPRs), notably developed in the research of Elinor Ostrom and colleagues in *Governing the Commons* (1990) that explores non-hierarchical management structures for commonly owned resources and the resolution of disputes to ensure equity – innovative work for which she was awarded the Nobel Prize in 2009 – or approaches in Strathern (2004) regarding the 'ownership' of intellectual labour. There is also a growing literature on the idea of commonfare regarding knowledge commons, for example in the work of Vercellone and others (Fumagelli et al., 2018). An interesting wide-ranging though reformist viewpoint, developed in Parance and Saint Victor and colleagues' analysis of common goods, explores 'the triptych of juridical modernity: state/market/property' (2014: 22) to argue for a limit to property in the context of 'economies of scarcity' because of resource depletion. There are also different notions of commons in Latour (2010, 2012), where it is framed in relation to the concept of 'nature/culture' and the socio-technical status of objects, and in Hardt and Negri's *Commonwealth*, where commons is understood by reference to concepts of 'multitude', biopolitics and altermodernity, positions that become problematic when proposing different and dissident property regimes and the philosophical and ontological grounds underpinning such alternatives.

The point is that the growing inequality and destitution we have witnessed over the last 30 years is one consequence of the elimination, and increasing privatisation and subversion of public interest as well as of institutions like friendly societies, mutuals, credit unions, co-operatives, the non-profit sector generally, that is, institutions and organisations that practise forms of common ownership and management and make a surprisingly large contribution to the economy through providing employment as well as a significant proportion of services, goods and support for communities, even in the USA, as Wilkinson and Pickett have pointed out (2010: 252–254). Such public institutions function to constitute the public as an independent domain of life in common. Their 'liberalisation' and marketisation amounts to the failure by governments to 'protect social and ecological goals' and 'ensure that long-term public goods are not undermined by short-term private interests' (Jackson, 2009: 166), with adverse effects for the poor – and indeed for the whole of society – since 'inequality tends to be higher in liberalized market economies than in coordinated market economies' (Jackson, 2009: 164). The arguments I have been developing about the specificity of capitalism with regard to its property regime and its project of unlimited commodification mean that a politics of the commons necessarily undermines capitalism.

It should be clear then that the degradation and plunder of the environment and its consequences like climate change, loss of biodiversity, the exhaustion of essential resources, and growing inequality and insecurity worldwide are directly connected to the failure of the private sector to take responsibility for safeguarding not only vital elements of common assets, but the things that make life worth living. An important conclusion is that the essential difference between public and private interest must be maintained as condition for an equitable system of distribution of resources and life chances. It is a struggle about competing values and worldviews. For all the reasons sketched so far, it is clear also that the developments brought about by neoliberal and neoconservative doctrines reinforce the judgement that capitalism, and all that underlies it, is fundamentally destructive, undemocratic and unethical; it is incapable of resolving the crises which now beset us.

Notes

1 The notion of associated milieu developed in Gilbert Simondon's work refers to the kind of dynamics whereby several elements in the formation of an entity are conjoined in the process of the reciprocal becoming or actualisation of the entity. As an example, he explains how, in the process of making a brick, the system hand-clay-mould can be considered as forming an associated milieu (Simondon, 2005: 42, 43; see my extended account in Venn, 2010).

2 It is important to underline that for humans as a species, these forms of life include the technicised milieux and the technical objects to which we are coupled and that are themselves now subject to profound changes. This aspect of humans as 'technical beings' (Stiegler, 1998) brings to mind Simondon's arguments against the neglect of technical objects in the understanding of human culture, for he proposed that '(I)n order to restore to our understanding of culture the truly general character that it has lost, one must be able to reintroduce within it the awareness of the nature of machines, of the relations which they entertain amongst themselves, of their relations to man, and the recognition of the values implied in these relations' (1989 [1958]: 13). One could point to the discovery and applications of electricity and electro-magnetism which have completely revolutionised all aspects of life across the planet, whilst nowadays digital and cybernetic technologies are altering conditions of existence in fundamental yet unpredictable ways that we are still trying to fathom. This material aspect of human culture, increasingly thought in terms of the technology–nature–culture dynamics, implies the necessity of reorganising and inventing new technologies as central objectives for constituting alternatives to capitalism.

3 Regarding scarce critical materials, see for example, Ridgway and Webb (2015) on rare earths in the South China Sea, particularly since it highlights the link between geopolitical conflicts and the competition for resources for the industrial–military–media complex.

4 Indeed, as many have argued, a disturbing feature of the essential conflict of interest is the extent to which trade agreements such as the now defunct NAFTA, or those now vetoed by the Trump Administration, namely, Transatlantic Trade and Investment Partnership (TTIP) and Trans Pacific Trade (TPP), include, or included, dispute settlement mechanisms between investor and state that cede power to transnationals and effectively by-pass state sovereignty and established transnational regulatory mechanisms and bodies. The likelihood is that now such agreements will be between the (economically dominant) USA and individual states, yet carrying the same crucial implications for citizens' rights and liberties, and for commons; the proposed Comprehensive Economic and Trade Agreement (CETA) between Canada and the EU carries the same political and economic risks. Monbiot (2013: 33) has argued that investor-state rules could be used to make it impossible for governments to renationalise public assets such as railways or ban specific pesticides,

etc., the implication being that '(T)hese rules shut down democratic alternatives'. Such agreements would institutionalise the shift in the balance of power between the state and capital, between the people and the enterprise, and in terms of geopolitical interests, to the benefit of already dominant nations and corporations (see also Chapter 1).

5   One should shun the term capital when applied to such commons because it converts these forms of public goods into the categories that belong to the conceptual structure of liberal capitalism and thus already corrupts and commodifies them by bringing them within the sphere of calculation of value consistent with the interest of 'enterprise' and the accounting practices of business.

6
New Foundations for Postcapitalist Worlds

Philosophical displacements

In addressing the issues of the grounds for breaking away from the assumptions and claims to truth invested and inscribed in the current order of things, I shall examine three theoretical displacements which are necessary as basis for imagining alternatives. The first concerns the rejection of any understanding of the worlding of a world that neglects its essentially co-implicate character, that is, involving all forms of life in the choreographic processes involved. Second, the displacements reject the still resilient concept of the autonomous, egocentric, self-interested subject as agent of history and of rational action, and the 'metaphysics of individualism' that underlie it. Third, they signal a break with anthropocentrism, to which egocentrism is affiliated, and which is freighted with attitudes to other beings and nature that support their domination and exploitation. The different ontological, epistemological and ethical standpoints which relate to these displacements have been alluded to at various points in the book. Together they outline perspectives that are antithetical to the assumptions about the social order, subjectivity, rationality, governance, embedded in and cashed out in capitalism and other economies founded on institutionalised inequalities and oppressive power. And they announce a worldview in which solidarity, empathy, being-with and being-for-the-other and an heteronomous ethics are prioritised. Basically, the displacements and decentrings will help to clear the grounds for considering what postcapitalist and post anthropocentric/racist/patriarchal societies entail. Besides, this line of questioning follows from the arguments that the problems we face are far from being purely economic or political and so require reflections that problematise the ways of life and values which have become normalised, though they are inimical for convivial socialities.

Underlying the perspective I am developing is an ontology grounded in the idea of the essentially co-implicate and composable character of forms of life. Jean-Luc Nancy (2000: 3) signals such a view when he says:

> Being cannot be anything but being-with-one-another, circulating in the with and as the with of this singularly plural coexistence ... But this circulation goes in all directions at once ... opened by presence to presence: all things, all beings, all entities, everything past and future, alive, dead, inanimate, stones, plants, nails, gods – and 'humans', that is, all those who expose sharing and circulation as such by saying 'we'.

I will explore the broad ontological framework in Nancy and in the standpoint of co-implication through the idea of epigenesis for it can act as a relay-concept to link the different thematics relating to the displacements I have suggested, and it helps to widen the scope of analysis beyond the philosophical. This is because epigenesis theorises the idea of an attunement linking organism and environment in a reciprocal dynamics, and so echoes the perspective in Nancy's statement whilst providing a material counterpart to anchor the alternative conception of life and of the social which the project of constituting postcapitalist worlds entails, and that I address in this chapter.

I have been arguing in previous chapters that economies and political systems invariably authorise themselves ultimately by appeal to an idea of the common or greater good which they all claim to be able to uphold. Whether the claim asserts that this goal is to be achieved through establishing greater efficiency, productivity and growth, a more stable social order, a more equitable distribution of wealth and powers, greater levels of freedom, more widespread liberties, or by ensuring the virtuous community of believers or of those who belong as the authentic people, the underlying argument is always that the preferred system deserves the public's support because it more effectively secures these goals and values than competing systems. What is privileged is the priority granted to the values themselves and their central role in the narratives of legitimation of whichever social order, though this is not often explicit in political discourse or in the discourse of social policy.

This is true of capitalism as much as it is of any other economy. Indeed, the arguments of Adam Smith and of the Physiocrats at the birth of liberal political economy foregrounded the moral economy underlying 'free market' when they argued for its greater ability to protect individual freedoms whilst being a more effective and objective mechanism for the equitable distribution of wealth. Furthermore, the title of key works which have inspired the neoliberal reconstitution of society, notably, Hayek, Friedman or Rand explicitly appeal to values such as freedom, liberty, individualism and rationality in support of the socio-economic system they advocate as Curtis (2013) and others have shown. Rand and Branden's *Virtue of Selfishness* (1964) is the exemplary case. The thinking of postcapitalist worlds likewise must start with the question of social goods which are desired because they are grounded in a moral order or in the anticipation of an ethical sociality.

In an important sense then, an idea of a dominant or organising narrative – or grand narrative in Lyotard's (1984 [1979]) vocabulary – implicitly or explicitly enframes the preferred politico-economic system. They are the narratives that provide answers to the 'big questions' concerning the basis of social order, the foundation of law, the fulfilled life, proper conduct, or the ultimate purpose of existence. In order for such narratives to have authority, they also must lay claim to a truth, whether divinely or transcendentally sanctioned or grounded in a secular rationality – as also the discourse of modernity is supposed to do. Epistemological, ontological and theological issues are thus involved in the foundation of these legitimising narratives inscribing visions of the good life, though the founding metaphysical assumptions are either placed beyond question by being displaced onto sacred texts, or some essentialised notion of 'Nature', or else by appeal to the people as agency and telos in populist rhetoric. Power is visibly or invisibly inscribed in these foundations, which accounts for why the assumptions are often hidden or erased, whilst the coincidence of 'Truth' and Faith that they secrete easily slips into fundamentalisms and their violent exclusions (as arguments in Derrida and others have shown, and as I established in Venn, 2000). Radical change in the way we live implicates reflection upon such fundamental questions with the aim of finding new foundations, ones which dethrone the narratives that throughout history have authorised systems of exploitation and forms of violence, or that have failed to provide clear enough principles for opposing systemic inequalities and the mindless plunder of the earth. In their contemporary refigurations, principally in the discourse of neoliberal political economy, they have hastened the confluence of crises with which we are now familiar.

Another major consideration when thinking about abandoning the established 'grand narratives' arises from the recognition that the motivations for such overarching discourses are driven by the cruel limits inherent in the human condition, relating to our experience of temporality, specifically the foreknowledge of finitude ('being-towards-death'), the experience of loss as an existential given (of loved ones, of the flight of the past into the dimness of memory, of youthful vitality, innocence, opportunities), the fragilities and the unpredictabilities or chance that govern each life, and the limitations which historically specific circumstances place on what it is possible for individuals to achieve and do. In all cultures, a sacred dimension, or the anticipation of an emancipation, has emerged to give heart to the calculus of hope without which life would truly be meaningless and prey to a soulless cynicism that would allow every kind of despotism. Indeed, the abiding attraction of capitalism is the knowledge that it creates possibilities for winners in the lottery of life, yet could mitigate the harshest deals of fate. Its alliance with the project of modernity promised progress, equity and opportunity in equal measure for humanity as a whole. My analysis in previous chapters has established that in most societies the winners are few and the losers many and mostly drawn from the same populations. Today in the midst of plenty, capitalism is the wound that oozes poverty and misery as signs of a terminal sickness.

From anthropocentrism to the co-implicative web of life

In order to both understand the underlying assumptions yet challenge them, we could start by identifying features constitutive of the conceptual framework sustaining liberal capitalism that continue to act as obstacles to the radical shifts in foundation which have become necessary. Central to modernity as a discourse, we find one defining feature, perhaps more specific to

Western modernity than other features of modernity, namely, the location of the (male, 'Western'/'Westernised') individual subject as the autonomous, rational, self-sufficient, self-interested agent or entity at the centre of the epistemological system underwriting the discourse of truth. Its exemplar is the rational 'man' of science, now largely regarded as an idealised construct belonging to a rationalist epistemology. One encounters its modern foundation in the Cartesian discourse of a self-affirming mind, casting aside doubt at the cost or erasing the other in the elaboration of reliable knowledge. Arendt, in her critique of Descartes' circular affirmation of the cogito as the self-evident foundation of reliable knowledge, argued instead that 'our certainty that what we perceive has an existence independent of the act of perceiving, depends entirely on the object's also appearing as such to others and being acknowledged by them' (1978: 46). And she adds:

> all solipsistic theories – whether they radically claim that nothing but the self 'exists' or, more moderately, hold that the self and its consciousness of itself are the primary objects of verifiable knowledge – are out of tune with the most elementary data of our existence and experience. Solipsism ... has been ... the most pernicious fallacy of philosophy even before it attained in Descartes the high rank of theoretical and existential consistency. (ibid.)

This cognitivist agent or hero of science has been the subject of extensive critiques in science and technology studies, for instance in the work of dissident theoreticians of science like Canguilhem and Bachelard, and in feminist and decolonial philosophy, for example, in Sandra Harding, Karen Barad, Donna Haraway, Walter Mignolo. The counterpart of this agent of modern epistemology and ontology is the subject inscribed in the idea of possessive individualism and the rational legal subject, or encountered in the autonomous subject which conventional psychosciences presuppose. They are conceptually in solidarity with the notion of the self-interested individual at the heart of capitalism and (neo)/liberal political economy – and in cultures in which the human being is thrown onto its own resources, condemned according to the fiction of destiny or fate, thus placed outside one's responsibility or care.

The important point is that although the historical specificity and flawed or partisan character of these paradigms of a discrete and autonomous subject of knowledge and agent of history have been amply demonstrated, they have nevertheless remained resilient and central in a good deal of political economy, and in economics, political philosophy, law, psychology and assumptions about mind and self (for a critique see Henriques et al., 1998 [1984]). With the rise of neoliberalism, the privileging of individualism and subject-centredness has been asserted almost as dogma, underwriting the idea of the individual as the 'enterprise subject' driven by innate self-interest and self-seeking passions. Besides, it operates as the 'rational' consumer who is supposed to 'freely' choose amongst options, and it is the economic agent at the heart of the 'individual social policy' which ordoliberals promote. Equally, the individualist spirit of capitalism has found fertile soil to grow in cultures in which inequalities have become naturalised in the form of fixed hierarchies, however legitimated, say, in terms of differences of gender or race or caste or rank or religion.

A new decentring of this subject therefore is a first step in reorienting social and economic policy in accordance with principles that challenge existing systems of values and capitalist and proto-feudal regimes of power and property. This broader aim of radical transformation means that previous decentrings that had relied mostly on philosophical arguments deployed for example in critical theory, structuralism and poststructuralism, have limited purchase. The argument which will be developed here is that research across a diversity of sciences, say in biology, critical psychology, quantum physics, radical ecology, radical anthropology and cognate sciences, and some perspectives in the neuro and cognitive sciences, are increasingly framed by approaches that emphasise relationality, co-emergence, co-constitution, complexity, cooperation, that is, they assert the co-implication of all beings in a world in common. Together they suggest new ways of grounding ontology, epistemology and ethics, and thus new points of departure for rethinking the relation of being and knowing, being and acting. They thus provide appropriate grounds for inventing ways of living compatible with postcapitalist societies, that is, compatible with a cosmopolitical project aligned with a politics of the common.

The kinds of shifts which this corpus signals can be gleaned from the following perspectives. Karen Barad, thinking through the implications of aspects of quantum physics in *Meeting the Universe Halfway*, and referencing the views of Niels Bohr about Heisenberg's uncertainty principle (regarding the calculation of momentum and position for particles) writes that what Bohr is doing contra Heisenberg is to follow the logic of complementarity rather than that of uncertainty, and thus that he is saying something about how 'particles do not have determinate values of position and momentum simultaneously' (2007: 19). The implication for Barad is that Bohr's 'counterintuitive' interpretation,

> is calling into question an entire tradition in the history of Western metaphysics: the belief that the world is populated with individual things with their own independent sets of determinate properties. The lesson that Bohr takes from quantum physics is very deep and profound: there aren't little things wandering aimlessly in the void that possess the complete set of properties that Newtonian physics assumes ... rather, there is something fundamental about the nature of measurement interactions such that, given a particular measuring apparatus, certain properties become determinate, while others are specifically excluded. (2007: 19)

One of her conclusions from this episode in the history of quantum physics – apart from implications regarding the objectivity of experiments, or about causality and the intentionality of the experimenter – is that,

> (P)erhaps intentionality might be better understood as attributable to a complex network of human and nonhuman agents, including historically specific sets of material conditions that exceed the traditional notion of the individual ... it is less that there is an assemblage of agents than there is an entangled state of agencies. (Barad, 2007: 23)

She goes on to point to the broader challenge which the principles of complementarity and entanglement announce, for, not only do we have to recognise that the binary between free will and determinism is flawed, but 'if causality is reworked, then power needs to be rethought ... Agency needs to be rethought. Ethics needs to be rethought. Science needs to be rethought' (ibid.). This calls for a reexamination of 'the very terms of the question about the relationship between science and ethics. Even beyond that, it undermines the metaphysics of individualism and calls for a rethinking of the very nature of knowledge and being' (ibid.).

Much the same kind of challenge applies about scientific observations of the behaviour of humans and other animals, regarding the effects of the conceptual and technical apparatus both for recording and interpreting the observations, implying the evacuation of the anthropocentric subject from one's understanding of living systems. Just as importantly, the rejection of 'the metaphysics of individualism' means the rejection not only of the idea of individuals as independently contained or bounded entities however conceptualised – for instance, as the autonomous subject of (logocentric) reason, or as metaphoric 'monads' (Tarde) and the like – but entails instead the prioritising of relationality which is implied in the standpoint of co-implication and compossibility, and thus the point of view of co-constitution, of becoming-with through complex processes of development in which living being and environment constantly and reciprocally determine each other (details in Venn, 2010). Concepts of epigenesis (or the developmental process whereby elements from 'outside' come to be interiorised as an integral part of a living entity) and symbiogenesis, elaborated in the work of Lynn Margulis (2009) and Dorion Sagan (2003), cometo mind in support of the radical ontological shift which is proposed by Barad.

Indeed, it is possible to propose a view of the universe of things according to which mutual entanglement and co-dependence are seen as fundamental characteristics in all existence, a proposition that could appear to lend support to ideas such as supersymmetry – that is, the idea that every particle has a heavier partner, but invisible for existing measuring instruments (say, quark and squark). This view could, as Stephen Hawking (2012) suggests, resolve inconsistencies in the standard model relating to the observed mass of atomic particles and the Higgs field (the Higgs field is theorised as what imparts mass to fundamental particles; the Higgs boson is the sub-atomic particle which theoretically implicates the existence of the field). Supersymmetry, though now fraught with its own problems, may also provide an elegant solution for dark matter by showing how all matter and the four principal forces in the universe (gravitational, electromagnetic, strong nuclear and weak nuclear) are co-implicated as part of fields. This is of course far from the relativist position, a position that slides back onto the terrain of individualism.

Or, consider Clark and Chalmers' thesis of an 'extended mind', that is, the idea of an 'active externalism' whereby 'the human organism is linked with an external entity in a two-way interaction, creating a coupled system that can be seen as a cognitive system in its own right' (in Clark, 2011: 222). This means that 'the relevant external features are active, playing a crucial role in the here-and-now ... the relevant parts of the world are in the loop, not dangling at the other end of a long causal chain' (2011: 222, 223). What is recognised is the decentring of mind, specifically its cognitive capabilities, away from the brain as container and mind as the privileged inner site of cognition. The 'environment' in this account fully participates in the development and evolution of cognition. Furthermore, the body too is considered as an integral part of the coupled system, acting in accordance to 'ecological control', that is, control in terms of 'relevant order in the bodily or worldly environment' (Clark, 2011: 6). Clark refers to Pfeifer and Bongard's (2007) principle of 'ecological balance' to explain this dynamic and epigenetic coupling, whereby 'given a certain task environment there has to be a match between the complexities of the agent's sensory, motor, and neural systems ... there is a certain balance or task-distribution between morphology, materials, control and environment' (2011: 7). One encounters this kind of extended epigenetic process in the way an infant learns to use initially unresponsive limbs to achieve its goals through the 'inhabited interaction' between its body and the environment. For Clark, the body becomes 'transparent equipment' by reference to world, that is, its relationship to world is shaped in terms of habituated and nonconscious deployment of acquired skills whereby a body inhabits a task-oriented world; in doing so, it relies on 'minimal memory strategies' – which minimises energy expenditure through habit formation – to achieve desired ends, for example, organised in terms of 'small-world networks', as I explained in the Introduction.

Another or a second order of the coupling of body and world takes place when new information is generated altering 'the particular mixes of biological memory and active, embodied retrieval recruited to solve different versions' of a problem (Clark, 2011: 13). In such cases, embodied, embedded cognition makes use of 'whatever mix of problem-solving resources yield an acceptable result with a minimum effort' (ibid.). Clark links this kind of 'active sensing' to the 'principle of ecological assembly', a principle understood in terms of efficacity as the central measure whereby neural, bodily and environmental resources are assembled. In such strategies, the combination of active sensing and 'perceptual coupling', often taking place at a liminal level, acts 'as an open conduit allowing environmental magnitudes to exert a constant influence on behavior' (ibid.: 16). Embodied cognition thus enables subjects to nonconsciously select strategies that simplify neural problem solving by making the most efficacious use of freely available information and environmental opportunities (or affordances, as Gibson, 1977 and 1979, calls them in his anti-cognitivist 'ecological psychology').

Time is another component of the kinds of structural couplings between mind, body and environment, particularly in cases of what Clark calls 'continuous reciprocal causation', when changes occuring in either the local environment or in the brain–body system affect each other in terms of feedback and feed-forward pathways, as in a dance. In those situations of coupled unfolding, 'two or more systems engage in a continuous, real-time, and effectively instantaneous dance of mutual codetermining interaction' (2011: 25). Clark's point is that 'appeals to the body, to the environment, and to embodied action' show the essential role of active sensing and strategies of 'ecological assembly' in the dynamic loops whereby material artifacts, language, and symbolic culture open up transformative potential for agents. His analysis leads to 'the suggestion that mind itself leaches into body and world' (2011: 29).

A story which Clarke tells at the beginning of *Embodied Mind* illustrates this point whilst providing an opening for my next example which will be about the epigenetic relation binding being and technics in the process of hominisation, that is, the evolution of the human. He recounts the encounter between Richard Feynman (Nobel prize-winner for his work on quantum electrodynamics) and the historian of physics Charles Weiner who described Feynman's notes and sketches as 'a record of [Feynman's] day-to-day work'. Feynman however, rejecting Weiner's view that the paper is a 'record' of the work he had done in his head, asserted that he 'actually did the work on the paper', emphasising the working itself: 'No, it's not a *record*, not really. It's *working*. You have to work on paper and this is the paper' (in Clark, 2011: xxv, italics in original). Clark goes on to say that 'Feynman was actually *thinking* on the paper' (ibid.) and not just in his head.

The idea of active externalisation of mind is nicely captured in this example, yet there is more: for the important feature of the process of externalisation involves (in this case) the invention of writing and paper and pen on the one hand, and, on the other hand, the way that such prosthetic devices or technical apparatuses, invented by humans, actually transform human capabilities in an alloplastic manner, as the work of Leroi-Gourhan demonstrates. The idea of the active dynamism whereby mind, body and environment are coupled, that is, act as an 'associated milieu' (Simondon, Stiegler, below), goes beyond the case of noting one's thoughts down so that one can return to it at a later date to continue the work. That point refers to an example given by Husserl to underline the role of writing in the development of thought, the argument being that it makes possible the recording of thought or its externalisation in the form of messages to oneself (or anyone) to enable one to begin again where one left off. The example is used by Bernard Stiegler (2007: 339) as a starting point to argue for the crucial importance of such retentional devices as both an inscribed memory and a prosthetic tool which extends human evolution through feed-back loops. Both time (as memory, as history) and technology (as the intentional setting to work [*agencement*] of technics) are relayed in this becoming of the human. According to this different history of human evolution, thought is already technological; in Stiegler they are features of what he calls 'epiphylogenesis' (Stiegler, 1998).

The new theory of mind emerging in works such as Clark's is in line with other approaches that explicitly or implicitly decentre the subject in their rejection of species of cognitivism, geneticism and behaviourism. An influential position elaborated in Varela et al.'s *The Embodied Mind* (1993) concerns the enactive approach to embodied cognition. This perspective is grounded in the 'mutual enfoldment view of life and world' (1993: 200), a view that asserts the 'complicative nature of organism and environment' (1993: 200). They draw from (Nobel prize-winner) Lewontin's claim that 'Just as there is no organism without an environment, so there is no environment without an organism' (Lewontin, 1983, cited in Varela et al., 1993: 198) to argue that neither organism nor environment should be conceptualised as pre-given entities that only subsequently enter into relation. Instead:

> ... living beings and their environments stand in relation to each other through mutual specification and codetermination. Thus ... environmental regularities are not external features that have been internalized, as representationism and adaptationism both assume, [but] the result of a conjoint history, a congruence that unfolds from a long history of codetermination ...[T]he organism is both the subject and the object of evolution. (1993: 198, 199)

This view finds support in Oyama's (2000 [1985]) *The Ontogeny of Information*, which, among other things, rejects the 'separation of form and matter [that] underlies all the versions of the nature–nurture antithesis that have so persistently informed our philosophical and scientific approaches to the phenomena of life' (2000: 1). The privilege of form is too often today re-inscribed in the guise of information, replacing 'God, a vitalistic force, or the gene as Nature's agent that is the source of the design of living things' (2000: 1). It prevents one from breaking the spell of the dualism of matter and form. Oyama contends that all these metaphors for a determining agent share 'a "preformationist" attitude toward information, that is, the assumption is that information exists before its utilization or expression' (2000: 2). She proposes instead the view of an ontogeny (the process of development of an organism, e.g. from fertilised egg to mature form) whereby ontogenesis applies 'not only to bodies and minds, but to information, plans, and all the other cognitive-causal entities ... that supposedly regulate their development. This means that developmental information itself ... has a developmental history. It neither preexists its operation nor arises from random disorder' (2000: 3).

These arguments, incidentally, problematise the cybernetic model of information widely accepted across the social sciences, a critique first formulated by Bateson (1980) and MacKay (1969), and that we find in Gilbert Simondon also (2005; see additionally the arguments in Hayles, 1999). Applied to the organism–environment coupling, they lead us to conceptualise both as 'mutually unfolded and enfolded structures' (Varela et al., 1993: 199), for 'genes and gene products are environments to each other' (Oyama, 1985, cited in Varela et al., 1993: 199; see Venn, 2010 for details).

The upshot is that ontogenesis (the process whereby an individual of a species develops) and phylogenesis (the process whereby a species or population evolve) come to be seen as co-related processes. It is worth noting that the emergent approach in the life sciences is for the integration of specialisms that had addressed questions of epigenetic development in isolation from contiguous sciences. Thus, today the field of ecological developmental biology brings together the concerns of epigenesis and embryology to present an integrated approach that recognises more clearly the mutual effects of environment and organism in terms of a plastic history of development, as Gilbert and Epel (2009) have established.

An example to illustrate the practical implications is the report of findings by Anthony Auger that if a female rat is treated like a male (different licking and grooming patterns by the mother, according to sex), brain changes occur that make it look more like a male brain, specifically, resulting in a lower number of oestrogen receptors in the hypothalamus of stroked females (reported in Powell, 2009); in other words, epigenetic action has ontogenetic effects. This is in line with another argument of Oyama who supports the idea of blurring the distinction between inherited and acquired characteristics, suggesting that we regard evolutionary change in terms of 'functioning developmental systems: ecologically embedded genomes' (2000 [1985]: 138).

Another example to illustrate the thesis of dynamic co-implication is one given by Varela and colleagues of the case of the match between honey bees and flowers, given that the former are known to be trichromats sensitive to the ultraviolet end of the spectrum, while flowers have contrasting reflectance patterns in ultraviolet light. Avoiding either the dead end of a chicken-and-egg conundrum or the circularity that the concept of affordance can harbour, they explain the 'fit' between honey bees and flowers in terms of co-evolution: 'colors of flowers appear to have coevolved with the ultraviolet sensitive, trichromatic vision of bees' (Varela et al., 1993: 201). More generally, it would seem that 'environmental regularities are not pre-given but are rather enacted or brought forth by a history of coupling' (1993: 202), an argument supporting the idea of the co-determination of environment and organism implied for instance in symbiogenesis. The issue of the sentience of honeybee and flower could suggest also a sense of interconnectedness – or Gaian dynamics or cosmology – that would support a cosmopolitical becoming (Stengers, 2009).

So, if we set aside pre-formationist views and see the environment–organism complex as one of mutual constitution and processual becoming, how does one account for individuation, individual differences, as well as collective becoming or acting? I want to argue that what the analysis so far indicates is that before moving on to these questions, two further breaks with dimensions of subject-centredness are required, namely, with anthropocentrism and its privilege of the concept of the solipsistic human individual as model and starting point for theorising forms of life generally, and with the neglect of the technical in conventional accounts of the evolution of the human. In constructing this different epistemological and ontological terrain, it is important to avoid any species of sociobiologism, geneticism or other monocausal and monological paradigms that would simply reinscribe the older conceptual frameworks and their ontological presuppositions. These paradigms are still dominant across the social sciences and much popularising science writing – for instance, in the search for a 'thinking conscious machine', the android dream of science fiction, that tends to assume the Cartesian model of minds as autonomous and discrete entities, neglecting entirely the epiphylogenetic and socio-historically embedded character of minds and what they are able to do. Yet, as we can infer by reference to Clark's notion of an extended mind, what is the subject without an environment that includes others and a symbolic universe, or without a technical world (Stiegler, 1998, 2005; also the work of Latour and others)? And, what is the mind without the senses, without, in other words, both the active participation of the body in cognition and without affective economy as one of its fundamental components?

The core of the post-anthropocentric standpoint I am outlining is strikingly summarised in Haraway's notions of companion species and significant otherness. She has this to say about living things that resonates with much of what I have trailed above:

> Through their reaching into each other, through their 'prehensions' or graspings, beings constitute each other and themselves. Beings do not preexist their relatings. 'Prehensions' have consequences. The world is a knot in motion ... There are no pre-constituted subjects and objects, and no single sources, unitary actors, or final ends. In Judith Butler's terms, there are only 'contingent foundations'; bodies that matter are the result ... For me, that is what companion species signifies. (2003: 6)

Her emphasis on 'emergence, process, historicity, difference, specificity, co-habitation, co-constitution, and contingency' (2003: 7) is precisely the conceptual markers that we find in the authors and positions that I have sketched.

This approach to the relationality of the living – of players as 'neither wholes nor parts' (Haraway, 2003: 8) – and to the human as but one entity intertwined amongst the cohort of organisms and objects of the world, and as always more-than-one, implies the co-implication of vulnerabilities. An important consequence entails the rejection of all forms of colonialism and anthropocentrism, that is, of difference-as-antagonism or as excuse for ontological violence through exploitation of one kind or another. It suggests a politics of 'significant otherness' oriented to 'on-the-ground work that cobbles together non-harmonious agencies and ways of living that are accountable both to their disparate inherited histories and to their barely possible but absolutely necessary joint futures' (Haraway, 2003: 7; see also Haraway, 2016). This politics – of generosity, of welcoming the other, of indebtedness, which I've examined in Venn (2000) and (2002) – is allied to a politics of 'naturecultures', breaking with the dichotomies separating the human and other animals and the human and the technical that

Leroi-Gourhan (1964, 1971 [1943]), Simondon (2005), Latour (2010), Latimer and Miele (2013) amongst others, have also challenged. It is in solidarity with a politics of the common and an heteronomous ethics that rejects any populist politics of identity founded on an essentialist us/them distinction and the pathologies and violences it incites.

Common ground: Being-with and an ethics of responsibility

One of the central issues underlying Haraway's counter-anthropocentric and anti-solipsistic ontology is the question of the relation of the human to nature and, as a supplement to this relation, that between humans and other animals. The issue opens up the question of the human to the problematic of a 'flat ontology' and to the regrounding of the human in relation to the rest of the world, with implications for an ecological/environmental politics, particularly the possibility of a politics which rejects the imperialist thrust immanent in the idea of a mastery of nature, mastery over the animality of human beings, and dominion over other animals and those beings classified as 'other'. There is much to unpack here for the problem trails the whole history of philosophy, metaphysics and theology in the West and elsewhere.

The question of the animal, so central within species of humanism (a term which it is difficult to use without qualification), hangs on the different ways in which a range of key concepts such as reason, the soul, consciousness and conscience, nature, instinct, intentionality, and the experience of pain and suffering have been deployed either to distinguish the specificity of the human, or else to locate the human and other animals within the same order of a harmony that may be conceptualised as grounded on either divine or 'natural' foundations. Simondon's brief survey in his lectures 'on the animal and man', points to a long history of such reflections, though for our purposes it is sufficient to signal a number of positions in his analysis that encapsulate the main standpoints. He notes the cosmological and anti-dualist universe of Giordano Bruno for whom 'life and consciousness have an existence that begins at a cosmological level', implying that animals equally share in this 'universal force' and 'must not be considered inferior beings' (Simondon, 2004 [1967]: 69); indeed, pointing to the closeness of animals to nature, Bruno grants the animal an exalted place above humans in the scheme of things (2004 [1967]: 68).

Related in some way to this view, one finds a pantheistic perspective, notably in the idea of the divine complementarity of all living things, as in St Francis of Assisi for whom animals, humans and plants share faculties and a world in common framed by the thought that 'it is the whole of Creation which is harmonious, man's [sic] place complements that of animals and plants' (Simondon, 2004 [1967]: 70). Another perspective is represented by the monism of those like Montaigne according to whom 'the psychical faculties existing for animals are the same as those that exist in the human being' (2004 [1967]: 71); besides, for Montaigne, human beings are more destructive and violent than other animals, for they wage religious wars and inflict the most depraved cruelties on their fellows. Research today in animal studies increasingly establishes that various species show so-called human attributes such as point of view (bonobo, chimps), rational thinking (elephants, many birds), grieving (elephants), social organisation, and so on. In Simondon's outline, it is with Descartes' dualism that the animal is most intransigently consigned to the status of a machine, to *res extensa*, without intelligence or soul or consciousness/conscience, directed purely by instincts. Within the Cartesian system, the automatism of instinctual behaviour means that non-human animals have no 'plasticity' or 'mind'; it implies the 'denial of consciousness, the denial particularly of the acquisition of rationality, intelligent apprenticeship, of the intelligent resolution of problems' (2004 [1967]: 78). Doctrinaire Cartesians such as Malebranche have concluded from this that only human beings are able to suffer, a commonly shared argument that has endorsed the disregard of our responsibility or care for all animals and that has legitimised untold cruelties to this day.

The enduring dilemmas in the dichotomy splitting the 'human' from the 'animal' linger even in analyses that intend to overcome them, say, in Agamben's different point of view of the relation to the other that he develops in *The Open: Man and Animal* in order to mark out a space for rethinking the question of ethical responsibility. Yet his idea of anthropogenesis resonates sufficiently with the project of overcoming anthropocentrism to provide a handle on what is at stake ethically and politically. Anthropogenesis in his text is the idea of a discourse that accounts for the process of emergence of the human in terms of a genesis characterised by the gradual emancipation from the world of nature. Crucially, this would involve the overcoming by humans of the limits that the animality of 'man' places upon him, that is, the process whereby humans open themselves to an historical becoming.

In the background to the way Agamben (2004) poses the question of the relation of the animal to humans – though one should avoid this slippage into a dichotomy – are the issues which surface when he distinguishes between the animality or 'bare life' of humans and the polis as terrain upon which the process of an historical becoming for humans has a purchase. Already this distinction, recast as between *zoe* and *bios* (Agamben, 1998), muddies the waters between the animality of humans (or *animalitas*) and their political being (or *humanitas*), for there is a suggestion of both a relationship and a split, the latter returning the discussion to the older problems when understood according to what he calls the 'anthropological machine' that invented the split. As we saw, one finds this opposition notably in the Cartesian ontology, and that Agamben finds still at work in Heidegger's thinking of 'a historical mission of being' (2004: 75), that is, the idea that the becoming of the human being uncovers the different relations that humans have with world compared to that of non-human animals. The context here is Heidegger's (problematic) view that non-human animals are lacking in world and lack access to other beings, whilst an inanimate object like the stone is 'worldless'; thus for Heidegger, the process of worlding widens the gap between humans and other beings (see Heidegger, 2001).

For Agamben, the split in the light of the events of the 20th century and the 'end of history' entails that 'for a humanity that has become animal again, there is nothing left but the depoliticization of human societies by means of the unconditional unfolding of the *oikonomia*, or the taking of the biological life itself as the supreme political (or rather impolitical) task' (1998: 76). There is not much traction here for a project of transformation, given the slippage in his discourse into anthropocentrism, except that the terms of his critique of historical becoming resonates with the argument that neoliberalism attempts to complete the economisation of society that began with liberal capitalism. His pessimism however reinforces my argument that neoliberal political economy establishes a neo-biopolitical governmentality that 'depoliticises' society through the elimination of public interest, the elevation of the competitive and self-interested individual and the reduction of persons to things in social policy, as arguments of Esposito would suggest, as I noted in Chapter 1.

Agamben's conclusion from his examination of 'Western philosophy's anthropological machine' offers more rewarding openings for the broader linkages I am trying to outline. For, he claims that 'anthropogenesis is what results from the caesura and articulation between human and animal' (1998: 79), and that 'ontology ... is not an innocuous academic discipline, but in every sense the fundamental operation in which anthropogenesis, the becoming human of the living being, is realised' (ibid.). The anthropological machine, that is, the discourse that separates out the human from nature and animality in order to present emancipation as the effort to overcome the animal in the human, is allied to a metaphysics that seeks the 'overcoming of animal *physis* in the direction of human history. This overcoming is not an event that has been completed once and for all, but an occurrence that is always under way' (ibid.).

Agamben's discussion of 'overcoming' brings into the open the relationship of becoming with respect to nature, particularly by reference to technology, to passivity and to a different articulation of the 'animal' and the 'human'. He points first to Walter Benjamin's view that '(F)or modern man the proper place of this relationship is technology. But not ... a technology conceived, as it commonly is, as man's mastery of nature' (Agamben, 2004: 82). It is instead 'the mastery of the relation between nature and humanity' (2004: 83) that does not suspend or capture the inhuman but establishes a betweenness in which the two terms remain open. What is implied is the emergence of an attitude, that of letting be, which relinquishes the ambition of the anthropological machine to prioritise the destiny of the human. Agamben's reflection however is inconclusive, for it seeks to put an end to anthropocentrism without investigating what an alternative would be, that is, without addressing the question of the politico-ethical task of managing the openness.

What is missing is any idea of, first, the closeness of animals to humans at the level of characteristics and faculties, now established in a vast literature that shows animals as social beings often capable of empathy and collective ways of surviving; second, the utter dependence of human history on the relation to the animal and to animality (as discussed above); third, a different history of becoming, a different anthropogenesis that takes account of both the relation to animals and the relation to technics as part and parcel of a history of becoming. The latter suggests the recognition of epiphylogenesis as in Stiegler's (1998) and Leroi-Gourhan's (1964) analysis of hominisation and individuation, and the recognition of a transindividual dimension in the constitution and becoming of beings, that is, a dimension which is at once historical, developmental, collective and enactive, as elaborated in Simondon's work. We encounter various approaches in the works of other thinkers such as Ettinger and Merleau-Ponty, amongst a corpus that foregrounds an aspect of being that in a sense is both transcendent and immanent, belonging at once to world (and worlding) and the here and now (that I examined in Venn, 2010). This is perhaps the approach that opens up a different space for posing the question of new grounds for an ethics that regards the commonality of existential conditions such as suffering and fragility as basis for responding to fellow creatures in accordance with a duty of responsibility.

It is precisely this question of the suffering of the other that we encounter in Derrida's reflections on the question of the animal, in *The Animal that Therefore I am* (2008), alongside the critique of that other key element of Cartesian thought, namely, 'logocentrism' and the violences it inflicts on non-human animals (and 'othered' humans), for behind this juncture one finds the interminable question of 'who I am' (2008: 3), calling in its wake issues of 'technics ... evil and history, and work', and 'shame' (2008: 5). What is at stake for Derrida, and the reason for interposing his text here, is his argument that in the everyday world, the fact of living alongside an animal, and thus of being locked into a series of interactions with it, prompts the question of 'who I am' since this situation leads me either to cast the animal companion as unresponding machines as Descartes thought, or to recognise it as 'this irreplaceable living being that one day enters my space ... (and) is an existence that refuses to be conceptualized' (2008: 9). His account draws attention to the fact that living alongside a non-human animal, and generally of being in the same space as another being, elicits responses to that being which entail a questioning of the who and the what of existence. This is because 'Being *after*, being *alongside*, being *near* [prés] would appear as different modes of being, indeed of *being-with*' (2008: 10, emphases in the original). Derrida presses the point when he says that these questions 'involve thinking about what is meant by living, speaking, dying, being, and world as in being-in-the-world or being-within-the-world, or being-with ...' (2008: 11). The upshot of this line of questioning is that it brings into view what it means to recognise the gaze of the other, even those deemed wholly other such as the non-human animal, and therefore having to respond to the gaze, that is, to the call of the other, to what follows once one includes all others within the sphere of being-with and of those to whom responsibility is owed.

It is because of this pivotal implication that Derrida's discourse foregrounds the standpoint of suffering and anguish, proposing an ethics that, in grounding responsibility for the other in the ontological condition of being-with, refuses all forms of subjection and violence, as in cases where the denigration, abjection or objectification of the other precedes and authorises all forms of violence inflicted upon them: killing, exclusion, exploitation and so on. By contrast, for Derrida, the recognition of the suffering of the other opens up the problem of both pathos and the pathological, that is, 'of suffering, pity, compassion; and the place that has to be accorded to the interpretation of this compassion, to the sharing of this suffering among the living, to the law, ethics, and politics that must be brought to bear upon this experience of compassion' (2008: 26).

And so, the coupling of humans and all other beings within the sphere of responsibility (and passivity or letting be) makes visible what is at stake in terms of two options. On the one hand, the standpoint of care for the other, of responding to the call of the other (say, as theorised in terms of the face relation in the work of Levinas), and thus of conceptualising the 'open' as a response to fragility, suffering and vulnerability, one's own and that of all other beings (as I have discussed in Venn, 2000). The inclusion of all creatures in a way extends but does not undermine the Levinasian problematic of ethical being, for, whilst his discourse focuses principally on the responses which are triggered when I encounter an other human being, the standpoint of the primacy of the ethical emphasises an idea of justice and conscience, linked to 'signification, teaching, and justice' (Levinas, 1969: 79) that could encompass all. Besides, the 'ethical relation to the other is ultimately prior to his ontological relation to himself (egology)' (Levinas, 1984: 57); thus heteronomy precedes autonomy, that is, it indicates a principle that once more suggests a sense of the fundamental relationality or co-implicate character of being and the world as a commonality that both exceeds yet contains all creatures within the scope of generosity, gift, care. By contrast, on the other hand, we confront a biopolitics founded on dominion over the other, that is, that thereby fails to respond to the call of the other, and that thus disregards the despotisms imposed by those who are given or have seized power and authority over those deemed lesser beings for one reason or another.

I am arguing therefore that the way that Derrida has set up the problem of the relation of the human to the animal suggests that the problematic of epigenesis – or the constitutive matrix binding humans and other animals and the environment generally, expressed in the concept of 'naturecultures' – extends onto the terrain of ethics by way of the recognition of being as always-already being-with and being-in-the-world, an idea one finds also in the discourse of writers who seek to redefine the grounds of a new politics of the common that does not forget ethical responsibility, as I have examined in Venn (2010).

One could juxtapose here the work of Bracha Ettinger who also emphasises the point of view of compassion and responsibility (or com-passion and co-response-ability in her vocabulary), starting from a similar recognition of the primacy of being-with, of co-emergence, of co-affecting in the formation of subjectivity from birth and before that, that is, from the uterine experience of co-existing and co-constituting infant and mother (Ettinger, 1992, 1995; Pollock, 2004). Ettinger argues that the reality of this 'matrixial substratum' as a primary and necessary condition of our emergence as humans entails a response to the other which is at once ethical and affective, and for Ettinger aesthetic (Ettinger, 2006; Venn, 2004, 2009b, 2014). The addition of the affective and ethical dimensions to the questioning of being broadens the problem of ontology, making visible the point of view of the who of action and responsibility. There are problems though in formulating an ethics on the basis of the epigenetic and symbiogenetic character of the formation of subjects generally. The difficulty is that one cannot directly derive an ethics from an ontology – though the latter can provide foundational support. There is thus a gap between ontology and ethics which needs thinking through if one is to address the issues inscribed in the question of the 'who', thus also of singularity, and of the one who is answerable, that we find in Derrida or Levinas. Issues of solidarity, altruism and compassion arise that refer to a history of responsibility for the other and to an apprenticeship whereby one learns to become an ethical being. The point of view of responsibility and answerability entails the difficult duty of having to make (perhaps undecidable) judgements about the balance of harm in any particular case, taking into account the priority of protection for the vulnerable, humans as well as all forms of life. So, the complicated problem of justice comes into view.

Elements for postcapitalist life in common

What the philosophical reflections above open up is a perspective regarding the relation to the other and to all living beings, an attitude to the earth, and a system of values that break with those which underlie capitalism and other zero-sum economies and their affiliates, principally socialities premised on the naturalisation of inequalities and the pathologisation of differences of one kind or another. It is clear that we face two related sets of problems. On the one hand, the arguments above show why the problem is much larger than a purely economic or political one since it involves issues about foundations guiding the remaking of world and subjectivities according to the values and ways of life appropriate for addressing the consequences of the convergence of crises which we have been analysing. Equally these foundations and values could provide common ground for cosmopolitical agreements encompassing local and regional polities, as I argued in the Introduction. On the other hand, the problem is the practical one of what is possible in terms of technologies, institutions, political, economic and social arrangements that would accord with the alternative view of the place of the human in the scheme of things as implied in the decentrings and delinkings which I have been outlining.

Clearly, scenarios which aim to save capitalism by tweeking existing systems either through technological fixes or through a recallibrated meritocratic society that could work only for a small minority – such as the 10% in the 19th century – would change little in terms of avoiding the tipping points many now recognise. Such strategies fail to address the forces underlying the problems identified so far and make invisible underlying unequal relations of power and iniquitous property regimes, and their effects in sustaining systematic exclusion, denigration and pauperisation of the different 'other' and the 'losers'. Besides, as I have been arguing, the quest for profit maximisation and private accumulation tends to promote disregard for ecologies, environmental degradation and social justice. Thus, saving capitalism would merely delay the coming of the worst in the form of despotisms, extinctions, or the breakdown of the conditions supporting liveable existence for humans and many species. So, if one were to start from the alternative premise outlined above, namely, an ontology grounded in the idea of being as being-with and being alongside extended to all life, an ethics of co-responsibility for the other consistent with such an ontology, an epistemology that departs from assumptions of mastery over others and over nature, and that rejects anthropocentrism, self-centredness and scientisms such as geneticism and biologisms, what options remain for the possibility of living well with and for others in just societies, as Ricoeur (1992: 351) has put it?

To begin with, one would have to acknowledge that the kind of massive transformation in society and subjectivities that many have called for could only happen over generations and would require constant inventive and experimental approaches consistent with the principles I have outlined. It would require another volume to properly address the social, political, economic, environmental, technological and cultural problems which will emerge. The likelihood is that as the tipping points approach, capitalism will not survive in its present form and the world could slip towards dystopia when lives would surely be nasty, brutish and short. Yet, there can be no blueprints. But a number of ideas can be presented here as indicative of the kind of agenda for debate and initiatives.[1]

A central problem is the establishment of a property regime that prioritises commons and common pool resources (CPRs), and that avoids the centralisation or bureaucratisation of decision-making processes. An increasing literature addresses the question of reconstituting commons and rethinking their scope and organisation, for example in analyses in Amin and Howell (2016); Gilbert (2014); Terranova (2015); Caffentzis and Federici (2014), extending earlier analyses by Hardt and Negri (2011). As

New Foundations for Postcapitalist Worlds

I have noted in the Introduction and Chapter 5, forms of governance that have emerged for such collective organisation of production in the context of collective ownership have been analysed by Ostrom and colleagues regarding the management of CPRs such as particular lakes, stretch of rivers, woods, pastures, and so on. The studies have examined their efficacity as organisations that have both economic and social goals, including the need to build trust amongst all participants and to deal with the problem of free riders within flat organisational structures (Ostrom, 1990; Poteete et al., 2010). In spite of the wide range of commons involved, Ostrom derived from the many cases studied a number of design principles consistent with long-enduring CPR institutions, namely, clearly defined boundaries, rules regarding appropriation, collective participation in making and changing operational rules, the monitoring of behaviour, graduated sanctions for those disregarding agreed rules, conflict-resolution mechanisms, independence from governmental bodies, organisation in multiple layers for nested larger commons. One conclusion is that such collective resources are better managed than by governmental bodies. Of course some collectively 'owned' and managed resources will experience failure mainly due to the fact that goodwill doesn't always succeed and humans do not necessarily follow the kind of rational rules of conduct Ostrom advises.

Furthermore, property regimes that prioritise common ownership would need to foster appropriate subjectivities since collaborative work requires an apprenticeship and appropriate values (Gibson-Graham, 2006), especially as one moves from possessive individualism and ego-centric attitudes. The issue of scale is important regarding trust and solidarity as basis for successful commons. For example, the small town of Marinaleda in Spain is organised as a collectivist economy and polity, where most people work for the town co-operative which is run according to direct democracy; there is no unemployment, no police, no violence (Hancox, 2014). But, would this work when scaled up? The broad approach could be extended for example to problems of generating electricity using renewable resources at the local level yet organised as part of a shared wider grid. Nevertheless, systems such as national transport networks and the supply of potable water would require establishing coordinating mechanisms operating across a host of similar heterogenous communities whilst avoiding the centralisation of power we associate with the model of the nation-state. Other resources, notably minerals, may be the object of leasehold arrangements with private firms, with democratic decision-making boards ensuring transparency and social and environmental responsibility.

From the point of view of radical democracy, one could imagine decentralised networked arrangements that try to find a balance between the efficacity of systems and autonomy at the regional or localised level of decision-making. Perhaps new forms of federalism could emerge, depending on conditions, yet constrained within the principles and values indicated above, say regarding the system of laws. One would have to think through the implications for the kind of international institutions and binding agreements that would be needed for tackling the big issues like climate change and resource management at the global level.

Effort directed at establishing alternative or appropriate technologies, for instance, away from fossil fuels and non-renewable resources, should be a central concern. I have suggested the idea of the future as ambient to indicate the need for humans to tap more intelligently into the affordances existing in the natural environment, but to do so whilst overcoming the impulse to dominate or tame the environment and the creatures which co-habit it. It means learning from and respecting the vital and natural qualities and properties that have co-evolved symbiotically over time as a consequence of the organism/environment couplings. It is another, extended, sense of co-implication. For familiar examples, one could point to the fact that ultimately our energy sources come mainly from the burning sun and from gravity, harvested directly through solar panels obviously, but also indirectly by way of photosynthesis producing biofuels, or through harnessing the potential energy due to the effects of gravitational force, for example, tides, waves, dams, and indirectly windmills.

Ways of utilising such energies would need to be consistent with a 'green technology' such as by further developing fourth generation biofuels or solar-to-fuel technologies using synthetic microorganisms in combination with sunlight and waste CO_2. There are many more examples, many at an experimental or trial stage, such as the use of vertical temperature differentials in the oceans to power turbines, or techniques for growing food that tap more inventively into photosynthesis, or that extend hydroponics, and so on. The general approach should include humans learning from and co-habiting with other species, given that much research in ecologies and biotechnologies already shows what is possible in terms of producing materials inspired by what other species produce for their own needs. Yet, the postcapitalist standpoint means altering the direction and constraints of such research, particularly regarding the ownership of knowledges, data and technologies, and generally prioritising renewable and safe technologies consistent with ambient energy. It suggests the emergence of a scientific-technological-environmental productive complex of a new kind responding to the new needs and the recognition of limits to the planet and human capabilities.

A crucial aspect concerns the 'liberation' of knowledges that have been captured by the appropriation machine to thus constitute cognitive commons which sustain the education and training of populations to equip them with appropriate capabilities and knowledges that will be a vital necessity for survival in the future. This training would include an apprenticeship in participatory democratic institutions, and learning to live in collectivities whilst also developing values and activities that feed the spirit. Clearly the difficult and non-coercive work of changing subjectivities is an integral part of such programmes, requiring the emergence of a new political culture and language consistent with a postcapitalist vision.[2]

Note

1 I had originally envisaged discussing the practical dimension of postcapitalist transformations in an eventual Part 2 of *After Capital*. For health reasons, I cannot now do this.
2 This project has been the subject of ongoing collaborative research by the group originally involved in writing *Changing the Subject* (1984, reprinted 1998), consisting of Julian Henriques, Wendy Hollway, Cathy Urwin, Couze Venn, Valerie Walkerdine.

References

Adee, Sally (2017) 'The money machine', *New Scientist*, 3147: 22–23.
Agamben, Giorgio (1998) *Homo Sacer: Sovereign Power and Bare Life*, trans. Daneil Heller-Roazen. Stanford: Stanford University Press.
Agamben, Giorgio (2004) *The Open: Man and Animal*. Stanford: Stanford University Press.
Agamben, Giorgio (2005) *State of Exception*, trans. Kevin Attell. Chicago: University of Chicago Press.
Agamben, Giorgio (2013) *The Highest Poverty. Monastic Rules and Form-of-Life*. Stanford: Stanford University Press.
Ahmed, Kamal (2015) 'Shell stops Arctic activity after "disappointing", tests', *BBC News*, 28 September. Available at: www.bbc.co.uk/news/business-34377434.
Allen, Katie (2010) 'The land rush doesn't have to end in a poor deal for Africans', *The Guardian*, 16 August. Available at: www.theguardian.com/business/2010/aug/16/foreign-land-grab-threat-to-africa.
Amin, Ash and Philip Howell (eds) (2016) *Releasing the Commons: Rethinking the Futures of the Commons*. London: Routledge.
Amin, Samir (1974) *Accumulation on a World Scale. Critique of the Theory of Underdevelopment*, trans. Pearce Broan. New York: Monthly Review Press.
Amin, Samir (1977) *Imperialism and Unequal Exchange*. New York: Monthly Review Press.
Amos, Jonathan (2017) 'Antarctic iceberg: Giant "white wanderer" poised to break free', *BBC News*, 5 July. Available at: www.bbc.co.uk/news/science-environment-40492957.
Ananthaswamy, Anil (2015) 'The methane apocalypse', *New Scientist*, 3022: 38–41.
Appiah, Kwame (1992) *In My Father's House: Africa in the Philosophy of Culture*. Oxford: Oxford University Press.
Arendt, Hannah (1978) *The Life of the Mind*. New York: Harcourt Brace Janovich.
Arendt, Hannah (2000) 'The social question', in Peter Baehr (ed.), *The Portable Hannah Arendt*. Harmondsworth: Penguin.
Armitage, David (2000) *The Ideological Origin of the British Empire*. Cambridge: Cambridge University Press.
Arnoldi, Jakob (2004) 'Derivatives: Virtual values and real risks', *Theory, Culture & Society*, 21(6): 23–42.
Arrighi, Giovanni (1994) *The Long Twentieth Century*. London: Verso.
Ashurst, Francesca (2010) 'A genealogy of school exclusion', unpublished PhD Thesis, Cardiff University.
Ashurst, Francesca and Couze Venn (2014) *Inequality, Poverty, Education: A Political Economy of School Exclusion*. London: Palgrave Macmillan.
Atkinson, Anthony (1999) 'Income inequality in the UK', *Health Economics*, 8(4): 283–288.
Atkinson, Anthony (2013) 'Reducing income inequality in Europe', *IZA Journal of European Labor Studies*, 2(1): 12.
Atkinson, Anthony (2015) *Inequality: What Can Be Done?* Cambridge, MA: Harvard University Press.

References

Barad, Karen (2007) *Meeting the Universe Halfway: Quantum Physics and the Entanglement of Matter and Meaning*. Durham, NC: Duke University Press.
Bateson, Gregory (1980) *Mind and Nature*. London: Fontana/Collins.
BBC News (2015) 'ECB unveils massive QE boost for eurozone', 22 January. Available at: www.bbc.co.uk/news/business-30933515.
Bebbington, Jan, Jeffrey Unerman and Brendan O'Dwyer (eds) (2014) *Sustainability Accounting and Accountability*. London: Routledge.
Beveridge, William (1942) *Social Insurance and Allied Services*. London: HMSO.
Birla, Ritu (2009) *Stages of Capital: Law, Culture, and Market Governance in Late Colonial India*. Durham, NC: Duke University Press.
Blaser, Mario (2013) 'Notes towards a political ontology of environmental conflicts', in Lesley Green (ed.), *Contested Ecologies: Dialogues in the South on Nature and Knowledge*. Cape Town: HSRC Press, pp. 13–28.
Blyth, Mark (2013) *Austerity: The History of a Dangerous Idea*. Oxford: Oxford University Press.
Brahic, Catherine (2017) 'Living with climate change: Turning the corner', *New Scientist*, 3131: 32.
Braudel, Fernand (1974 [1967]) *Capitalism and Material Life: 1400–1800*, trans. Miriam Kochan. New York: Fontana.
Braudel, Fernand (1977) *Afterthoughts on Material Civilization and Capitalism*. Baltimore: Johns Hopkins University Press.
Braudel, Fernand (1984) *Civilization & Capitalism. The Perspective of the World*, trans. Sian Reynolds. London: Collins and Sons.
Braudel, Fernand (1986 [1979]) *The Wheels of Commerce. Civilization & Capitalism. 15th–18th Century. Vol. 2*, trans. Sian Reynolds. New York: Harper & Row.
Brown, Wendy (2003) 'Neo-liberalism and the end of liberal democracy', *Theory & Event*, 7(1): 1–19.
Brown, Wendy (2015) *Undoing the Demos: Neoliberalism's Stealth Revolution*. New York: Zone Books.
Brundtland Commission (1987) *Our Common Future. The World Commission on Environment and Development*. Oxford: Oxford University Press.
Buchanan, Mark (2014) *Forecast: What Physics, Meteorology and the Natural Sciences Can Teach Us About Economics*. London: Bloomsbury.
Burgis, Tom (2015) *The Looting Machine: Warlords, Tycoons, Smugglers and the Systematic Theft of Africa's Wealth*. London: HarperCollins.
Caffentzis, George and Silvia Federici (2014) 'Commons against and beyond capitalism', *Community Development Journal*, 49(1): 92–105.
Chakrabortty, Aditya (2015) 'Now Tories are allowing big business to design their own tax loopholes', *The Guardian*, 13 October. Available at: www.theguardian.com/commentisfree/2015/oct/13/tories-big-business-tax-loopholes.
Chakrabortty, Aditya (2017) 'How could we cope if capitalism failed? Ask 26 Greek factory workers', *The Guardian*, 18 July. Available at: www.theguardian.com/commentisfree/2017/jul/18/cope-capitalism-failed-factory-workers-greek-workplace-control.
Chang, Ha-Joon (2010) *23 Things They Don't Tell You About Capitalism*. London: Allen Lane.
Clark, Andy (2011) *Supersizing the Mind: Embodiment, Action and Cognitive Extension*. Oxford: Oxford University Press.
Clark, Nigel and Kathryn Yusoff (2014) 'Combustion and society: A fire-centred history of energy use', *Theory, Culture & Society*, 31(5): 203–226.
Coghlan, Andy and Debora MacKenzie (2011) 'Revealed – the capitalist network that runs the world', *New Scientist*, 2835: 8–9.
Colebrook, Claire (2014) *Death of the PostHuman: Essays on Extinction, Vol. 1*. London: Open Humanities Press.
Colley, Linda (2002) *Captives: Britain, Empire and the World, 1600–1850*. London: Cape.

References

Conio, Andrew (2015) *A People Yet to Come*. London: Open Humanities Press.
Crutzen, Paul (2002) 'Geology of mankind', *Nature*, 415(6867): 23.
Curtis, Neal (2013) *Idiotism: Capitalism and the Privatisation of Life*. London: Pluto Press.
Daly, Herman (1991 [1977]) *Steady-State Economics: With New Essays*. Washington, DC: Island Press.
Daly, Herman (1997) *Beyond Growth: The Economics of Sustainable Development*. Boston: Beacon Press.
Dardot, Pierre and Christian Laval (2010) *La nouvelle raison du monde: Essai sur la société néolibérale*. Paris: La Découverte.
Dardot, Pierre and Christian Laval (2014) *Commun. Essai sur la révolution au XXIe siécle*. Paris: La Découverte.
Davis, Nicola (2017) 'Giant iceberg poised to break off from Antarctic shelf', *The Guardian*, 6 January. Available at: www.theguardian.com/world/2017/jan/06/giant-iceberg-poised-to-break-off-from-antarctic-shelf-larsen-c.
Deffeyes, Kenneth S. (2006) *Beyond Oil: The View from Hubbert's Peak*. New York: Hill & Wang.
Deleuze, Gilles (1990) 'Post-scriptum sur les Société de Controle', *L'autre Journal*, 1 (Mai).
Deleuze, Gilles and Félix Guattari (1988) *A Thousand Plateaus*, trans. Brian Massumi. London: Athlone Press.
Derrida, Jacques (1982 [1972]) *Margins of Philosophy*, trans. Alan Bass. Brighton: The Harvester Press.
Derrida, Jacques (1997a) *Cosmopolites de tous les pays, encore un effort*. Paris: Éditions Galilée.
Derrida, Jacques (1997b) *Le droit à la philosophie du point de vue cosmopolitique*. Paris: Éditions Unesco/Verdier.
Derrida, Jacques (2008) *The Animal that Therefore I Am*, trans. David Mills. New York: Fordham University Press.
Descola, Philippe (2011) *L'Écologie des autres*. Versailles: Éditions Quae.
Donovan, Paul and Julie Hudson (2011) *From Red to Green? How the Financial Credit Crunch Could Bankrupt the Environment*. London: Earthscan.
Donzelot, Jacques (1979) 'The poverty of political culture', *Ideology and Consciousness*, 5: 71–86.
Elden, Stuart (2007) *Space, Knowledge and Power: Foucault and Geography*. London: Routledge.
Elden, Stuart (2009) *Terror and Territory. The Spatial Extent of Sovereignty*. Minneapolis: University of Minnesota Press.
Elliott, Larry and Dan Atkinson (2008) *The Gods that Failed: How the Finanical Elite Have Gambled Away Our Futures*. London: Vintage Books.
Emmanuel, Arghiri (1972) *Unequal Exchange: A Study of the Imperialist Trade*, trans. Brian Peace. New York: Monthly Review Press.
Engels, Friedrich (1969 [1887]) *The Conditions of the Working Class in England*. London: Panther Edition.
Esposito, Roberto (2015) *Persons and Things: From the Body's Point of View*, trans. Zakiya Hanafi. London: Polity.
Ettinger, Bracha (1992) 'Matrix and metramorphosis', *Differences: A Journal of Feminist Cultural Studies*, 4(3): 176–209.
Ettinger, Bracha L. (1995) *The Matrixial Gaze*. Leeds: University of Leeds.
Ettinger, Bracha L. (2006) *The Matrixial Borderspace*, edited and with an Afterword by Brian Massumi. Minneapolis: University of Minnesota Press.
Evans, Simon (2016) 'Shell outlines "below 2C" climate change', *Oil and Gas*, 11 May.
Ferguson, Adam (2007 [1767]) *An Essay on the History of Civil Society*. Ann Arbour: University of Michigan Library.

References

Forshaw, Jeff (2013) 'Why do physicists gravitate towards jobs in finance?', *The Guardian*, 20 July. Available at: www.theguardian.com/science/2013/jul/21/physics-graduates-gravitate-to-finance.
Foucault, Michel (1970) *The Order of Things*. New York: Pantheon Books.
Foucault, Michel (1975) *Discipline and Punish: The Birth of the Prison*, trans. Alan Sheridan. London: Penguin.
Foucault, Michel (1979) 'On governmentality', *Ideology & Consciousness*, 6: 5–21.
Foucault, Michel (1984) *Histoire de la sexualité. Vol. 2. L'usage des plaisirs*. Paris: Gallimard.
Foucault, Michel (1991) 'What is enlightenment?', in Paul Rabinow (ed.), *The Foucault Reader*. London: Penguin.
Foucault, Michel (2000) *Power: Essential Works of Michel Foucault: 1954–1984. Vol. 3*, ed., James D Faubion. New York: New Press.
Foucault, Michel (2003) *Society Must be Defended: Lectures at the Collège de France, 1975–76*, trans. David Macey. New York: Picador.
Foucault, Michel (2004a) *Sécurité, territoire, population: Cours au Collège de France, 1977–1978*. Paris: Gallimard.
Foucault, Michel (2004b) *Naissance de la biopolitique: Cours au Collège de France, 1978–1979*. Paris: Gallimard.
Foucault, Michel (2007) *Security, Territory, Population*, trans. Graham Burchell. Houndmills: Palgrave Macmillan.
Foucault, Michel (2008) *The Birth of Biopolitics*, trans. Graham Burchell. Houndmills: Palgrave Macmillan.
Friedman, Milton (2002 [1962]) *Capitalism and Freedom*. Chicago: University of Chicago Press.
Fryer, Peter (1984) *Staying Power*. London: Pluto Press.
Fumagelli, Andrea, Stefano Lucarelli, Carlo Vercellone and Alfonso Giuliani (2018) *Cognitive Capitalism, Welfare and Labour: The Commonfare Hypothesis*. London: Routledge.
Gabrys, Jennifer, Gay Hawkins and Mike Michael (eds) (2013) *Accumulation: The Material Politics of Plastic*. London: Routledge.
Galeano, Eduardo (1971) *Open Veins of Latin America*. New York: Monthly Review.
Gallese, Vittorio (2003) 'The roots of empathy: The shared manifold hypothesis and the neural basis of intersubjectivity', *Psychopathology*, 36(4): 171–180.
Gane, Nick (2015) 'Trajectories of liberalism and neoliberalism', *Theory, Culture & Society*, 32(1): 133–144.
George, Susan (1988) *A Fate Worse than Debt: The World Financial Crisis and the Poor*. New York: Grove Weidenfeld.
Gibson, J. James (1977) 'The theory of affordance', in Robert Shaw and John Bransford (eds), *Perceiving, Acting, and Knowing*. Hillsdale, NJ: Erlbaum, pp. 67–82.
Gibson, J. James (1979) *The Ecological Approach to Visual Perception*. Boston, MA: Houghton Mifflin.
Gibson-Graham, Julie Katherine (2006) *A Postcapitalist Politics*. Minnesota: University of Minnesota Press.
Gilbert, Jeremy (2014) *Common Ground: Democracy and Collectivity in an Age of Individualism*. London: Pluto Press.
Gilbert, Scott and David Epel (2009) *Ecological Developmental Biology: Integrating Epigenetics, Medicine, and Evolution*. Sunderland, MA: Sinauer Associates Inc.
Gilroy, Paul (1993) *The Black Atlantic: Modernity and Double Consciousness*. Cambridge, MA: Harvard University Press.
Gilroy, Paul (2005) *Postcolonial Melancholia*. New York: Columbia University Press.
Glyn, Andrew (2007) *Capitalism Unleashed: Finance, Globalization, and Welfare*. Oxford: Oxford University Press.
Goldenberg, Suzanne (2015) 'Obama defends Arctic drilling decision', *The Guardian*, 29 August: 14.

References

Goldman, Lawrence (2002) *Science, Reform and Politics in Victorian Britain. The Social Science Association 1857–1886*. Cambridge: Cambridge University Press.

Gorz, André (1994) *Capitalism, Socialism, Ecology*, trans. Chris Turner. London: Verso.

Graeber, David (2011) *Debt: The First 5,000 Years*. London: Penguin. Reprinted in 2013 by Melville House Publishing.

Guardian, The (2015) 'Climate talks can't fail as there is no alternative planet, says French Minister', *The Guardian*, 18 May. Available at: https://www.theguardian.com/environment/2015/may/18/climate-talks-cant-fail-as-there-is-no-alternative-planet-says-french-minister.

Hacking, Ian (1981) 'How should we do the history of statistics?', *Ideology & Consciousness*, 8: 15–26.

Hall, Stuart (1979) 'The great moving right show', *Marxism Today*, January: 14–20.

Hallmann, Caspar A., Martin Sorg, Eelke Jongejans, Henk Siepel, Nick Hofland, Heinz Schwan, Werner Stenmans, Andreas Müller, Hubert Sumser, Thomas Hörren, Dave Goulson and Hans de Kroon (2017) 'More than 75 percent decline over 27 years in total flying insects biomass in protected areas', *Plos one*, 12(10): 2–17.

Hancox, Dan (2014) *The Village Against the World*. London: Verso Press.

Haraway, Donna (2003) *The Companion Species Manifesto: Dogs, People, and Significant Otherness. Vol. 1*. Chicago: Prickly Paradigm Press.

Haraway, Donna (2016) *Staying with the Trouble: Making Kin in the Chthulucene*. Durham, NC: Duke University Press.

Hardin, Garrett (1968) 'The tragedy of the commons', *Science*, 162: 1243–1248.

Hardt, Michael and Antonio Negri (2000) *Empire*. Cambridge, MA: Harvard University Press.

Hardt, Michael and Antonio Negri (2011) *Commonwealth*. Cambridge, MA: Harvard University Press.

Harvey, David (2003) *The New Imperialism*. New York: Oxford University Press.

Harvey, David (2005) *A Brief History of Neoliberalism*. New York: Oxford University Press.

Harvey, David (2010) *The Enigma of Capital*. London: Profile Books.

Hawking, Stephen (2012) 'Stephen Hawking at 70: Exclusive interview', *New Scientist*, 2846.

Hayek, Friedrich (1976) *The Mirage of Social Justice: Vol. 2 of Law, Legislation and Liberty*. Chicago: University of Chicago Press.

Hayek, Friedrich (2010 [1944]) *The Road to Serfdom*. London: Routledge Classics.

Hayles, Katherine (1999) 'Liberal subjectivity imperiled: Norbert Wiener and cybernetic anxiety', in Katherine Hayles, *How We Became Posthuman: Virtual Bodies in Cybernetics, Literature, and Informatics*. Chicago: University of Chicago Press.

Hefferman, Olive (2017a) 'Living with climate change. Can we limit warming to 2C', *New Scientist*, 24 June, 3131: 30.

Hefferman, Olive (2017b) 'Sustainability: A meaty issue', *Nature*, 544: 18–20.

Heidegger, Martin (2001) *The Fundamental Concepts of Metaphysics: World, Finitude, Solitude*. Indiana: Indiana University Press.

Heinberg, Richard (2007) *Peak Everything: Waking Up to the Century of Decline in the Earth's Resources*. Gabriola Island: Clairview.

Henriques, Julian, Wendy Hollway, Cathy Urwin, Couze Venn and Valerie Walkerdine (1998 [1984]) *Changing the Subject: Psychology, Social Regulation and Subjectivity*. London: Routledge.

Henry, James (2012) 'The price of offshore revisited', *Tax Justice Network*. Available at: www.taxjustice.net/cms/upload/pdf/Price_of_Offshore_Revisited_120722.pdf.

Hessel, Stéphane (2010) *Indignez-vous*. Montpellier: Indigene. Translated as *Time for Outrage* in 2011 by Charles Glass Books, London.

Hill, Joshua, S. (2017) 'India cancels 14 GW of new coal plants. Nobody wants coal but Trump', *Red, Green and Blue*, May 25.
Hochschild, Arlie (2012 [1983]) *The Managed Heart: Commercialization of Human Feeling*. Los Angeles: University of California Press.
Hochschild, Arlie (2016) *Strangers in Their Own Land: Anger and Mourning on the American Right: A Journey to the Heart of Our Political Divide*. New York: The New Press.
Holmes, Bob (2017) 'Living with climate change: Can I make a difference?' *New Scientist*, 234(3131): 35.
Home Office (1997) 'No More Excuses' (Cmnd 360). London: HMSO.
Hubbert, M. King (1956) 'Nuclear energy and the fossil fuel', in American Petroleum Institute, *Drilling and Production Practice*. New York: American Petroleum Institute.
Hui, Wang (2009) *The End of the Revolution. China and the Limits of Modernity*. London: Verso.
Hulme, Mike (2009) *Why We Disagree about Climate Change: Understanding Controversy, Inaction and Opportunity*. Cambridge: Cambridge University Press.
Institute for Energy Research (IER) (2017) 'Despite the Paris Agreement, China and India Continue to Build Cool Plants', 24 July.
IPCC (2014) *Fifth Assessment Report: Synthesis Report on Climate Change*. Geneva: IPCC.
Jackson, Tim (2009) *Prosperity without Growth*. London: Earthscan.
Jacquet, Jennifer (2015) *Is Shame Necessary? New Uses For an Old Tool*. London: Penguin.
Jalée, Pierre (1981) *Le Pillage du tiers monde*. Paris: Maspero.
Jose, Sajai (2015) 'India is now world's fastest-growing major polluter', *IndiaSpend*, 27 June. Available at: www.indiaspend.com/cover-story/india-is-now-worlds-fastest-growing-major-polluter-66600.
Joseph, Miranda (2014) *Debt to Society: Accounting for Life under Capitalism*. Minneapolis: University of Minnesota.
Joxe, Alain (2002) *Empire of Disorder*, trans. Ames Hodges. Los Angeles: Semiotext(e).
Kant, Immanuel (1992 [1784]) 'An answer to the question; "What is Enlightenment"', in Patricia Waugh (ed.), *Postmodernism: A Reader*. London and New York: Edward Arnold.
Keen, Andrew (2015) *The Internet is Not the Answer*. Bloomsbury: Atlantic Books.
Klein, Alice (2017) 'Will we have to geoengineer?', *New Scientist*, 3131: 34.
Klein, Naomi (2008) *The Shock Doctrine*. London: Penguin.
Klein, Naomi (2014) *This Changes Everything: Capitalism vs. the Climate*. New York: Simon & Schuster.
Knorr-Cetina, Karin and Urs Bruegger (2002) 'Traders' engagement with markets: A postsocial relationship', *Theory, Culture & Society*, 19(5–6): 161–186.
Kolbert, Elizabeth (2014) *The Sixth Extinction: An Unnatural History*. New York: Henry Holt.
Krugman, Paul (2015) 'The austerity delusion', *The Guardian*, 29 April. Available at: www.theguardian.com/business/ng-interactive/2015/apr/29/the-austerity-delusion.
Larkin, Amy (2013) *Environmental Debt: The Hidden Costs of a Changing Global Economy*. New York: St. Martin's Press.
Latimer, Joanna and Mara Miele (2013) 'Naturecultures? Science, affect and the non-human', *Theory, Culture & Society*, 30(7–8): 5–31.
Latouche, Serge (2009) *Farewell to Growth*, trans. David Macey. London: Polity.
Latour, Bruno (2003) *Un Monde pluriel mais commun*. La Tour d'Aigues: Éditions de l'Aube.
Latour, Bruno (2005) *Reassembling the Social: An Introduction to Actor-Network Theory*. Oxford: Oxford University Press.

References

Latour, Bruno (2010) *Cogitamus*. Paris: Editions la Découverte.
Latour, Bruno (2012) *Enquête sur les modes d'existence*. Paris: Éditions la Découverte.
Laurance, William (2015) 'Collision course', *New Scientist*, 226(3017): 26–27.
Lawrence, Amy (2017) 'For a fairer share of our resources, turn to the 13th century', *The Guardian*, 8 November: 32.
Lazzarato, Maurizio (2009) 'Neoliberalism in action: Inequality, insecurity, and the reconstitution of the social', trans. Couze Venn, *Theory, Culture & Society* 26(6): 109–133.
Lazzarato, Maurizio (2011) *La Fabrique de l'homme endetté: Essai sur la condition néolibérale*. Amsterdam: Éditions Amsterdam.
Lazzarato, Maurizio (2015) 'Neoliberalism, the financial crisis, and the end of the liberal state', trans. Couze Venn, *Theory, Culture & Society*, 32(7–8): 67–83.
Le Page, Michael (2015a) 'Earth now halfway to UN global warming limit', *New Scientist*, 227(3032): 8–9.
Le Page, Michael (2015b) 'Coal renaissance sets us for 4°C rise', *New Scientist*, 227(3030): 10–11.
Le Page, Michael (2016) 'UK has no good reason to approve fracking', *New Scientist*, 3095: 21.
Le Page, Michael (2017) 'Living with climate change: How to cope in a warmer world', *New Scientist*, 234(3131): 32–33.
Lee, Benjamin and Edward LiPuma (2002) 'Cultures of circulation: The imaginations of modernity', *Public Culture*, 14(1): 191–213.
Leroi-Gourhan, André (1964) *Le Geste et la parole, Vol. 1: Technique et langage*. Paris: Albin Michel.
Leroi-Gourhan, André (1971 [1943]) *L'Homme et la matière*. Paris: Albin Michel.
Levinas, Emmanuel (1969) *Totality and Infinity*, trans. Alfonso Lingis. Pittsburgh: Duquesne University Press.
Levinas, Emmanuel (1984) 'Ethics of the infinite', in Richard Kearney (ed.), *Dialogues with Contemporary French Philosophers*. Manchester: Manchester University Press.
Lewis, Michael (2010) *The Big Short: Inside the Doomsday Machine*. London: Allen Lane.
Locke, John (1959 [1896]) *An Essay Concerning Human Understanding*. New York: Dover Publications.
Locke, John (1963 [1690–1780]) *Two Treatises of Government*. New York: Cambridge University Press.
Luxemburg, Rosa (1968) *The Accumulation of Capital*, trans. Agnes Schwarzschild. New York: Monthly Review Press.
Luyendijk, Joris (2015) *Swimming With Sharks: My Journey into the World of Bankers*. London: Faber & Faber.
Lyotard, Jean-François (1984 [1979]) *The Postmodern Condition. A Report on Knowledge*, trans. Geoff Bennington and Brian Massumi. Manchester: Manchester University Press.
Lyotard, Jean-François (1993) *The Inhuman*. Cambridge: Polity Press.
Macalister, Terry (2015) 'Shell accused of strategy of risking catastrophic climate', *The Guardian*, 17 June. Available at: www.theguardian.com/environment/2015/may/17/shell-accused-of-strategy-risking-catastrophic-climate-change.
MacKay, Donald (1969) *Information, Mechanism, and Meaning*. Cambridge, MA: MIT Press.
Mackenzie, Adrian and Theo Vurdubakis (2011) 'Codes and codings in crisis: Signification, performativity and excess', *Theory, Culture & Society*, 28(6): 3–23.
MacKenzie, Donald (2006) *An Engine, Not a Camera: How Financial Models Shape Markets*. Cambridge, MA: MIT Press.
MacLean, Nancy (2017) *Democracy in Chains: The Deep History of the Radical Right's Stealth Plan for America*. London: Scribe Publications.

Malabou, Catherine and Xavier Emmanuelli (2009) *La Grande exclusion. L'Urgence sociale: Thérapeutique et symptomes*. Paris: Bayard Publishing.
Mandelbrot, Benoit (1997) *Fractales, hasard et finance*. Paris: Flammarion.
Marazzi, Christian (2008) *Capital and Language: From the New Economy to the War Economy*. Cambridge, MA: Semiotext(e).
Marazzi, Christian (2010) *The Violence of Financial Capitalism*. Cambridge, MA: Semiotext(e).
Margulis, Lynn (2009) 'Genome acquisition in horizontal gene transfer: Symbiogenesis and macromolecular sequence analysis', in Maria Boekels Gogarten, Peter Gogarten and Lorraine Olendzenski (eds), *Horizontal Gene Transfer: Genomes in Flux*. New York: Humana Press, pp. 181–191.
Margulis, Lynn and Dorion Sagan (2003) *Acquiring Genomes: A Theory of the Origin of Species*. New York: Basic Books.
Mark, Monica (2012) 'Slavery still shackles Mauritania, 31 years after its abolition', *The Guardian*, 14 August. Available at: www.theguardian.com/world/2012/aug/14/slavery-still-shackles-mauritania.
Marx, Karl (1959) *Capital, Book III*. Moscow: Progress Publishers.
Marx, Karl (1970 [1867]) *Capital, Book I*. London: Lawrence and Wishart.
Mason, Paul (2012) *Why It's Kicking Off Everywhere. The New Global Revolutions*. London: Verso Books.
Mathiesen, Karl (2015) 'Thinning Antarctic ice shelf could contribute to sea level rise, says survey', *The Guardian*, 12 May. Available at: www.theguardian.com/environment/2015/may/13/thinning-antarctic-ice-shelf-could-contribute-to-sea-level-rise-says-study.
Mazzucato, Mariana (2013) *The Entrepreneurial State: Debunking Private vs. Public Sector Myths*. London: Anthem.
Mbembe, Achille (2001) *On the Postcolony*. Berkeley, CA: University of California Press.
Mbembe, Achille (2008) 'Necropolitics', in Stephen Morton and Stephen Bygrave (eds), *Foucault in an Age of Terror: Essays on Biopolitics and the Defence of Society*. London: Palgrave Macmillan, pp. 152–182.
McNay, Lois (2009) 'Self as enterprise: Dilemmas of control and resistance in Foucault's *The Birth of Biopolitics*', *Theory, Culture & Society*, 26(6): 187–206.
McPherson, Crawford (1962) *The Political Theory of Possessive Individualism: Hobbes to Locke*. Oxford: Oxford University Press.
Meadows, Donella, Dennis Meadows, Jørgen Randers and William Behrens (1972) *The Limits to Growth*. New York: Universe Books.
Meadows, Donatella and Jorgen Randers (2004) *Limits to Growth: The 30-Year Update*. Chelsea Green Publishing Co.
Merefield, Matt (2004) 'The fortress, the siege and the haven: The British politics of mobility control within colonial-capitalism and globalization', unpublished PhD Thesis, Nottingham Trent University.
Mignolo, Walter (2011) *The Darker Side of Western Modernity: Global Futures, Decolonial Options*. London: Duke University Press.
Mill, John Stuart (1991 [1859]) *On Liberty and Other Essays*. Oxford: Oxford University Press.
Mirowski, Philip (2013) *Never Let a Serious Crisis Go to Waste: How Neoliberalism Survived the Finanical Meltdown*. London: Verso.
Mirowski, Philip and Dieter Plehwe (2009) *The Road From Mont Pelerin: The Making of the Neoliberal Thought Collective*. Cambridge, MA: Harvard University Press.
Monbiot, George (2013) 'This Transatlantic trade deal is a full-frontal assault on democracy', *The Guardian*, 4 November. Available at: www.theguardian.com/commentisfree/2013/nov/04/us-trade-deal-full-frontal-assault-on-democracy.
Monbiot, George (2017) *Out of the Wreckage: Finding Hope in the Age of Crisis*. London: Verso.

References

Moore, Jason (2015) *Capitalism in the Web of Life: Ecology and the Accumulation of Capital*. London: Verso.
Naess, Arne (1993) *Ecology, Community and Lifestyle*. Cambridge: Cambridge University Press, Reprint (1993-10-26).
Nancy, Jean-Luc (2000) *Being Singular Plural*, trans. Robert Richardson and Anne O'Byrne. Stanford: Stanford University Press.
Nancy, Jean-Luc (2012) *L'Équivalences des catastrophes*. Paris: Galilée.
National Oceanic and Atmospheric Administration (2015) *World of Change: Global Temperatures*. NASA: Goddard Institute for Space Studies.
Negri, Antonio (2015) 'On the constitution and financial capital', *Theory, Culture & Society*, 32(7–8): 25–38.
New Scientist (2015a) 'Upfront', 31 October (3045).
New Scientist (2015b) 'Obama's climate plans', 8 August, 277(3033): 6.
New Scientist (2017) 'Living with climate change: Can we limit warming to 2°C?', 24 June, 234(3131): 30.
Newsinger, John (2006) *The Blood Never Dried: A People's History of the British Empire*. London: Bookmarks.
Orléans, André (2014) *The Empire of Value*. Cambridge, MA: MIT Press.
Ostrom, Elinor (1990) *Governing the Commons: The Evolution of Institutions for Collective Action*. Cambridge: Cambridge University Press.
Oxfam International (2012) 'Left behind by the G20? How inequality and environmental degradation threaten to exclude poor people from the benefits of economic growth', 157 Briefing Paper, 4 January.
Oyama, Susan (2000 [1985]) *The Ontogeny of Information: Developmental Systems and Evolution*. Durham, NC: Duke University Press.
Pagden, Anthony (1993) *European Encounters with the New World: From Renaissance to Romanticism*. New Haven & London: Yale University Press.
Panitch, Leo and Sam Gindin (2013) *The Making of Global Capitalism: The Political Economy of American Empire*. London: Verso.
Parance, Béatrice and Jacques De Saint Victor (eds) (2014) *Repenser les biens communs*. Paris: CNRS éditions.
Pasquino, Pasquale (1978) 'Theatrum politicum. The genealogy of capital – police and the state of prosperity', *Ideology & Consciousness*, 4: 41–54.
Payne, Tony (2015) 'Melting Antarctic ice sheets could add up to 30 cms to sea levels by 2100', *CarbonBrief*, 18 November.
Pearce, Fred (2014) 'On the road to a climate fix', *New Scientist*, 224(2999): 8–9.
Pearce, Fred (2015) 'Negative emissions ahead', *New Scientist*, 207(3033): 8–9.
Pearce, Fred (2016) 'Capitalism must be re-imagined if we want a low-carbon world', *New Scientist*, 7 April: 30–33.
Pearce, Fred (2017a) 'We are on track to pass 1.5°C warming in less than 10 years', *New Scientist*, 11 May: 31.
Pearce, Fred (2017b) 'Talking to climate sceptics', *New Scientist*, 24 June, 3131 (33).
Peck, Jamie (2010) *Construction of Neoliberal Reason*. Oxford: Oxford University Press.
Pfeifer, Rolf and Josh Bongard (2007) *How the Body Shapes the Way We Think: A New View of Intelligence*. Cambridge: MIT Press.
Piketty, Thomas (2014) *Capital in the 21st Century*, trans. Arthur Goldhammer. Cambridge, MA: The Belknap Press of Harvard University Press.
Polanyi, Karl (2001 [1944]) *The Great Transformation. The Political and Economic Origins of Our Time*. Boston: Beacon Press.
Pollock, Griselda (2004) 'Thinking the feminine: Aesthetic practice as introduction to Bracha Ettinger and the concepts of matrix and metramorphosis', *Theory, Culture & Society*, 21(1): 5–65.
Pope's Encyclical Letter (2015) *Lauduto Si*, 24 May.
Poteete, Amy, Marco Janssen and Elinor Ostrom (2010) *Working Together: Collective Action, the Commons, and Multiple Methods in Practice*. Princeton: Princeton University Press.

References

Povinelli, Elizabeth (2016) *Geontologies: A Requiem to Late Liberalism*. Durham, NC: Duke University Press.

Powell, Devin (2009) 'Mum's behaviour may make young rats more butch', *New Scientist*, 7 January, Issue 2690.

Prakash, Gyan (1990) *Bonded Histories: Genealogies of Labour Servitude in Colonial India*. Cambridge: Cambridge University Press.

Puko, Timothy (2017) 'Trump plan for coal, nuclear power draws fire from environmental, oil groups', *Wall Street Journal*, 22 October. Available at: www.wsj.com/articles/environmentalists-energy-companies-unite-in-fight-against-electrical-grid-plan-1508677201.

Quiggin, John (2012) *Zombie Economics: How Dead Ideas Still Walk among Us*. Princeton: Princeton University Press.

Quijano, Anibal (2000) 'Coloniality of power, Eurocentrism, and Latin America', *Nepantla: Views from the South*, 1(3): 533–580.

Rajan, Sunder (2006) *Biocapital: The Constitution of Postgenomic Life*. Durham, NC: Duke University Press.

Ramesh, Randeep (2016) 'The inside story of the world's biggest financial scandal: How a jailed former banker and a lone British journalist broke a story that shook the world', *The Guardian*, 28 June. Available at: www.theguardian.com/world/2016/jul/28/1mdb-inside-story-worlds-biggest-financial-scandal-malaysia.

Rand, Ayn and Nathaniel Branden (1964) *The Virtue of Selfishness*. New York: New American Library.

Rebanks, James (2015) *The Shepherd's Life: A Tale of the Lake District*. London: Penguin.

Reed, Christina (2015) 'Plastic age: How it's reshaping rocks, oceans and life', *New Scientist*, 28 January: 28.

Rennison, Joe (2015) 'Exhanges vie for credit swaps trading', *Financial Times*, 8 September. Available at: www.ft.com/content/3d580b5e-5349-11e5-8642-453585f2cfcd.

Ricoeur, Paul (1992) *Oneself as Another*, trans. Kathleen Blamey. Chicago: University of Chicago Press.

Ridgway, Andy and Richard Webb (2015) 'Elemental risk: Securing the raw stuff of modern life', *New Scientist*, 225(3008): 35–41.

Robins, Kevin and Frank Webster (1988) 'Cybernetic capitalism: Information, technology, and everyday life', in Vincent Mosco and Janet Wasko (eds), *The Political Economy of Information*. Madison: University of Wisconsin, pp. 45–75.

Rose, Nikolas (2007) *The Politics of Life Itself: Biomedicine, Power and Subjectivity in the Twenty-First Century*. Princeton: Princeton University Press.

Rose, Stephen and Hilary Rose (2012) *Genes, Cells and Brains: The Promethean Promises of the New Biology*. London: Verso Books.

Roubini, Nouriel and Stephen Mihm (2010) *Crisis Economics. A Crash Course in the Future of Finance*. London and New York: Allen Lane.

Rousseau, Jean-Jacques (1998 [1762]) *The Social Contract and Other Later Political Writings*. Ware: Wordsworth Editions Limited.

Roy, Arundhati (2015) *Capitalism: A Ghost Story*. London: Verso Books.

Said, Edward (1978) *Orientalism: Western Concepts of the Orient*. Delhi: Penguin.

Said, Edward (1993) *Culture & Imperialism*. London: Chatto & Windus.

Schmidtko, Sunke, Lothar Stramma and Martin Visbeck (2017) 'Decline in global ocean oxygen content during the past five decades', *Nature*, 542: 335–339.

Schmitt, Carl (2007 [1932]) *The Concept of the Political*. Chicago: University of Chicago Press.

Semmel, Bernard (2004) *The Rise of Free Trade Imperialism*. Cambridge: Cambridge University Press.

Sen, Amartya (2009) *The Idea of Justice*. London: Penguin.

Sen, Amartya (2010) 'Beyond GDP: Measures of welfare and sustainability', Lecture, 24 May. Available at: www.youtube.com/watch?v=wtFmY68OQuc.

References

Sen, Amartya and Martha Nussbaum (1993) *The Quality of Life*. Oxford: Clarendon Press.

Shaxson, Nicholas (2012) *Treaure Islands: Tax Havens and the Men Who Stole the World*. London: The Bodley Head.

Shiva, Vandana (2002) *Biopiracy: The Plunder of Nature and Knowledge*. Cambridge, MA: South End Press.

Simondon, Gilbert (1989 [1958]) *Du mode d'existence des objets techniques*. Paris: Aubier.

Simondon, Gilbert (2004 [1967]) *Deux lecons sur l'animal et l'homme*. Paris: Ellipses Editions Marketing.

Simondon, Gilbert (2005) *L'Individuation á la lumière des notions de forme et d'information*. Grenoble: Millon.

Smith, Adam (1812 [1776]) *The Wealth of Nations*. London: Bradbury, Agnew & Co.

Smith, Adam (2009 [1759]) *The Theory of Moral Sentiments*. London: PenSmith.

Stengers, Isabelle (2009) *Aux temps des catastrophes*. Paris: La Découverte.

Stiegler, Bernard (1998) *Technics and Time: The Fault of Epimetheus. Vol. 1*, trans. Richard Beardsworth and George Collins. Stanford: Stanford University Press.

Stiegler, Bernard (2005) *De la misère symbolique, vol.2: La catastrophe du sensible*. Paris: Galilée.

Stiegler, Bernard (2006) 'De l'économie libidinale a l'écologie de l'esprit', *Multitudes*, 24: 85–95.

Stiegler, Bernard (2007) '"Technics, media, teleology": Interview with Couze Venn et al.', *Theory, Culture & Society*, 24(7–8): 334–341.

Stiegler, Bernard (2008) *Economie de L'hypermatériel et psychopouvoir*. Paris: Mille et Une Nuits.

Stiglitz, Joseph (2001) 'Foreword', in Karl Polanyi, *The Great Transformation*. Boston: Beacon Press, pp. vii–xvii.

Stiglitz, Joseph (2002) *Globalization and its Discontents*. London: Penguin.

Stiglitz, Joseph (2010) *Freefall: Free Markets and the Sinking of the Global Economy*. London: Allen Lane.

Stiglitz, Joseph (2013) *The Price of Inequality*. London: Penguin.

Stiglitz, Joseph, Amartya Sen and Jean-Paul Fitoussi (2011) *Mismeasuring Our Lives: Why GDP Doesn't Add Up*. New York: The New Press.

Strathern, Marilyn (2000) 'Audit cultures', in Alain Pottage and Martha Mundy (eds), *Anthropological Studies in Accountability, Ethics and the Academy*. London: Routledge, pp. 201–233.

Strathern, Marilyn (2004) *Commons + Borderlands*. Wantage: Sean Kingston Publishing.

Terranova, Tiziana (2009) 'The nature of political economy in Foucault's *Genealogy of Biopolitics*', *Theory, Culture & Society*, 26(6) : 234–262.

Terranova, Tiziana (2015) 'Introduction to Eurocrisis, neoliberalism and the common', *Theory, Culture & Society*, 32(7–8): 5–23.

Tett, Gillian (2010) *Fool's Gold: How Unrestrained Greed Corrupted a Dream, Shattered Global Markets and Unleashed a Catastrophe*. London: Abacus.

Tett, Gillian (2015) *The Silo Effect: Why Putting Everything in its Place isn't Such a Bright Idea*. London: Little, Brown.

Tiessen, Matthew (2014) 'Giving credit where credit's due: Making visible the ex-nihilo dimensions of money's agency', *Topia. Canadian Journal of Cultural Studies*, 30–31.

Todorov, Tzvetan (1992) *The Conquest of America*, trans. Richard Howard. New York: Harper Perennial.

Torres, Raymond (2015) 'Executive summary – the changing nature of jobs', *World Employment and Social Outlook*, (2): 1–7.

Townsend, Peter (2000) *Breadline Europe: The Measurement of Poverty*. Bristol: Polity Press.
Tsing, Anna (2015) *The Mushroom at the End of the World: On the Possibility of Life in Capitalist Ruins*. Princeton: Princeton University Press.
Tsonis, Panagiotis and Anastasios Tsonis (2004) 'A "small-world" network hypothesis for memory and dreams', *Perspectives in Biology and Medicine*, 47(2): 176–180.
United Nations Development Report (2015) 'Work for Human Development', ch. 21.
Urry, John (2011) *Climate Change & Society*. Cambridge: Polity Press.
Urry, John (2014a) *Offshoring*. Cambridge: Polity Press.
Urry, John (2014b) 'The problem of energy', *Theory, Culture & Society*, 31(5): 3–20.
Vallely, Paul (2011) 'Europe is facing a fate worse than debt', *The Independent on Sunday*, 20 November: 39. Available at: www.independent.co.uk/voices/commentators/paul-vallely-europe-is-facing-a-fate-worse-than-debt-6264954.html.
Varela, Francisco, Evan Thompson and Eleanor Rosch (1993) *The Embodied Mind: Cognitive Science and Human Experience*. Cambridge, MA: MIT Press.
Venn, Couze (1985) 'A subject for concern: Sexuality and subjectivity', *PsychCritique*, 1(2): 139–154.
Venn, Couze (2000) *Occidentalism, Modernity and Subjectivity*. London: Sage.
Venn, Couze (2002) 'Altered States: Post-enlightenment cosmopolitanism and transmodern socialities', *Theory, Culture & Society*, 19(1–2): 65–80.
Venn, Couze (2004) 'Post-Lacanian affective economy, being-in-the-world, and a critique of the present: Lessons from Bracha Ettinger', *Theory, Culture & Society*, 21: 149–158.
Venn, Couze (2006a) *The Postcolonial Challenge. Towards Alternative Worlds*. London: Sage.
Venn, Couze (2006b) 'The enlightenment', *Theory, Culture & Society*, 23(2–3): 477–486.
Venn, Couze (2009a) 'Neoliberal political economy, biopolitics and colonialism: A transcolonial genealogy of inequality', *Theory, Culture & Society*, 26(6): 206–233.
Venn, Couze (2009b) 'Identity, diaspora, and subjective change: The role of affect, the relation to the other, and the aesthetic', *Subjectivity*, 26(26): 3–28.
Venn, Couze (2010) 'Individuation, relationality, affect: Rethinking the human in relation to the living', *Body & Society*, 16(1): 129–161.
Venn, Couze (2011) 'Introduction: Reflections on Amin's "Remainders of Race": Culture, nature or the political economy of race?', *Theory, Culture & Society*, 28(1): 103–111.
Venn, Couze (2014) '"Race" and the disorders of identity: Rethinking difference, the relation to the other and a politics of the commons', *Subjectivity*, 7(1): 37–55.
Vercellone, Carlo (2015) 'From the crisis to the welfare of the common', *Theory, Culture & Society*, 32(7–8): 85–99.
Virno, Paolo (2008) *Multitude Between Innovation and Negation*, trans. Isabella Bertoletti, James Cascaito and Andrea Casson. Los Angeles: Semiotext(e).
Viswanathan, Guari (1989) *Masks of Conquest: Literary Study and British Rule in India*. New York: Columbia University Press.
Wachman, Richard (2011) 'New warning over exchange traded funds', *The Guardian*, 15 December. Available at: www.theguardian.com/business/2011/dec/15/exchange-traded-funds-warning.
Wadhams, Peter (2016) *A Farewell to Ice: A Report from the Arctic*. London: Allen Lane.
Wallerstein, Immanuel (1974, 1980, 1989) *The Modern World System. 3 Vols*. New York: Academic Books.
Weatherall, James Owen (2013) *The Physics of Wall Street: A Brief History of Predicting the Unpredictable*. Boston: Houghton Mifflin Harcourt.

References

Whyte, Chelsea (2017) '208 new rocks back case for Anthropocene', *New Scientist*, 3115: 11.
Wilkinson, Richard and Kate Pickett (2009) *The Spirit Level: Why Equality is Better for Everyone*. London: Allen Lane.
Wilkinson, Richard and Kate Pickett (2010) *The Spirit Level: Why Equality is Better for Everyone*, revised edn. London: Penguin Books.
Wilks, Stephen (2013) *The Political Power of the Business Corporation*. Cheltenham: Edward Elgar.
Williams, Eric (1964 [1944]) *Capitalism and Slavery*. London: Andre Deutsch.
Wolfe, Cary (2010) *What is Posthumanism?* Minnesota: University of Minnesota Press.
Wong, Sam (2016) 'Marks of the anthropcene: Seven signs we have made our own epoch', *New Scientist*, 3056: 14.
World Bank (2014) *World Development Indicators. Gross Domestic Product*, 9 June.
World Meteorological Organisation (2016) 'The state of greenhouse gases in the atmosphere based on global observations through 2015', *Greenhouse Gas Bulletin*, 12.
World's Oil and Natural Gas Scenario (2004) Springer, ch.2.
Zalasiewicz, Jan, Will Steffen, Reinhold Leinfelder, Mark Williams and Colin Waters (2017) 'Petrifying earth process: The stratigraphic imprint of key earth system parameters in the Anthropocene', *Theory, Culture & Society*, 34(2–3): 83–104.

Index

accounting practices 34–5, 42, 65, 100–1, 114–15
  critical perspectives 18, 34–5
accumulation 9, 10, 11, 14, 19, 20, 57, 66, 86, 93, 95, 96, 140
  and colonialism 41, 67–75
  continuity of 61, 72
  and the debt society 35, 37, 40
  long history of 41, 67
  new regime of 24–33, 74, 83, 118
  as vice or virtue 93
'accumulation by dispossession' 67
Adam Smith Institute 15
affordance 44, 129, 132, 129
Africa 20
  'development corridors' 59
  land grabs 74, 75
  new scramble for 7, 17
  scramble for (1880s) 71–2
Agamben, G. 77, 115, 135–7
agency 22, 128
  people as 125
  state as 30, 37–8, 51 n.2, 109, 119
algorithmic (algo) trading 26, 28, 47
altruism 94, 100, 139
aluminium 4, 71
Amazon (company) 33, 35
Amazon (region) 8, 59, 63
Ambani, Mukesh 83
ambient energy sources 17, 142
American Constitution 101
American Declaration of Independence 101
American Legislative Exchange Council 15
Americas
  colonisation 69, 71, 74, 75, 92, 96
  pre-colonial common pool resources 116
Amin, S. 69
animal–human relationship 134–8

answerability 22, 139
anthropocentrism 19, 45, 49, 123, 128, 133, 136, 140
anthropogenesis 5, 6, 20, 54, 59, 60, 64, 83, 135, 136
'apparatuses of capture' 10, 11
Arctic 52, 54, 55, 58, 59, 62
Arendt, H. 75, 126
Arnoldi, J. 28
Arrighi, G. 67, 69–70, 71, 72
Ashurst, F. 49, 50, 87, 92, 93, 99, 111, 113
'associated bodies' 14
'associated milieux' 12, 108, 121 n.1, 130
AstraZeneca 33
Athropocence 4
Atkinson, A. 72, 112
Atkinson Index 114
Atlantic Slave Trade 71
audit culture 34, 42, 82
Auger, A. 132
austerity programmes 3, 7, 10, 25, 27, 31–2, 35–6, 37, 101
Australia
  land grabs 74, 75
  pre-colonial common pool resources 116
Awajun people, Peru 116–17
Ayn Rand Institute 15

bailouts 3, 27, 35–6
banking crisis 3, 24–5
Barad, K. 49, 97, 126, 127–8
bare life 39, 135
Basel Accords 25, 34
Bateson, G. 131
Bebbington, J. 35
being-with 14, 22, 123, 137–8, 138–9, 140
benevolence 78, 91, 93

Index

Benjamin, W. 136
Bentham, J. 46, 93, 95, 96, 98, 99, 104
Berlin Wall, fall of 106
Beveridge, W. 103, 105
Beveridge Report (1942) 103
Big Bang (1986) 31
'big data' 10, 29, 101
biodiversity 4, 13, 55, 115, 120
biofuels 13, 142
biomass 56, 59
biomes 4, 12, 13, 53, 55, 56
biopiracy 17
biopolitical governmentality 18, 34, 43, 48, 86, 88, 105, 111, 112, 114
biopolitics 21, 39, 44, 46, 74, 65, 68, 80, 103, 109, 110, 120, 138
   vs. biopower 76
   coupling with capitalism and governmentality 91
biopower 76
Black-Scholes equation 27
Blair government 100
Blyth, M. 3, 34, 36
Bohr, N. 127
Bongard, J. 129
Booth, C. 103
Branden, N. 124
Braudel, F. 40, 67, 69, 70, 71, 72–3, 75
Bretton Woods institutions 25, 73
Britain, colonial exploitation and economic hegemony 69–70, 71
Brown, W. 51
Brundtland Commission 54
Bruno, G. 134
Buchanan, M. 27

capabilities 22, 96, 114, 115, 116
capital
   commons as 112, 119–20, 122 n.5
   relationship with labour 19, 29, 51, 61, 106
   relationship with the state 1, 20, 30, 36, 37–8, 40, 64, 87
   virtual 34, 47
capitalism
   alternatives 66–7, 84–5 n.2, 86
      see also postcapitalism
   and the Anthropocene 4
   antithetical perspectives 123
   attraction of 125

   as cause of convergent crises 1, 6
   and climate change 20, 52–3, 56, 58, 59, 63
   co-articulation with colonialism and modernity 65, 66, 107
   and colonialism 7, 19, 21, 42, 44, 67–75, 96–7
   common good as legitimation 124
   coupling with biopolitics and governmentality 91
   critiques of 4, 68, 97
   definition 44
   as democratic exemplar 104
   denunciation of counter-discourse 67
   destructive, undemocratic, unethical 121
   and environmental crisis 13
   equated to modernisation and development 78
   expansionary imperative 61
   genealogy of 21, 67–75, 79
   as greenhouse gas emitter 6, 52
   identification with the state 40
   individualist spirit 126–7
   likely non-survival 140
   'middle way' 103
   neoliberal faith in 7, 102
   new neoliberal modality 24–33
   as oozing wound 125
   and perpetual war 104
   political legitimacy 112
   post-crash strategies for saving 3
   property regimes 20, 42, 44, 66, 82, 86, 95, 96–7, 108, 109, 114, 119, 120, 140
   radical analyses 64
   reconstruction of regulatory framework to support 118
   role of new commons 109
   scaffolding upholding 14
   vs. socialism 61, 102–3, 111
   as specific form of market economy 6, 42–3
   tweaking to save 140
   undermined by politics of commons 120
   as zero-sum game 2, 24, 68, 84, 104, 139
   see also specific forms of capitalism
carbon-based economy 5, 52, 63

'carbon bubble' 57
carbon capture 6, 56, 59
carbon emissions 4, 53, 55, 58
carbon trading 2–3
care of the other 138
Carpenter, M. 98, 99, 103
Chadwick, E. 99
Chakrabortty, A. 33
Chalmers, D. 128
Chang, H.-J. 14, 29, 35, 68
Chicago School economics 27
China 58, 59
  as global player 106
  land grabs by 75
  non-privatised land 74
  pre-colonial market economy 70, 71
CIA 53
Clark, A. 128–30, 133
class 1, 21, 45, 51, 67, 77, 78, 98, 103, 107, 114
classical/neo-classical political economy 15, 66, 74, 80–1, 90–1, 97
Clean Power Plan, US 52
  cancellation 6, 58
Climate Action Trackers 53
climate change and global warming 3, 4, 5–6, 9, 14, 17, 19, 52–63, 68, 83, 107, 117, 120
  anthropogenic character 20, 54
  green/individual solutions 56
  inadequate government response 53
  main consequences 54–5
  market fixes 7, 57, 59, 63
  obstacles to progress 12
  as profit-generating opportunity 2–3, 10
  technological fixes 7, 56–7, 59, 60
  towards longer-term solutions 60–3
coal-fired power stations 58, 117–18
cobalt 72
Cochacamba rebellion, Bolivia 84
co-constitution 12–13, 15, 22, 42, 108, 109, 127, 133
Coghlan, A. 9
cognitive commons 142
cognitivism 131
co-implication 22, 108, 123, 124, 127–8, 132, 138, 142
Cold War 61, 67, 83, 103, 105, 106

collaborative practice 16, 17, 18, 50, 100, 119, 141
collateralised debt obligations (CDOs) 28
collateralised loan obligations (CLOs) 28
collective responsibility
  abnegated by neoliberalism 46, 48, 50, 79
  and the social bond 50–1
colonial capitalism 45, 111
colonialism 19, 21, 64–83, 87–8, 91, 98, 104, 133
  and accumulation 41, 68–75, 96
  and capitalism 7, 19, 21, 42, 44, 67–75, 96–7
  co-articulation with capitalism and modernity 65, 66, 107
  decolonial perspective 65, 68, 69, 71
  and the 'discourse of race war' 75–80
  and dispossession 65, 67–75, 76, 96, 109
  imperial governmentality 39–40
  and indebtedness 39
  rejection of 33
  see also imperial governmentality; postcolonies
coloniality of power 21
coltan 72
commodification 1, 20, 24, 46, 65, 86
  of debt 34
  'fetishism of the commodity' 42
  'fictitious commodities' 74, 116
  of knowledge 43
  of land 74–5
commodity capitalism 88
Commodity Futures Modernisation Act (2000), USA 25
common good
  abandonment/undermining 19, 20, 48, 49, 79, 102
  association with personal happiness 98
  balance with private/market interests 21, 49, 88–9, 98, 111
  centrality in legitimation 78, 124
  and common 'wealth' 116
  and conservative rhetoric 91
  and growth 111

Index

ignored by GDP 114
intensification of conflict with self-interest 87
vs. market interest 46
prioritisation of private interest over 4, 19, 37, 102
safeguarding 49
and social bond 50
state as arbiter 86, 88–9, 118
common pool resources (CPRs) 16, 22, 116, 120, 140, 141
commons 6, 12, 16–18, 22, 40, 108–22
infrastructure as 21–2, 109–13
privatisation 97
reframing value 34–5
see also postcapitalist (enlarged) commons
compassion 138, 139
competition 48, 50, 80–84
in classical political economy 74
effects 13–14
and the logic of war 83, 84
neoliberalism prioritisation 4, 8, 21, 47, 48, 50, 59, 78, 79, 80–4, 87, 101, 115
in ordoliberalism 80–1
and planetary exhaustion 83
complexity 10, 12–13, 27, 43, 64, 60, 127
compossibility 14, 42, 108, 123, 128
consumer capitalism 60
convergent crises 1–7, 19, 106–7
anthropogenic nature 64
conceptual roots 41–50
interconnections 13, 64–6
need for coordinated approach 64, 65–6
need for radical transformation 3–4
obstacles to change 7–13
as 'second order' systems 64
conviviality 2, 7, 15, 22, 50, 123
corporate capitalism 11, 20, 51, 62
and the 'postcolony' 82–3
cosmopolitics 12, 45, 88, 127, 132, 139–40
counter-discourse 67
counter-history 71, 87
credit default swaps (CDSs) 25, 28
critical genealogy, 87, 88, 107 n.1
Curtis, N. 3, 113, 124

cybernetic capitalisms 28
cybernetic technologies 9, 10, 19, 26, 34, 43–4

Dardot, P. 8, 15, 38, 82, 92–4, 95–6, 97, 102
dark matter 128
debt
and asset bubbles 25
and dispossession 77–8
institutionalisation and socialisation 37
as sin or 'trespass' 38–9
spread of 'odious' 32
virtualisation and securitisation 34
debt financing 25–6, 73
debt society 10, 20, 33–40, 42, 47, 86, 106
decolonial perspective 65
deforestation 4
dehumanising values 48
Deleuze, G. 10, 32, 38, 47, 79, 83
democracy 89, 101, 105
direct 141
erosion 20
radical 141–2
threats to 7, 19, 50, 83, 84, 90, 102
underlying values and principles 49
democratic institutions 1, 18, 19, 83, 142
depoliticization 136
deregulation 9, 25
derivatives 9, 20, 25, 26, 27, 28, 47
Derrida, J. 125, 137–8, 139
Descartes, R. 126, 135, 137
Descola, P. 14, 16
despotism and despotic regimes 22, 63, 64, 67, 125, 138, 140
development
as 'arrow of time' 13
association with modernisation/progress/growth 4, 46, 58, 65, 69
and climate change/environmental damage 58–9
decoupling from growth 40
and energy consumption 60–1
and natural necessity 78
as vehicle for wealth appropriation 73
disaster capitalism 10, 59
disciplinary techniques 76, 110

'discourse of race war' 21, 39, 40, 41, 69, 77–8, 84
dispossession 1, 66, 84
  'accumulation by' 66, 67
  as 'buried knowledge' 87
  colonial 65, 67–75, 76, 86, 96, 109
  continuity of 72
  and critique of capitalism 68
  legitimating 78, 96
  longevity of 67, 77–8
  new mechanisms of 3, 7, 19, 20, 21, 24–51
  neo-colonial 17
  progressive 119
Dissenter Christianity 89, 98, 100
divine vs. natural law 92–3
Donovan, P. 13

ecological assembly 129, 130
ecological balance 129
ecological developmental biology 132
ecological macro-economics 113
ecologically grounded technologies 12
ecology 6, 59
  transcolonial 117
economisation of knowledge 8
economisation of society 8, 136
egalitarian polities 40
egocentrism 47, 49, 101, 123
Elden, S. 8
emancipation 21, 28, 44, 45, 47, 48, 61, 88, 93, 100, 108, 125, 136
emancipatory politics 2, 11, 47, 88
Emmanuel, A. 69
emissions *see* carbon emissions; greenhouse gas emissions
empathy 93, 94, 123, 137
enclosures 7, 16, 20, 68, 73, 74, 77, 84, 96, 109, 119
Engels, F. 88
Enlightenment 45, 47, 48, 88, 93, 98
'enterprise man' 97
environmental damage 1, 13, 19, 55, 58–9, 68, 107, 109, 117, 120–1, 140
Epel, D. 132
epigenesis/epigenetic 5, 55, 124, 128, 129, 130, 132, 138, 139
epistemicide, 17
epistemology 22, 38, 100–1, 126, 127, 140

equality 2, 19, 45, 98, 102
equilibrium models 27
Esposito, R. 41, 136
ethics 15, 38, 67, 127, 139
  heteronomous 123, 134
  and science 128
ethics of responsibility 22, 46, 48, 137, 134, 138, 140
ethics of utility 89, 98
Ettinger, B. 137, 139
Euken, W. 81
Europe
  common land concept 75
  conquest and colonialism 69–70, 71, 92, 96, 116
  continuity of accumulation 71
  rise of mercantilism 70
  world as economic domain 74, 80
European Central Bank 8, 27, 36
European Commission 8
European Systemic Risk Board 57
Exchange Traded Funds 31
exclusion 17, 39, 41, 45, 77, 97, 100, 101, 125, 138, 140
exploitation 17, 19, 21, 24, 56, 61, 65, 68, 69, 70, 71, 75, 78–9, 83, 104, 110, 113, 123, 125, 133, 138
'extended mind' 128–30, 133
externalities 3, 13, 18, 103, 105, 108, 115–16, 118
  capabilities as 116
extinction 4, 6, 20, 61, 140
extractive industries 15, 20, 58–9, 60, 62

fair value accounting (FVA) 34
fascism 77, 103
Federal Reserve 36
Ferguson, A. 46, 47, 51, 93, 95, 99
Feynman, R. 130
financial capitalism 8, 11, 17, 19, 24–33, 29, 34, 42, 47, 57, 62–3, 71, 79, 81, 82, 91, 117, 118
  and co-articulation of information, money and the market 47
  and the debt economy 8, 32–40, 106
  emergence of 3, 43
  features of 26
financial crash (2008) 1, 20, 24–5, 30–1, 66
financialisation 24–33, 35, 65, 72, 118

161

Index

finitude 42, 125
Fitoussi, J.-P. 61
fossil fuels 6, 52, 56, 57, 59, 142
Foucault, M. 8, 21, 28, 30, 38, 39, 40, 41, 48, 49–50, 51 n.4, 66, 68, 69, 73–4, 75, 76–7, 79, 80, 81, 82, 91, 94, 107 n.1, 110, 118, 119
fracking 58, 62, 118
fragility 13, 15, 17, 53, 125, 137, 138
Francis, Pope 56
Francis of Assis, St 134
free market 30, 75, 87, 88
  balance with the common good 88–9
  as incarnation of acquisitive human nature 92
  moral economy underlying 124
  as motor of 'progress' 46
  as myth 14, 104
  state enforcement 79
free trade 75, 79, 104
  imposition in India 70, 73
freedom 18, 19, 104, 105, 124
French Declaration of the Rights of Man and the Citizen 101
Friedman, M. 30, 103, 104, 106, 124
Fryer, 71, 72, 85 n.3
fundamental rights 2, 19, 39, 45, 48, 49, 92, 95–6
fundamentalism 77, 125
futures market 26

G7/G20 73, 83
Gabrys, J. 5, 35
Galeano, G. 70
Gane, N. 89, 93, 101
GDP 59, 61
  derivatives market compared 28
  shortcomings as measure 60–1, 112, 113–14
gender 1, 21, 39, 45, 51, 77, 78, 98, 114, 127
genealogy 1
  of accumulation 24
  of capitalism 21, 67–75, 79
  of commons 14–21
  of conceptual shifts (1759–1850) 45–6
  critical, 87, 88, 107 n.1
  of governmentality 80, 91
  of liberal political economy 109–10
  of neoliberalism 21, 44, 49–50, 67–8, 74, 75, 90, 118, 102–7
  of power 76–7
  of varieties of liberalism 21, 49, 86–102
general equivalence 20, 26, 43–4, 65, 86
  information as mode of 20, 26, 43–4, 86
  instrumentalisation of modes 47–8
  integration of modes 47, 65
  market as mode of 20, 26, 44, 65, 86
  money as mode of 20, 26, 43, 65, 86
general interest
  as aggregate of private interest 90–1
  balance with private/self-interest 21, 88–9, 94, 98, 110, 111
  and commons 114, 116
  identified with growth 61, 112
  ignored by GDP 114
  principle eliminated 113
  private interest prioritised of over 4, 37
  safeguarding 49, 90, 99
  state as arbiter 90–1, 93, 94, 118
generosity 7, 133, 138
geneticism 140
genocide 77
geological changes 4
George, S. 38
Gibson, J. J. 44, 129
Gift 138
Gilbert, J. 15, 17, 93, 119, 132, 140
Gilroy, P. 7, 10, 48, 74
Gindin, S. 23
GINI coefficient 114
global capital 72, 82–3, 118
'global south' 83
global temperature 5–6, 53, 54–5, 57, 58, 59, 62
global warming *see* climate change and global warming
globalisation 71, 74, 79, 81, 84, 103
Glyn, A. 7, 82
GMO crops 13
Goldman, L. 99, 100, 110
Google 35
governmentality 73–4, 76
  coupling with biopolitics and capitalism 91

162

emergence of 110
genealogy of 80, 91
post-war 103
see also biopolitical governmentality; imperial governmentality; liberal governmentality; neoliberal governmentality
Graeber, D. 22, 38, 39, 42, 77
grand narratives 124–5
Great Crash (1929) 25, 26
Great Depression 103
Great Disinheritance 14
Greece 32
  neoliberal economic management 8
greenhouse gas emissions (GHG) 5, 6, 52, 53, 54, 56
Grotius, H. 95
growth
  as 'arrow of time' 4
  association with progress/development/prosperity 13, 44, 45–6, 58, 61, 66, 90, 111, 112
  and climate change 20
  and commodification 86
  and consent to the state 91
  consequences of ceaseless 13–14
  and convergent crises 106
  as crucial 19
  decoupling from energy-based emissions 57
  decoupling from prosperity and development 40, 66–7
  'hockey stick' diagram 61, 105
  identified with the common good/general interest 49–50, 111
  limits to 62
  as panacea 61
  and self-betterment 94
Guattari, F. 10, 47

Haiti, 'debt' to France 78
Hallmann, C. 4
Haraway, D. 126, 133, 134
Hardin, G. 16
Hardt, M. 23, 119, 120, 140
Harvey, D. 26, 30, 66, 67, 68, 106, 112
Hawking, S. 128
Hayek, F. 30, 89, 103–4, 106, 113, 124
hedge funds 26, 27, 33
Heidegger, M. 135–6

Henriques, J. 48, 110, 143 n.1
Heritage Foundation 15
Hessel 22, n. 1
heteronomous ethics 123, 134
heteronomy 138
Higgs boson 128
Higgs field 128
high frequency trading (HFT) 26
Hobbes, T. 95
Hochschild, A. 11
Holmes, B. 6
honey bee/flower 'fit' 132
Hudson, J. 13
Hui, W. 74
Human Development Index (HDI) 60, 114
human nature 92, 93, 97

ice cap and glacier melting 55
identity politics 15, 88
IMF 2, 8, 25, 73, 83
immunity from risks 37
imperial governmentality 21, 39–40, 44, 76–7, 79, 84, 110
indebtedness 38, 39, 42, 114, 133
Independent Petroleum Association 57
India
  coal-fired power stations 58, 117–18
  colonial wealth transfer mechanisms 73
  colonisation 69–70, 71, 74, 75, 98
  pre-colonial market economy 70
indigenous peoples 15–16, 116–17
individualism 49, 97, 100, 103, 119, 123, 124, 126, 128, 141
industrial capitalism 4, 45, 66, 71, 88
Industrial Revolution 6, 19, 21, 66, 79
industrialisation 71, 72
inequality/ies
  and austerity programmes 31–2
  global 3, 21
  increase in 1, 3, 68, 78, 112–13, 120
  intensification of 7, 86
  in liberalized market economies 120
  and market distortion 112
  mechanisms made invisible 87
  naturalisation of 96, 126–7, 139
  place of the poor/poorer economies in 68
  and the precarisation of labour 31
  production of 66, 72, 75, 88, 91

163

Index

and property 92
and 'social failure' 29
information
  control of 10
  cybernetic model 131
  and ecological assembly 129
  as mode of general equivalence 20, 26, 43–4, 86
  'preformationist' attitude 131
information technologies 3, 9, 10, 11, 12, 20, 28, 29, 72
informationalisation 20, 26, 34, 43, 46, 47, 65, 76
infrastructure 3, 12, 21–2, 108, 114, 117
  as new commons 21–2, 109–13
insecticides 13
Institute for Energy Research (IER) 58
insurantial technology 103
intangible assets 7, 9
intellectual property 73
intensive farming 4
International Energy Agency (IEA) 53, 58
International Labour Organisation (ILO) 78
'invisible hand' 90, 94–5
IPCC reports 12, 53, 54, 56
Ireland, colonial wealth transfer mechanisms 73

Jackson. T. 13, 66, 112, 113–14, 120
Jacquet, J. 93
Jalée, P. 69
Jefferson, Thomas 9101
John Law Mississippi Company (1719) 25
Joseph, M. 18, 34, 42
Joxe, A. 38
juridico-political discourse 41, 87
justice 138, 139

Kant, I. 45
Keen, A. 35
Keynes, J. M. 103
Keynesianism 106, 112
Klein, N. 2, 9, 10, 27, 32, 52, 59
kleptocracies 17, 19, 73, 83
Knorr-Cetina 27

'knowledge economies' 29
Krugman, P. 36
Kyoto Protocol 12

laissez-faire 69, 79, 104
Lake District Fells 16
land grabs 20, 73, 74–5, 109, 116–17
Landless People's Movement, South Africa 16
Landless Workers Movement, Brazil 15
Larkin, A. 13
Larsen C ice shelf 55
Latin America, destabilising military force 67
Latouche, S. 66
Latour, B. 17, 120, 134
Laval, C. 8, 15, 38, 50, 82, 92–4, 95–6, 97, 102
Lawrence, A. 16
Lazzarato, M. 35, 38, 50, 64, 119
Lee, B. 28
Le Page, M. 5, 6, 13
Leroi-Gourhan, A. 130, 134, 137
Levinas, E. 138, 139
Lewis, M. 26, 34
Lewontin, R. C. 131
liberal capitalism 47, 50, 66, 68, 69, 74, 75, 76, 86, 87, 96, 97, 110–11, 125, 136
liberal governmentality 19, 21–2, 98, 103, 109
liberal political economy 18, 21, 44, 45, 49, 61, 66, 93, 110–11
  co-emergence with industrial capitalism and biopolitical governmentality 68, 88
  emergence of 75, 124
  genealogy of 68, 109–10
liberal political philosophy 47, 90, 94, 105, 111
liberalisation 7, 10, 72
  of common assets 117, 119
  of Indian trade 69–70
  of public institutions 120
  and subjugation 65
liberalism 40, 45–6, 86–107, 109
  dilemmas of 97–102
  emergence of 86–8
  problems of legacies 88–97

radical/utilitarian split 21, 49, 93, 98–100
shift to neoliberalism 21, 41, 49, 90, 102–7
liberty 18,19
Library of Things 16
LiPuma, E. 28
lithium 59, 72
Locke, J. 46, 50, 92, 95, 96, 101
logic of growth 18
logic of war 39, 83, 84
logocentrism, and violence 137
looting machines 7, 71
Lyotard, J.-F. 10, 23, 43, 44, 46, 48, 65, 93, 105, 124

Ma, Jack 83
MacKay, D. 131
Mackenzie, Adrian 27
MacKenzie, Deborah 9
MacKenzie, Donald 27
MacLean, N. 3, 6, 11, 102
mafia capitalism 29
mafia economy 2
'magical' thinking 11
Malebranche, N. 135
Malthus, T. R. 46, 93, 96, 98, 99, 104
management-speak, 8
managerial compensation schemes 29
Mandelbrot, B. 28
manufacture of consent 8
manufacture of distrust 11
Marazzi, C. 10, 24, 33, 37
margin trading ('gearing') 31
Margulis, L. 128
Marinaleda, Spain 141
market
  vs. common good 46
  'despotism' 94
  as enabling mechanism and governing idea 47
  generalization of 81
  globalisation of 74
  justification by 'common welfare' 110–11
  as mode of general equivalence 20, 26, 44, 65, 86
  as motor of progress 46
  reconstruction of regulatory framework to support 118
  as transcendental force 46
  see also free market
market/'free' market capitalism 40, 46, 66, 79, 98
market fixes 7
  and climate change 7, 57
market fundamentalism 9, 24–5, 46
market rationality 42, 43
  alignment with state rationality 86
marketisation 43, 47, 120
Marshall Plan 61
Martineau, H. 98, 99
Marx, K. 32, 33, 42, 67
Matrixial 139
Mazzucato, M. 82
Mbembe, A. 67
Meadows, D. 62
mercantilism 79
Merefield, M. 73
Merton, R. C. 27
Methane 5
Met Office Handley Centre 54
metaphysics of individualism 49, 97, 123, 128
metastability 12, 23 n.7, 27
methane 52, 53, 54, 55, 58
'middle way' 46, 98, 103
Mignolo, W. 16, 65, 126
Mihm, S. 23, 24–5, 29, 34
Miles, W. A. 99–100
militarisation of society 20, 79, 83
militaristic logic 39–40
Mill, J. S. 49, 51, 88–90, 93, 97–8, 99, 101, 102, 103, 105, 113
mind/body/world 22, 128–30
Mirowski, P. 2, 10
model of growth 4, 9, 20
modernisation 65, 78
  association with development and progress 4, 45–6, 60
modernity 124
  association with growth/development/progress 44, 66, 125–6
  and the autonomous subject 125–6
  co-articulation with capitalism and colonialism 65, 66, 107
  epochal shifts announcing 70
  and genealogy of capitalism 79
  as grand project 44
  triptych of juridical 120

165

Index

Monbiot, G. 6, 11, 121–2 n.4
monetisation 29, 43, 47, 65
money
  and debt 38
  invention of 95, 96
  as mode of general equivalence 20, 26, 43, 65, 86
  virtual 35
money-capital 9, 33, 34, 47, 63
monism 134–5
Mont Pelerin Society 15, 30, 84 n.1, 89, 101
Montaigne, M. de 134–5
Moore, J. 4
moral economy 21, 46, 47, 51, 87, 91–2, 93, 111, 124
Mossack Fonseca 37

NAFTA 2
'naïve naturalism' 81
Nancy, J.-L. 43, 44, 46, 65, 123
National Association for the Promotion of Social Science 99
National Oceanic and Atmospheric Administration (NOAA) 54
natural rights 92, 95–6
naturecultures 115, 120, 133–4, 138
negative emission 6, 56, 59
Negri, N. 51, 119, 120, 140
neo-biopolitical governmentality 8, 20, 106, 136
neo-biopolitics 11, 79, 116, 119
neo-colonial 17
neo-fascism 48
negative emissions 6
neoliberal capitalism 13, 24–33, 36, 37, 42, 51, 63, 68, 74, 103
neoliberal governmentality 81–2, 98
neoliberal orthodoxy 7
neoliberal political economy 15, 20, 21, 24, 40, 68, 75, 97, 106, 111, 118, 125
  collective responsibility abnegated 46, 48, 50, 79
  self-referential character 66
  state intervention opposed 92
neoliberal political philosophy 24, 93
neoliberalism
  as authority for new modality of capitalism 24

common good undermined or abandoned 19, 20, 48, 49, 79, 102
common goods misappropriated 119
competition prioritised 4, 8, 21, 47, 48, 50, 59, 78, 79, 80–4, 87, 101, 115
conflict between common good and corporate/self-interest intensified 87
as counter-emancipatory project 47, 48
discourse of legitimation 78
doublespeak about the state 119
early theoreticians 89
economic management 2–3, 8, 24–33
economisation of society 136
emergence of 30
faith in capitalism 7, 102
fixation with the market 46
genealogy of 21, 44, 49–50, 67–8, 74, 75, 90, 102–7, 118
general interest eliminated 113
growth prioritised 49–50
'guilt' and debt 39
'individual social policy' 115
individualism privileged 97, 126
market generalisation 81
monetisation of the ethical 111
moral economy abandoned 47, 92
naturalising of existing social relations 97
and neo-biopolitical governmentality 8, 20, 136
as neo-biopolitics 79
new relations of force favouring capital 102
and 'postcolonial' inequality and planetary destruction 68
private interests prioritised 4, 19, 37, 102, 105, 119
repositioning of the state as an enterprise 38
and the right to property 96
shift from liberalism to 21, 41, 49, 90, 102–7
and state/capital realignment 40
state responsibility abnegated 100
strategic and pragmatic character 8
technological tools for 44
transformation of minds by 108–9
values of 8

166

New Deal 103, 105, 112
New Poor Law Act (1934) 99
New Right 3, 11, 62
new scramble for Africa 7
Newsinger, J. 70, 74
nitrogen, soil levels 4
non-renewable resources 1
normalisation 76, 79, 83, 88
Nussbaum, M. 12, 96

Obama, Barack 52, 58
'occidentalism' 66, 97
Odum, Marvin 53
offshoring 7, 32–3, 37, 65, 68, 73, 74, 83
oil crisis (19702) 106
oil drilling, Arctic 52, 53
1MDB (1 Malaysia Development Berhad) 73
ontogenesis 132
ontological security 11
ontological violence 133
ontology/ies 44, 49, 56, 93, 97, 117, 126, 128, 133, 136
  Cartesian 135
  egocentric 101
  and ethics 139
  'flat' 22, 134
  post/counter-anthropocentric 18, 22, 66–7, 127, 134
  relational ('being-with') 14, 15–16, 22, 123–4, 138, 140
openDemocracy 22
oppression 1, 19, 39, 42, 45, 75, 92, 104, 107
ordoliberalism 80–1, 98, 104, 116, 118, 119, 126
organism–environment coupling 131–2, 142
Ostrom, E. 16, 120, 141
othering 77, 78, 79
outsourcing 82–3
ownership of data 10
Oyama, S. 108, 131, 132

Pagden, A. 74, 96
Paine, T. 45, 88, 98
Panitch, L. 23 n.5
pantheism 134
Paradise Papers 33

Parance, B. 120
Paris conference, 2016 (COP21) 5, 53, 59
'pastoral power' 91, 110
pauperisation 3, 14, 51, 66, 67, 68, 71, 75, 79, 84, 91, 104, 111, 140
Pax Britannica 70
'peak oil' 62
Pearce, F. 57
performativity 43, 46
pesticides 13
petrochemical industries 5, 52, 58, 71
Pfeifer, R. 129
phosphorous, soil levels 4
photosynthesis 142
phylogenesis 132
Physiocrats 75, 94, 97, 124
Pickett, K. 29, 66, 68, 72, 78, 120
Piketty, T. 36, 68, 88, 113
planet Earth 6, 15, 17, 44, 56, 59, 83, 95, 106, 107, 108, 139
  destruction of 59
  exhaustion of 83
  limits 1, 2, 18, 19, 45, 51, 132
  plunder of 1, 58, 84, 125
  ravages of 19
  transformation of 4–5
plantation economy 72–3, 110
Plasticene 5, 55
plasticity 18, 135
plastics 4, 5, 52, 55, 58
'plastisphere' 5, 55
Polanyi, K. 23, 25, 67, 69, 72, 74, 79, 116
polar ice 6
political economy 86, 87, 109
  and the autonomous subject 126
  connection with moral economy 93
  discourse of legitimation 78
  'economic man' tropes 97
  emergence 110
  relationship to government 92–3
  see also classical/neo-classical political economy; liberal political economy; neoliberal political economy
political philosophy 86, 93, 126
  radical vs. liberal 105–6
politics of commons 2, 6–7, 14, 15, 16, 17, 19, 42, 84, 86, 88, 120, 127, 139, 140–1
pollinator decline 4

Index

pollution 1, 4, 20, 55, 58, 113, 115
Poor Law Acts (1834) 25
population 8, 110, 118
  biopolitics of 21
  increases 55, 56, 61, 66, 84
  neo-biopolitics of 11
  us/them division 20, 39, 76, 78, 79
populism 2, 11, 90
post-anthropocentrism 12, 15, 18, 22, 49, 86, 108, 133
postcapitalism 7, 13–19, 22, 40, 44, 63, 66–7, 86, 87, 93–4, 123–43
postcapitalist (enlarged) commons 6, 12, 16–17, 21–2, 40, 109, 114, 119–20, 139–42
postcolony 13, 68, 73, 80, 81, 82–3, 106
  locating 64–7
post-Enlightenment outlook 45–6
postliberalism 39, 87, 88
post-war political settlement 61, 87, 103, 104–5
poverty 11, 47, 68, 70, 78, 125
  and 'accelerated wealth' 38, 83
  blaming the poor 99–100
  and 'insurantial technology' 103
  link with precarisation and inequality 31, 78
Povinelli, E. 117
power
  concentration of 10
  correlation with accumulation, dispossession and property 41, 67
  genealogy of 76–7
  and grand narratives 125
  and hostility to change 10
  and lack of accountability 31
  limits to political 89–90, 102
  oppressive 21
  relationship with political economy and governmentality 68, 69
  and 'small-world networks' 9–10, 31, 83
  spatial dimensions 7–8
  transnational dimension 32
  verticality of 10
  see also biopower; soft power
power relations
  breaking with existing 6, 14, 106
  colonial legacy 65
  forces maintaining existing 1, 10, 19, 31, 67, 106
  geopolitical 83
  global 79
  and resistance to change 11, 12
  and state policies 91
power relations, asymmetrical/unequal 31–2, 38, 89, 113, 140
  and authorisation of 'killing' 77
  between capital and labour 19, 51, 106
  challenging 2
  and class, gender and race 39, 51, 114
  inscribed in capitalism 4
  institutionalisation 9, 50
  and us/them binary 39
Prakash, G. 73
precariat 3, 36,
precarisation 1, 8, 11, 31, 32, 48, 78, 83, 91
primitive accumulation 69, 96
principle of utility 89
private accumulation 2, 11, 19, 20, 60, 72, 73, 140
private interest
  aggregate equated with general interest 90–1
  balance with general interest 21, 87, 88–9, 98, 102–3, 110
  differentiated from public interest/common good 98, 121
  prioritised over public interest 4, 19, 20, 37, 102, 105, 119
private equity acquisition 26
privatisation 1, 42, 50, 65, 66, 72, 96
  of common wealth 22, 38, 97, 117, 119
  of land 74–5
  mythical assumptions 7, 82
  overturned 84
  of the providential state 99, 112
  of public assets 7, 30
  of public institutions 120
  of public utilities, UK 82
  of social services 28–9
profit maximisation 2, 4, 11, 24, 26, 29, 83, 140
progress
  association with growth/development/modernisation 13, 44, 45–6, 60, 61, 65, 66, 69, 71, 90, 111
  and competition 47

conflicts over 'motor' of 46
conventional narrative 87
legitimating dispossession 78
property
  and inequality 92
  vs. wealth 75, 119
property regimes 16, 28
  challenging existing 2, 19, 21
  alternative 119, 120, 140, 141
  capitalist 20, 42, 44, 66, 82, 86, 95, 96–7, 108, 109, 114, 119, 120, 140
property rights 95–6, 101
  and rationality 95, 96–7
prosperity 70, 74, 80, 101, 103, 111, 112
  association with growth/progress/development 13, 45–6, 61, 66, 69, 112, 113
  decoupling from growth 18, 40, 66
  indebtedness and 38
  indices of 114
providential state 45, 50, 87, 99, 101, 103
public interest
  and the 'invisible hand' 90–1
  distinction from private interest 121
  subversion and elimination of 120, 136

Quantitative Easing 30, 31, 35–7
quantum physics 127–8
Quijano, A. 65

race 1, 21, 39, 78, 98, 114, 127
  see also, 'discourse of race war'
racism 41, 77, 79, 107
radical democracy 19, 113
radical liberalism 21, 98, 99, 104, 111
Radical Right 90, 104
radioactive isotopes 4
Rand, A. 97, 124
rational subject 45, 48, 49, 126
rationality 24, 44, 45, 69, 78, 90, 123, 124, 135
  market 7, 42, 43, 46, 74, 86
  and the right to property 95, 96–7
  state 80, 86, 93
Reaganism 106
Rebanks, J. 16
reciprocity 14

redistributive justice 91, 96
reform through education 99
regime of accumulation 24–33
regimes of truth 14–15, 17, 44, 46, 48, 109
regulatory frameworks 32, 82, 118
relationality 51 n.4, 127, 128, 133, 138
religion 45, 48, 77, 78
renewable energy 16, 52, 56, 57, 58, 62, 63, 141, 142
rent-seeking mechanisms 9, 10, 20, 26, 35, 37, 63, 72
resource depletion 1, 3, 14, 17, 19, 68, 107, 120
resources for living 115
responsibility for the other 22, 48–9, 138, 139, 140
Ricardo, D. 46, 98
rich minority 2, 20
Ricoeur, P. 18, 140
rights 11, 51, 86, 87, 88, 89, 90, 93, 97, 101, 102, 115 see also fundamental rights; natural rights; property rights
risk
  corporate reduction 9, 83
  and financialisation 27, 28, 30, 31, 32
  and fossil fuel reserves 57
  management 27, 38
  shared 50
  transferal 2, 7, 35, 37, 51
  welfare state reduction 103
robotisation 24
role of law 94
Ropke, W. 81
Roubini, N. 24–5, 29, 34
Rousseau, J.-J. 50, 110
Russian Revolution 103

Sagan, D. 128
Said, E. 65, 78
Saint Victor, J. de 120
scalar disjuncture 63, 117
scarcity 3, 55, 115, 120
Scholes, M. 27
securities 26, 34, 35, 36
sea level rises 4, 6, 55
second industrial revolution 71–2
self-interest 56, 100, 123, 126

Index

aggregated into public interest 78, 90–1, 94
balance with general interest 88–9, 98
co-existence with empathy 93
conflict with general interest intensified 87
dire effects of 95
and inequality 91
prioritised 101
self-interested subject 49, 50, 97, 119, 123, 126, 136
Sen, A. 61, 96, 114
shadow banking 25, 47
shareholder value maximisation 29
Shaxson, N. 32, 37
Shell (Royal Dutch Shell) 52, 53, 62
short-termism 2, 11, 29, 53, 56, 117, 120
silver circulation, pre-colonial 70–1
Simondon, G. 108, 121 n.1, 131, 134, 135, 137
singularity 49, 139
slave trade 41, 71, 72
slavery 42, 91, 98, 101
Slim, Carlos 83
small-world networks 9, 31, 83, 85 n.2, 129
Smith, A. 40, 46, 47, 51, 69, 78, 90–2, 93, 94–5, 99, 101, 104, 106, 110–11, 112, 124
social bond 19, 38, 50–1, 101, 115
social cohesion 1, 87, 94, 119
social contract 50, 103, 110, 113
social justice 2, 14, 19, 40, 61, 88, 96, 98, 110, 140
social scientific knowledge 100–1
socialism 40, 51, 89, 101, 103–4
vs. capitalism 61, 102–3, 111
and collective responsibility 50
'societies of control' 32, 38, 79, 84, 861
soft power 7, 12, 47, 67, 73
solipsism 126
South America
extraction and dispossession 17, 20, 72
pre-colonial silver production 70–1
sovereignty 8, 10, 93, 94
of capital 40
classical theory 45, 76
current stratagems 8
'modes of limitation' 89
new anti-democratic and totalitarian 10

solidarity 7, 22, 24, 50–1, 94, 119, 123, 134, 139, 141
spatial disjuncture 12, 63, 118
spiritual dimensions 18, 118
Stalinism 106
state
as agency/relay 30, 37–8, 51 n.2, 109, 119
as arbiter of general interest/ common good 46, 86, 88–9, 90–1, 94, 118
contribution to corporate profits 115–16
and the debt economy 20, 35–8
economic intervention seen as against 'natural' order 94
encouraging 'affective bonds' 95
as enterprise 38
as facilitator for transnationals 32–3
and infrastructure development 21–2, 109–10
institutionalizing unequal power relations 9, 50
intervention for equitable distribution 91, 103
intervention to favour competition 81
'laissez-faire' enforced by 79
legitimacy 87, 90–1, 105, 113, 118
limits to 94, 95
neoliberal doublespeak about 119
neoliberal opposition to intervention 92
relationship with capital 1, 20, 30, 36, 37–8, 40, 64, 87
role in balancing public/private interest 21, 87
shrinking 10
'social contract' with citizenry 50–1, 113
us/them relationship with polity 84
state capitalism 61
state of exception 39
state rationality 80, 90, 93
alignment with market rationality 86
Statistical Society 99
Stengers, I. 3, 13, 66, 132
Stiegler, B. 23, 42, 115, 121 n.2, 130, 133, 137
Stiglitz, J. 3, 9, 10, 30–1, 35, 61, 68, 72, 78, 89, 112

170

stock markets and exchanges 11, 28, 31, 33, 34, 82
  Shanghai crashes (2015) 31
'strategic universalism' 48–9
Strathern, M. 18, 34, 120
structural adjustments 7, 73, 99
struggles 2, 18, 19, 21
subjectivity/ies
  formation of 139
  and the needs of capital 110
  neoliberal reconstitution 48
  postcapitalist transformation 15, 108–9, 127, 140, 141, 142
  responses to insecurity 11
subjugated people 19, 39, 41, 69, 72, 74, 76, 77, 79, 87
subjugation 21, 38, 39, 41, 45, 65, 71, 77, 86
suffering 9, 134, 135, 137, 138
suffrage 45, 90, 98, 99, 101, 113
super entity 9, 23 n.7
supersymmetry 128
suppression of dissent 8
surveillance 8, 32, 38, 39, 84
sustainability 12, 19, 35, 59, 62, 114, 118
symbiosis, 14,15, 142
synthetics 26

tax havens 32–3, 37, 115
Taylor, H. 89, 98, 99
technologies of the social 28, 44, 76, 99, 105, 110, 119
technology–culture–nature dynamics 121 n.2
technological climate change fixes 7, 56–7, 59, 60
technological transfer 7
temporal disjuncture 11–12, 63, 117–18
Terranova, T. 86, 119, 140
terra nullius 41, 74, 96, 116
territory, and power 8
Tett, G. 26, 34
thanatopolitics 77
Thatcherism 106
third industrial revolution 72
tipping points 17, 54, 57, 62, 64, 67, 109, 140
Todorov, T. 69
Torres, R. 31

totalitarianism 104
trade agreements 121–2 n.4
trade networks, pre-colonial 70–1
transindividual dimension 48, 49, 137
transnational corporations
  conflict with the common good 87
  and economic/political power nexus 9
  externalisation of costs 117
  global operation 12
  and GMO crops 13
  new scramble for Africa 7
  short-termism 11–12, 117
  and 'small-world' power networks 9–10, 31, 83
  tax avoidance 32–3, 115
  and 'trickle-down' myth 112
  wealth expropriation 3
  see also offshoring
Treaty of Westphalia 80, 119
Triangular Trade system 72–3, 85 n.3
trickle down 35, 50, 91, 112, 113
Trump, Donald 118
Trump Administration 3, 5–6, 52, 58
Tsing, A. 5
'tulip mania' (1630) 25

UK Central Bank 36
unequal exchange 69, 71, 73, 83
Unitarianism 89, 98, 99, 100
United Nations 62
  Commission on Sustainable Development 60
  Development Report 60
  Environment Programme 55
Urry, J. 7, 32, 61, 65, 66, 74
us/them binary 20, 21, 39, 41, 76, 79, 84
utilitarianism 21, 36–7, 46, 47, 49, 89, 91, 92, 93, 95, 96, 98, 99–100, 101, 112

value
  commons standpoint 34–5
  creation, and informational technologies 28
  destabilisation of 35
  extraction from commodified humans 42
  and interest on capital 33
  production through commodities (M-C-M) 33, 34

Index

production through debt (M-D-M) 34
production through 'fictitious capital' (M-M) 33
'vanquished ones' 77
Varela, F. 131, 132
Venn, C. 7, 14, 15, 17, 23, 28, 38, 50, 64, 68, 74, 79, 87, 104, 133
Vercellone, C. 120
verticality of power 10
Via Campesina Movement 16
Viome factory, Greece 16
von Mises, L. 89, 101
vulnerability 1, 138
'vulture' funds 26
Vurdubakis, T. 27

Wallerstein, I. 69
Wang, Jianlin 83
'war economy' 10
'war machine' 39, 42
wealth (re)distribution 30, 40, 49, 61, 79, 87, 88, 91, 92, 101, 104, 105, 106, 110, 112–13, 124

wealth transfer 3, 8, 19, 20, 36, 66, 68, 72, 73, 75, 87–8, 91
web of life 5, 125–34
Weatherall, J. O. 27
Weiner, C. 130
welcoming the other 133
welfare state 10, 30, 50, 61, 87, 89, 101, 103, 104, 105, 106, 112, 118
Whyte, C. 4
Wilkinson, R. 29, 66, 68, 72, 78, 120
Williams, E. 7, 69, 71
Wollstonecraft, M. 88, 98
Wong, S. 4
workers' rights 87, 101
World Bank 25, 53, 62, 83
World3 model 62
WTO 2, 73

Zalasiewicz, J. 4
zero-sum economies 2, 17, 19, 24, 68, 84, 101, 104, 139
'zombie economics' 36